Elements of Accounting, Delegation of Authority and Financial Management in the Government of Canada

Basic Government Accounting

Glyden O. Headley
Basement Apartment
667, Vanalman Avenue
Saanich Peninsula
Victoria V8Z 3B3
British Columbia, CANADA

GLYDEN O. HEADLEY

Printed in Victoria, BC, Canada.

ISBN: 978-1-4251-6267-2 (sc)
ISBN: 978-1-4251-7897-0 (e-book)

*Our mission is to efficiently provide the world's finest, most comprehensive book publishing
service, enabling every author to experience success. To find out how to publish your book, your
way, and have it available worldwide, visit us online at www.trafford.com*

Trafford rev. 4/8/2010

www.trafford.com

North America & international
toll-free: 1 888 232 4444 (USA & Canada)
phone: 250 383 6864 ♦ fax: 812 355 4082

The author assumes full responsibility for the accuracy
of quotations cited in this book

Contents

PART II The Theories Associated with GAPSAP

PART III The Practice of Implementing Generally Accepted Accounting Principles (GAAP)

PART IV PRACTICAL APPLICATION OF GENERALLY ACCEPTED ACCOUNTING PRINCIPLES (GAAP) AS INTRODUCED EARLIER IN PART III

PART V Accounting Procedures and Systems for Operating a Business

Dedication

This book is dedicated to Marcia Selma, a close and wonderful friend, to whom I owe an enormous debt of gratitude. I fully appreciate Marcia's caring, emotional, financial, physical, spiritual and unfailing support, particularly during those difficult times. Then her help with my successful efforts to rebuild my confidence and to complete this small textbook are very much appreciated.

Acknowledgements

Of all those who inspired me to write book this book, I am especially indebted to Mrs. Lucy Mae Kum, my first accounting teacher at Caribbean Union College on the island of Trinidad; my niece Mrs. Jean V. Greaves, who is a banker; Monsieur Daun Diffey, Manager, Logistics, Advanced Leadership Program at the Canada School of Public Service and the Honourable Dennis Kellman, M.P., the elected parliamentary representative for the parish of St. Lucy on the island of Barbados for their unwittingly being the four main catalysts, from totally differing fields of endeavour, living thousands of miles apart, and partially unacquainted with each other, for my being able to begin, continue to working on and eventually completing this small educational and professional work. Finally, I am grateful to a number of accounting students and fellow practitioners, particularly Mrs. Rosalind Ho, Certified Management Accountant.

Glossary or Some Commonly Used Accounting, Delegation of Authority and Financial Management Terminology

The accountancy profession and accountants who practice in private and public sector organizations, in some aspects, do not differ very much from many other professional bodies and fellow practitioners when it comes to mode of speech. For instance, accountants speak their own language which often seems intended to bemuse or befuddle the non-accountant, both public servant and non-public servant alike. The definitions of commonly used accounting, delegation of authority and financial management terms which follow may help a bit to solve this age old problem.

Authority: The power delegated in the government of Canada by Cabinet Ministers which provides the said power to temporary and positions held by decision makers at varying levels of responsibility. These in turn effect changes and make significant decisions in the government. In addition, one financial classification is designated as authority.

Absorption costing: A system of costing which is designed to attribute overhead or burden costs, also known as indirect costs, to a particular product, service or cost centre.

Account: A separate record which shows the changes in each asset, liability, owners' equity, revenue or expense item.

Accounting equation: The equation which states that assets must always equal owners' equity plus liabilities held by a firm. [*Assets = (Owners' Equity + Liabilities)*].

Accounting period: The period of time which is covered by the income statement and other financial statements which report a firm's operating results.

Accounts payable: Those to whom a firm or individual owes money. In the balance sheet, the accounts payable balance is the amount owing by the firm to individuals and other firms. In the United Kingdom these customers are called 'creditors' on companies' balance sheets.

Accounts receivable: Those who owe money to the business, for example, customers who buy on credit terms. In the balance sheet, the accounts receivable balance is the total amount owing by those who owe the firm money. In the United Kingdom, on companies' balance sheets, these clients are known as 'debtors'.

Accrual basis of accounting: Recognizes the effect on which those transactions and events occur, whether there has been a receipt or payment of cash or its equivalent. Accrual accounting encompasses deferrals that occur when a cash receipt or payment occurs prior to the criteria for the recognition of revenue or expense being satisfied. (*CICA Handbook* 1000.46)

Accruals: The accruals concept requires that a business take account of all expenses incurred in the period, whether or not they have been actually paid for. This generally accepted accounting concept is also known as the 'matching concept'. In the 1984 Report to Parliament, the Auditor General for Canada recommended that departments and agencies comply with the concept of applying full accrual accounting to their financial records. Previous to that, the partial accrual concept had been applied.

Accrued expenses: These are expenses that have been incurred but not paid as yet. They include employee salaries, commissions, taxes, interest, etc.

Accrued revenues: These are incomes that have been earned but for which cash has not yet been received.

Activity-based costing: A system of costing that is *designed* to relate overhead costs to their use by the products of activities which drive those costs in a business. In the government of Canada, the *Treasury Board* has issued its own policy, *"Guide to the Costing of Outputs",* to apply this concept in public sector organizations.

Aging accounts receivable: The classification of accounts receivable according to how long they have been outstanding. An appropriate amount of loss may be applied to each age group in order to estimate probable loss from non-collectable accounts.

Amortization: Sometimes used synonymously with the term depreciation, this term denotes the allocation of the historical cost of a capital asset over its useful life. It may be also described as the gradual planned reduction in the value of capital expenses.

Annual Appropriation Act: An appropriation Act is a legislative motion (or bill) which authorizes the government to spend money. It is a bill that provides the ultimate authority for individuals with the delegated authority to spend specific monies. In most democracies, approval of the legislature is necessary for the government to spend money. In a parliamentary system, the defeat of an appropriation bill in a parliamentary vote generally necessitates either the resignation of a government or the calling of a general election.

Annual Reference Level Update (ARLU): The Annual Reference Level Update (ARLU) is an annual process where three-year forecasts are revised and agreed upon by departments and the Treasury Board of Canada Secretariat.

Appropriation: Oftentimes known as a "vote", this term denotes any authority of Parliament to pay money out of the Consolidated Revenue Fund (CRF) [See *Financial Administration Act* - definitions].

Assets: Assets are what an individual or business **owns.** Assets include current assets, long term assets, financial assets, fixed assets and non-financial assets. They are also economic resources controlled by a government. Assets have three essential characteristics: (1) They embody future benefits which involve a capacity, singly, or in combination with other assets to provide future net cash flows, or to provide goods and services. (2) The government can control access to such a benefit. (3) The transaction or event giving rise to the government's rights to, or control of the benefit has already occurred. [*PSAAB Handbook* 3150.04]

Audit: An examination of the financial status and operations of an enterprise, mostly on the books of account, and undertaken to secure information or to check the accuracy of the enterprise's balance sheet, income statement or surplus statement.

Audit report: Every limited company and public sector organization is subject to an annual audit. An audit is an independent examination of the financial records and statements of the business by an auditor. In an audit report, usually completed after the audit is finished, the auditor expresses an opinion as to the truth and fairness of the financial statements.

Audit trail: A chain of events and references which make it possible to trace information about transactions through an accounting system.

Bad debts: Debts which are irrecoverable and charged to revenue in the profit and loss account as an expense.

Balance Sheet: A statement showing the financial position of a business as at a certain point in time. The balance sheet lists the various open balances on the ledger accounts found in the general ledger at the year end. These balances may be assets, liabilities or owners' equity. The balance sheet may also be described as an accounting statement which displays the assets, liabilities and owners' equity balances of a firm.

Bills payable: Technically, these are unconditional orders in writing upon the enterprise by another enterprise or person for the payment of a sum of money. In practice they usually represent bank loans payable.

Book value (of a firm): Assets minus liabilities.

BOSR: The Treasury Board of Canada in 2008 approved the Budget Office Systems Renewal (BOSR) Project. BOSR is designed to replace various legacy information systems that support critical government-wide expenditure management processes such as Main Estimates and Annual Reference Level Updates (ARLU).

Bottom line: A business's net profit or loss after taxes for a specific accounting period.

Break-even point: That point at which a business no longer incurs a loss but has not yet made a profit. The break-even point can be expressed in total dollars of revenue exactly offset by total expenses or total units of production, the cost of which equals exactly the income derived from their sale.

British North America Acts 1867: A set of ancient legislation, more recently repatriated to become the *Constitution Acts 1867*, which governed the fledging Dominion of Canada and nowadays the independent nation of Canada. The focus on the Consolidated Revenue Fund (CRF) remains one of the key components for accounting, delegation of authority and financial management in the government of Canada.

Budget: The development of a set of financial goals. A business is then evaluated by measuring its performance in terms of these goals. The budget contains projections for cash inflows and outflows and other balance sheet items.

Capital: The net worth of a company's assets.

Capital assets: Comprising mainly property, plant, equipment and intangible properties, these identifiable assets meet the following criteria. (1) They are held in use for producing or supplying goods and services, for rental to others, for administrative purposes or for developing, constructing, maintaining or repairing other capital assets. (2) They have been acquired, constructed or developed with the intention of being used on a continuing basis. (3) They are not intended for sale in the ordinary course of business. (*CICA Handbook* 3060.04)

Capital employed: This is the effective amount of money that is being used in the business. This can be the total of owners' equity funds plus long term debt. It may be also referred to as fixed assets plus net current assets.

Capital expenses: Expenses incurred on acquiring fixed assets. In addition, in the government of Canada, they may comprise one of the five classes of votes or appropriations, called a capital expenditure vote, approved by Parliament in the *Annual Appropriation Acts.*

Capital invested: The actual amount of money, or 'money's worth', brought into a business by the proprietor, other investors or owners from their outside interests.

Cash budget: A calculation of expected future receipts and payments to determine the net inflows and outflows for each future period (for example, annually, monthly or quarterly or weekly).

Chart of accounts: A list of number and titles of a business's general ledger accounts.

Closing entries: Entries made at the end of an accounting period to reduce the balances of revenue and expense accounts to zero. Most businesses close the books at the end of each month and at the end of the year.

Conservatism: An accounting concept whereby revenues and profits are not anticipated, but provision is made for all known liabilities. This is also known as the 'prudence' concept.

Consistency: An accounting concept which requires that there should be consistency of accounting treatments with items within each accounting period from one period to the next.

Consolidated Revenue Fund (CRF): The aggregate of all monies on deposit, managed by the federal Minister of Finance and controlled by the Receiver General for Canada. Legislated authority is required under the *Annual Appropriation Acts*, the *Financial Administration Act* and other legislation controlling individual departments and agencies, to withdraw monies from the CRF.

Contingent liabilities: Obligations that may materialize sometime in the future, but relate to transactions that have occurred on or before the accounting report date (that is, the balance sheet date). These potential obligations or liabilities depend on some uncertain future event. Some appear as notes to financial statements such as the cost of cleaning up mine tailings in Canada's cold north or the cost of possible lawsuits the government may have to settle out of court. Others represent funds collected from third parties in advance, with whom the Treasury Board has authorized via one of its five specified purpose accounts.

Contract: An agreement between two or more parties containing clear economic consequences that the agreeing parties have little, if any, discretion to avoid, usually because the agreement is enforceable at law. Contracts, and thus financial instruments, may take a variety of forms and need not be in writing. (*CICA Handbook* 3860.06)

Control account: A control account usually summarizes individual accounts receivable [sales ledger control] or individual accounts payable [purchases ledger control]. They are also certain kinds of bank or reconciliation accounts. The Receiver General for Canada, plus all departments and agencies maintain approximately six (6) debit and credit control or bank accounts.

Cost centre: A business, or a part thereof, that operates within a cost budget, being the purchase cost or cost of manufacture. The cost of sales [also called the cost of goods sold – COGS] may be calculated as: opening inventory plus purchases minus closing inventory.

Credit: An amount entered on the right side of an account in double-entry accounting. A decrease in asset and expense accounts; and an increase in liability, capital and income accounts.

Creditor: A company or individual to whom the business owns money. [See accounts payable]

Current asset: Any asset other than a fixed asset. Current assets are either cash or can be reasonably expected to become cash or be converted to cash within one year from the date of the balance sheet. Examples include accounts receivable, loans receivable, inventory and prepaid items.

Current ratio: A dependable indication of liquidity computed by dividing current assets by current liabilities. A ratio of 2.0 may be considered acceptable for most businesses.

Current liabilities: Claims on the business by outsiders, which are payable within twelve months of the balance sheet date. Examples include accounts payable, loans payable and tax liabilities.

Debit: An amount entered on the left side of an account found in double entry accounting. A decrease in liabilities, capital and income accounts; and an increase in asset and expense accounts.

Deficit: When appearing in the balance sheet, represents the amount by which assets fall short of equaling the sum of liabilities (creditors' claims) and owners' equity. When appearing in an income statement, usually represents the amount which revenues fall short of equaling expenses and charges. An "operating deficit" means a loss before deducting fixed charges.

Deferred revenue: A local government may receive amounts before the transactions or events that give rise to the revenues. These amounts should not be included in revenue, but would not be considered a revenue until the local government discharges the obligations that led to the collection of refunds. For example, depending on the underlying agreement or legislation, some development changes, fees, tariffs and other contributions may be deferred revenues. (*PSAB Handbook,* 1800.40)

Delegated authority: The process where authority is delegated from a minister to his or her deputy head and subsequently to positions in the government department or agency. *Delegatus non potest delegare* emphasizes that delegated authority cannot be re-delegated without the permission of the one who has first delegated such a level of authority.

Depreciation: A measure of wearing out, consumption or other loss of value of a fixed asset arising from its use, passage of time or obsolescence through technology and market changes.

Depreciation should be allocated to accounting periods so as to charge a proportion of cost to each accounting period during the expected useful life of each fixed asset.

In his 1984 Report to Parliament, the Auditor General for Canada recommended that fixed assets owned by government departments and agencies be capitalized and depreciated instead of being charged to expense.

Direct costs: These costs, also known as **variable costs,** can be identified with specific products or services, for example, direct materials, direct labour and direct overhead.

Double entry: An ingenious system of accounting or bookkeeping purported to have been invented by Father Luca Pacioli, for recording business transactions in journals and ledger accounts. Broadly speaking, **increases** in assets and **decreases** in liabilities and capital items are known as *debits*, and **increases** in liabilities and capital items and **decreases** in assets are known as **credits.**

Drawings: Cash or goods withdrawn from a business by a sole proprietor or partner for his or her own use.

EID: The division of the Treasury Board of Canada referred to as EMIS (Expenditure Management System) has been renamed the Expenditure Information Division (EID). This name change better reflects the division's fundamental mandate: to provide enhanced financial, management and performance information.

Entity concept: The concept that the business entity should be considered as separate from the owners of such a business.

Expenses: The cost of resources consumed in and identifiable with the operations of the accounting period. [*PSAAB Handbook,* 1500.93]

Federal Accountability Act: Enacting the *Conflict of Interest Act,* this piece of legislation also makes consequential amendments in furtherance of that Act. That Act sets out substantive prohibitions governing public office holders. Compliance with the Act is deemed a term and condition of a public office holder's appointment or employment. The Act also sets out a detailed regime of compliance measures to ensure conformity with the substantive prohibitions, certain ones of which apply to all public office holders and others of which apply to reporting to public office holders. The Act also provides for a regime of detailed post-employment rules. Finally, the Act established a complaints regime, sets out the powers of investigation of the Commissioner and provides for public reporting as well as a regime of administrative monetary penalties.

Financial planning: The process of estimating a firm's funding needs and deciding how to finance those funds.

Financial statements: The periodic reports that summarize the financial affairs of a business.

Fiscal year: Any 12-month period used by a business as the basis for computing and reporting profits or losses.

First in, first out method (FIFO): A method of valuing inventory which assumes that the first items purchased are the first items to be sold. When ending inventory is computed the costs of the latest purchases are used.

Fixed assets: These assets are intended for use on a continuing basis in a business's activities. For example, they include land, buildings, plant, machinery, furniture and fixtures. In the government of Canada, the Treasury Board of Canada has recommended in its Accounting Standards that a threshold of $10,000.00 be used to determine whether these kind of items be capitalized and depreciated.

Fixed costs: Costs that do not vary in total during a period even though the volume of goods manufactured may be higher or lower than anticipated. It should be remembered, however, that all fixed costs vary in the long run. [See definition of variable costs].

Foreign exchange rate: The price at which a currency of one country can be bought or sold with the currency of another country. For example, on average, it takes two Canadian dollars to purchase one pound sterling in the United Kingdom.

General journal: Used to record all the transactions of a business. Transactions are listed in chronological order and transferred or posted to individual accounts in the general ledger. Specific numbers are usually assigned to each account in a general ledger.

Generally Accepted Accounting Principles (GAAP): A set of accounting principles which have been researched, developed, commented on, generally accepted and documented by professionally qualified accountants the world over. In the public sector, specific kinds of generally accepted accounting principles also exist.   [See GAPSAP].

Going concern concept: With this concept, normally adopted in drawing up the accounts of a business, one assumes that the enterprise will continue in operational existence for the foreseeable future. The profit and loss account and balance sheet are based on the assumption that there is no intention or necessity to liquidate assets and liabilities prematurely. [The foreseeable future is generally taken as being a minimum of six months following the date of the audit report or one year after the balance sheet date, whichever period ends on the later date]. For example in recent times, firms such as Altmans and Arthur Anderson in the United States have ceased to be going concerns. The governments of Indonesia and New Zealand seemed to have come quite close to no longer being going concerns also.

Goodwill: The value of a business over and above the value of its tangible net assets, for example, the value placed on a business's reputation or the worth of a skilled, well-motivated workforce. [See paragraph on 'Human Resource Accounting' which appears in Chapter 25 of this text]. This calculation normally appears in the accounts of companies as a result of takeover activity, when it represents a calculated difference between the amount paid and the net intangible assets acquired.

Gross profit: The excess of sales revenue over the cost of sales.

Gross profit margin: An indicator of the percentage of each sales dollar remaining after a business has paid for its goods. This margin is computed by dividing the gross profit by the sales.

Guide to Financial Administration: A document in which a detailed series of policies on financial administration were developed and documented by the Treasury Board of Canada. *The Financial Information Strategy Manual* and the *Comptrollership Manual* replace this policy document.

Indirect costs: Those costs that cannot be identified with particular products or services, for example, the rates on a factory building. Those are considered a fixed cost as they do not vary directly with the level of production. [See direct costs]. It must be once more remembered that **all** fixed costs vary in the long run.

Interest: The price charged or paid for the use of money or credit. For example, financial institutions and the Canada Revenue Agency tend to be consistent when calculating interest to be paid or received.

Intangible assets: These assets have long term value to the business, but have no physical existence. For example, intangible assets include goodwill, copyrights and patents.

Inventories: Stores supplies of goods or raw materials. Inventories are usually broadly classified as materiel, work in progress and finished goods.

Investment centre: An investment centre comprises a business unit in which the manager is normally accountable for sales revenue and expenses but in addition is responsible for some capital investment decisions.

Invoice: A bill for the sale of goods or services sent by the seller to the purchaser.

Last in, first out method (LIFO): A method of valuing inventory which assumes that the last items purchased are the first items to be sold. The cost of the ending inventory is computed by using the cost of the earlier purchases. [See Average and FIFO methods]

Liabilities: Amounts **owed** by an individual or a company. They may be payable within twelve months of the balance sheet date or after twelve months. These are financial obligations to outside individuals and organizations as a result of transactions and events which occurred on or before the accounting date. They are usually the result of contracts, agreements and legislation in force at the accounting date that require the government to repay borrowings or to pay for goods and services acquired or provided prior to the accounting date. [*PSAAB Handbook*, 1500.39]

Long term liabilities: Liabilities that will not be due for more than a year in the future.

Luca Pacioli: Fifteenth century Roman Catholic friar and purported father of the concept of debit and credit.

Matching: See 'accruals'.

Mesopotamia: Reputed ancient birthplace of accounting.

Management, Resources, and Results Structure (MRRS): Originally brought into effect on April, 2008, the MRRS reinforces the government's commitment to strengthen its management and accountability of public expenditures by providing a modern expenditure management framework.

Net book value: The balance sheet value of an asset, that is, cost less accumulated amortization or depreciation.

Net current assets: Current assets minus current liabilities.

Net loss: The amount by which expenses are greater than revenue. On an income statement this figure is usually listed as both a pre-tax and an after-tax figure.

Net profit margin: The measure of a business's success with respect to earnings on sales. It is derived by dividing the net profit by the sales. A higher margin means the firm is more profitable.

Net realizable value: The actual or estimated selling price of an asset, net of the expenses of sale.

Net sales: Gross sales less returns and allowances and sales discounts.

Net working capital: Defined as current assets minus current liabilities; it may be used as an indication of the liquidity of a business from one year to another.

Net worth: See owners' equity.

Operating Cycle: The period of time that it takes a business to buy inputs, make or market a product and collect the cash from the customer.

Operating profit margins: The rates of profits earned from operations, excluding taxes and interest from consideration.

Owners' equity: The financial interest of the owner(s) of a business. The total of all owners' equity is equal to a business's assets minus its liabilities. The owners' equity represents total investments in the business plus or minus any profits or losses the business has accrued to date.

Partnership: The form of a business whose legal structure is owned by two or more persons.

Percentage of completion method: A method of accounting that recognizes revenue proportionately with the degree of completion of goods or services under a contract. [*CICA Handbook* 3400.05]

Petty cash fund: A fund from which non-cheque expenditures are reimbursed.

Posting: This is the process of transferring data from a journal to a ledger.

Program Activity Architecture (PAA): The PAA is a structured inventory of a department's programs. These programs are arranged in a hierarchical manner depicting the logical relationship between each program and the department's Strategic Outcomes to which they contribute. In Section 6.1.12 of its policy on MRRS, the Treasury Board of Canada defines the requirements for a PAA as follows: (a) Identify and group related program activities and link them logically to the Strategic Outcomes which they support. (b) Provide the framework to link planned resource allocations to each program activity at all levels of the PAA and against which financial results are reported. (c) Provide the framework to link expected results to each program activity at all levels and for which actual results are reported. (d) Provide the framework for those responsible for program activities at each level of the PAA so they can commit to the results they intend to achieve with the resources they have been allocated and for which they report inside and outside departmental management. (e) Establish the structure for Estimates display and parliamentary reporting. (f) Serve as the basis for resource allocation by Parliament, Treasury Board and departmental management. (g) Provide the foundation for constructing those horizontal program activity architectures involving more then one department.

Prepaid expenses: Expense items that are paid for prior to their use. Some examples are insurance, rent and prepaid inventory purchase.

Profit and loss account: Statement of the revenue, expenses, profit or loss of a company for a particular period. [See income statement].

Profit centre: A business unit for which the manager is accountable for the sales revenue and expenses. For example, a division of a company is responsible for the selling and production of a product. [See for contrast the definition of a cost centre].

Provision for bad and doubtful accounts: An amount set aside out of profit, in line with the concept of prudence, to allow for possible non-payment by some of the firm's current debtors. In the simplest procedure the provision is a fixed percentage, say 5%, being in line with the past experience of the business with accounts receivable.

Prudence: See definition of conservatism.

Public money: All monies belonging to Canada received or collected by the Receiver General for Canada or any other public officer in his or her official capacity or any person authorized to receive or collect such monies, and includes: (1) Duties and revenues of Canada; (2) Money borrowed by Canada or received through the sale of securities; (3) Money received or collected for or on behalf of Canada; and (4) All money that is paid to or received or collected by a public trust officer under or pursuant to any Act, trust, treaty, undertaking or contract and is to be disbursed for a purpose specified in or pursuant to that Act, trust, treaty, undertaking or contract. [See *Financial Administration Act* definitions].

Ratio analysis: An analysis involving the comparison of two individual items on financial statements. One item is divided by the other and the relationship is expressed as a ratio.

Residual value: The estimated net realizable value of a tangible capital asset at the end of its useful life to a government. [*PSAAB Handbook*]

Responsibility Centre: A segment of an organization where an individual manager is responsible for the segment's performance. [See cost centre, profit centre, investment centre]. Responsibility is also one of the four main areas of classification used in the government of Canada. [See other classifications].

Revenue: The income that results from the sale of products or services or from the use of investments or property. In essence, revenue may be defined as that which a business **earns.**

Salvage value: The estimated net realizable value of a capital asset at the end of its useful life. Salvage is normally negligible [*CICA Handbook* 3060.15]

Scotland: The birthplace of accounting in the western world.

Standardized financial statements: These comprise a method of comparing the balance sheets and income statements of departments and agencies which may have different sizes of assets, liabilities, incomes and expenses.

Statement of funds flows: A financial statement that traces funds inflows and outflows originating in operating, capital and transfer payment financing activities.

Straight-line depreciation: Depreciating an asset by dollar amounts each year over the estimated life of the asset. [This is the method recommended for use in the government of Canada by the *Treasury Board Standards* whenever the historical cost of a particular fixed asset is at or above the suggested threshold of $ 10,000].

Tangible capital assets: Non-financial assets having physical substance acquired, constructed or developed that: (1) Are held for use in production or supply of goods and services; (2) Are intended to be used on a continuing basis with their useful lives extending beyond an accounting period; and (3) Are not intended for sale in the ordinary course of operations. [*PSAAB Handbook* 3150.04]

Trial balance: A memorandum listing all of the ledger account balances. Under the **double** entry system, the total of **debits** equal the **credits**---hence the notion of balancing.

Useful life: The estimate of either the period over which a tangible capital asset is expected to be used by a business, or the number of production or similar units that can be obtained from the tangible capital asset by the firm. The actual life of a tangible capital asset, other than land, is finite. It is normally the shortest of the physical, technological, commercial and legal life. [*PSAAB Handbook,* 3150.04]

Variable costs: Costs that vary in total directly with the level of output. [Please remember that **all** fixed costs become variable in the long run]

Westminster Model: A democratic system of government bequeathed to and practiced in varying forms by Commonwealth nations, including Canada, originating in the United Kingdom whose seat is located in Westminster, London, England.

Work in progress: Manufactured products that are only partially completed at the end of the accounting cycle.

Working capital: Inventories, called stocks in United Kingdom, plus accounts receivable, listed as debtors in the United Kingdom, minus accounts payable, known as creditors in the United Kingdom. This is the capital required to fund the firm's operating cycle. When computing the amount of working capital required, it is usual to exclude cash, whereas in assessing the amount of working capital in use, cash is normally included.

Introduction

OBJECTIVES OF THE TEXTBOOK

The objectives of this accounting, delegation of authority and financial management textbook are to:

1. Introduce the reader and course or workshop participant to the individual and combined concepts which remain to this day the government of Canada's general approach to accounting, delegation and financial management. To exercise and implement these concepts economically, effectively, efficiently and with excellent quality also remains paramount.

2. Provide the reader and course or workshop participant with imaginary, practical examples of this inter-related core concept.

3. Allow the reader and course or workshop participant to implement these ideas and concepts in her or his day to day function as an accountant, bookkeeper, consultant, financial officer or any decision maker who is either in the employ of or contracted with a particular firm.

INTRODUCTION

Some years ago the Public Accounts Committee of the government of Canada summoned an elected official to answer the following loosely paraphrased question:

"…Did you, honourable sir, have the authority to make certain decisions and take certain actions on behalf of the government of Canada, which may have both resulted in the spending of the government of Canada's public monies?…"

The answer to that fundamental question and its authoritative and practical application, both remain paramount to private and specifically public sector decision makers. While exercising delegated authority, combined with applying the basic accounting concept that in each bookkeeping entry *left must always equal right,* and while managing government finances, the suggested answers provided in this textbook comprise a joint fundamental accounting, delegation of authority and financial management principle. These answers attempt to form the central core of a combination of accounting, delegation of authority and financial management functions in the government of Canada. This principle core helps to work as a fiscal catalyst to effective decision making.

In most private sector business environments, and even more so in those surrounding public sector organizations, especially government departments such as the Department of National Defence, whose annual budget exceeds 10 billion of Canadian taxpayers' dollars, the application of these fundamental concepts have sometimes proven not only to be unnecessarily complicated, but also very challenging, fiscally and politically rewarding. Complications arise because the combination of exercising delegated authority, complying with generally public sector accounting principles and effective financial management produces the type of information which one middle level manager in the Canadian government described as:

"...almost akin to possessing raw political power..."

However, the users, and unfortunately often abusers, of delegated authority who are usually the government of Canada's vital decision makers are often motivated to manage their organizations by methods and motives by which they use the very information reported on their firms' accounting, financial and operational systems. This information needs not only to be accurate; it must be also complete, free from the bias of undue influence, precise, relevant and timely.

Canadian governments started with rule making, the primary focus of this accounting textbook. The *British North America Acts of 1867*, repatriated to become the *Constitution Acts of 1867*, remain one of the first. This rule making leads next to policy setting. Hence the Treasury Board of Canada created the *Guide to Financial Administration.* In later years, this policy setting evolved to standard setting, found in such standards which formed a part of the old *Comptrollership Manual*, the latter giving way to the current *Financial Information Strategy Manual.* Now, standard setting and rule making have resulted in the creation of various types of regulations. Regulations, in turn, have become the basis of generally accepted public sector accounting principles, recommended by the *Canadian Institute of Chartered Accountants' Public Sector Accounting and Auditing Board.* The second part of the three dimensioned focus of this accounting text describes the absolute necessity for compliance by government departments and agencies to generally accepted public sector accounting principles.

This entire inter-related concept, in addition to the actual spending of pubic monies in the government of Canada, may be seen to work during the process of the management and control of the Consolidated Revenue Fund (CRF), bequeathed to Canadians by the *British North America Acts.*

OUTLINE OF THE TEXT

The division of this textbook into five parts attempts to achieve the above-mentioned ideas and goals. Part I presents the theories and practices of exercising delegated authority. Part II comprises the theories associated with generally accepted public sector accounting principles. Part III details the practical application of Parts I and II. Part IV describes those systems and procedures designed for operating a business. The final part, Number V, also includes a chapter comprising present issues and topics which have continued and will continue to make an impact on financial management in the government of Canada. Twenty five chapters make up this accounting text. The author has attempted gradually and progressively to show how these key inter-related concepts have worked, now work, and will in all likelihood continue to work together in reality to benefit most Canadian accounting principles. (GAPSAP) A bibliography, case studies, a glossary, problems, quizzes and solutions all support this textbook.

ORGANIZATION OF THE TEXT

This introduction to the textbook sets the tone of the book's objectives. These objectives depend on the history of how the exercise of delegating authority surfaced, and how the history of accounting came into being. The history of the latter is older but not as profound as that of the former. These two histories, which started about two centuries from each other, merged as the keeping of records, of collecting and expending funds was first approved by a British Parliament, later on by a Dominion of Canada Parliament. Finally, an independent Canadian nation continued to follow the same model of delegating authority and disseminating power as its ancient fiscal mentor, the government of the United Kingdom. The concept of a constitutional monarchy which rules indirectly or directly still influences to a significant degree the manner in which Canada is now governed, how authority is exercised, and how GAAP and GAP-SAP are applied. The text not only attempts to narrate the merging of these two histories, it also describes how the practices of exercising delegated authority and implementing GAAP and GAPSAP obtain both in private and public sector firms. Practical examples are given in an attempt to follow the majority of these concepts. In addition, a step by step review of applying the more salient features of GAAP and GAPSAP, as recommended by the *Canadian Institute of Chartered Accountants* (CICA), the *Public Sector Accounting and Auditing Board* (PSAAB), The Receiver General for Canada, and The Treasury Board of Canada appears in practical examples. These examples in turn demonstrate the use of accounting principles in each transaction for accrual accounting, authority (appropriations or votes) and objects of expenditure. Selected practical examples appear detailing day-to-day operations of an imaginary accounting practice, Samuel L. Bell, Chartered Accountant. An alphabetical bibliography and glossary provide the reader and course or workshop participant with access to the principle idea(s) propounded in the text. However, the classroom or workshop instructor or co-coordinator needs to select and assign those relevant practical exercises as the latter becomes needed by participants to enhance the learning process.

The Reader Must Remember: that exercising delegated authority and implementing GAAP or GAPSAP while financially managing are inexorably linked as decision makers in the government of Canada help to provide goods and services, control and donate contributions to Canadian taxpayers, pensioners and non-Canadians. Acts of Parliament, ancient and modern, all contribute to this inter-related catalyst which drives this complex day-to-day provision of goods and services.

PART I

The Theory and Practice of Exercising Delegated Authority

This first part, on exercising delegated authority in the government of Canada, comprises Chapter One of this accounting, delegation of authority and financial management text.

Exercising Delegated Authority In the Government of Canada

OBJECTIVE OF CHAPTER ONE

The objective of this chapter is to provide the reader and course or workshop participant with the key tenets of exercising authority which have been delegated to various and sundry positions occupied permanently and temporarily by employees in the government of Canada.

INTRODUCTION

Chapter one attempts to cover the main functions of exercising delegated authority in the government of Canada. The chapter comprises its objective; a definition of authority, the theory (ies) which purport to support the exercise of delegated authority; a summary on the *British North America or Constitution Acts*; the application of the Westminster Model in the Canadian government; and a definition of the Consolidated Revenue Fund (CRF).

DEFINITION OF AUTHORITY

Authority may be defined as:

Power to enforce laws and regulations, exact obedience, command, direct or judge;

One that invested within this power, especially a government or body of government officials;

Power assigned to another or authorization;

A public agency or organization with administrative powers in a specified field—for example, city or transit authority;

An accepted source of expert information or advice;

A quotation or citation from such a source;

Justification grounds;

A conclusive statement or decision that may be taken as a guide or precedent;

Power to influence or persuade resulting from knowledge or experience;

Confidence derived from experience or practice and self assurance by such an administrative unit of government as the Central Intelligence Agency, the Bureau of Statistics, the Treasury Board Secretariat, the Office of the Comptroller General and the Receiver General for Canada;

Official permission or approval: for example, "...authority for the program was renewed several times..."

An authoritative published work: for example, *The Guide to Financial Administration, The Treasury Board Comptrollership Manual, The Financial Information Strategy Manual, The Canadian Institute of Chartered Accountants Handbook; The Public Sector Accounting and Auditing Board Handbook, and The Receiver General for Canada Directives;* and

An authoritative statement: for example, "...the Minister approved in principle...", "... the Treasury Board approved in principle...", "...Parliament voted..." and "...the responsibility centre manager, the chief of administration, exercised her delegated authority..."

THEORIES SUPPORTING THE EXERCISE OF DELEGATED AUTHORITY

Introduction

In private sector organizations, authority may be derived from the executive committee minutes. In the government of Canada, authority is delegated outwards from each elected minister of government via an appointed public servant, usually the deputy minister or president, to various positions held temporarily or permanently by one or more public servants in each department and/or agency.

The legal theories revolving around this delegation of authority often focus on this maxim: *"...delegatus non potest delegare..."* This delegated authority to spend public monies out of the CRF originally derived its legal power from the *British North America or Constitution Acts, 1867.*

The British North America or Constitution Acts, 1867

The British North America Acts 1867 to 1975, comprises a series of Acts of Parliament passed by the government of the United Kingdom dealing with the Dominion of Canada, the territory formerly known as "British North America" until 1867. The first and foremost important act in the series, the *British North America Act, 1867* (now repatriated as *The Constitution Act, 1867*), was passed in 1867, and created the self-governing Dominion of Canada. Canada and other British dominions achieved full legislative sovereignty with the passage of the *Statute of Westminster, 1931,* but prior to the *Canada Act 1982;* the *British North America Acts* were excluded from the *Statute of Westminster* and could only be amended by the British Parliament. This long delay was in a large part due to the inability to create a constitutional amendment procedure which was acceptable to all of the provinces, particularly Quebec.

In 1982, spearheaded by the then Prime Minister, Pierre Elliott Trudeau, Canada repatriated its constitution and entrenched it within the *Charter of Rights and Freedoms,* through the *Constitution Act, 1982,* which established a procedure for the amendment of the Canadian Parliament. The *British North America Acts 1867 to 1975* were generally named the *Constitution Acts* in Canada and together with the *Constitution Act, 1982,* are collectively known as the *Constitution Acts 1867 to 1982,* though in the United Kingdom they remain named as they originally were.

Delegation of Authority

A department or agency head (deputy minister or president) may delegate in writing the authority delegated to him or her by a department's minister, by Public Works and Government Services Canada (PWGSC), or by the Treasury Board of Canada. Authority which has been delegated cannot be re-delegated without the direct and indirect written authority of the deputy minister or president himself or herself or some individual superior to the individual wanting to re-delegate his or her authority temporarily or permanently. A department or agency head may also authorize the dollar amount and level of a contract as per the authority (ies) delegated to him or her by PWGSC or by the Treasury Board of Canada, and also, under Section 7 of the *Financial Administration Act*.

Limits on Exercising Authority

Authority may be limited to a dollar maximum amount (sometimes referred to on a delegation instrument as "full") and to the level of the position as documented in the department or agency's delegation of authority document or chart as approved and authorized by the deputy head and the Minister for which such a department or agency he or she is ultimately responsible.

Basic Responsibility of Individuals Exercising Delegated Authority in Government Organizations

With the exercise of delegated authority comes a commensurate, basic responsibility of all decision-makers in organizations. In this textbook, part of the focus intended for decision-maker falls on financial managers. Financial management is a very challenging and rewarding field. It is an exciting area because financial managers the world over, and particularly those in government organizations, assist ably in having been assigned part of the responsibility in planning the future growth and direction of a business---which can greatly affect the community in which it is based. For example, the military bases in Esquimault, British Columbia and Gagetown, New Brunswick, both operated by the Department of National Defence, along with the medium correctional facility in Springhill, New Brunswick, operated by Correctional Services Canada, the Experimental Farm operated by Agribusiness and the Agrifood Canada in Ottawa, Ontario, can all attest the positive effect they have had, and most likely continue to have on the communities in which they are located. Decisions reached by the financial managers ultimately represent a blend of the theoretical, technical and judgmental matters which reflect the concerns of the hinterlands of operations such as those mentioned above.

The burden of the costs associated with the environmental, ethical, moral and social considerations fall unevenly on Parliament, central agencies, departments, other agencies and subordinate organizations. For example, the Department of National Defence in any one fiscal year has had significantly more resources voted for its spending by Parliament than say, Agriculture Canada or Correctional Services Canada. Within this framework, governmental financial managers are obligated to those entrusting them with a significant share with managing their organizations by using responsibility centres. This situation the textbook will attempt to demonstrate later in further detail as to how the exercise of delegated Spending Authority by those responsibility centre managers is inextricably linked to the exercise of delegated Payment Authority either by financial officers or other decision makers at varying levels. More specifically, financial managers cannot work in a vacuum concerned only with the actual payment of cash to customers, public servants and other service providers. This approach may cause them to overlook equally important aspects of their need to assist providing those goods and services the taxpayer needs. A good decision-maker knows how to use the factors discussed above in arriving at final decisions.

APPLYING THE WESTMINSTER MODEL WHILE EXERCISING DELEGATED AUTHORITY

Introduction

The Westminster Model, a democratic parliamentary system of government modeled after that of the United Kingdom, still functions in the palace of Westminster, the location of the Parliament of the United Kingdom. This system comprises a series of procedures for operating a legislature. The system continues to be used in most Commonwealth and ex-Commonwealth countries. The practice began with the Canadian provinces in the mid-19th century. It also currently obtains in Australia, India, Ireland, Jamaica, Barbados, Malaysia, New Zealand, Singapore and Malta.

KEY CHARACTERISTICS OF THE WESTMINSTER MODEL

Important features of the Westminster Model include:

A head of state, the nominal or theoretical source of executive powers, holds numerous reserve powers, but in practice functions as a ceremonial figurehead. Such examples include the British Sovereign and the President of India.

A *de facto* head of the executive and also the Prime Minister, for example, George Brown in the United Kingdom, David Thompson in Barbados and Stephen Harper in Canada, who officially receive their appointment from the Head of State which currently is the Sovereign in the United Kingdom and the Governor General in Barbados and Canada. In practice, the Prime Minister usually functions as the leader of the largest elected party in Parliament.

A *de facto* head of the executive branch usually made up of members of the legislature with the senior members of the executive forming a Cabinet chosen and led by the Prime Minister, such members executing executive authority on behalf of the nominal or theoretical executive authority.

'Her Majesty's Opposition' which usually functions.

The ability of the lower house of Parliament, House of Commons, to, by default, dismiss a government which is in power by withholding, or blocking, "Supply", hence a rejecting a budget, by passing a no-confidence motion, or by defeating a confidence motion. Funds needed to run the government's operations may then be approved by the Governor General via the issuance of a special warrant. The Westminster Model enables a sitting government to be defeated, or forced into a general election, independently of a new government being chosen.

An elected legislature, with two houses in which at least one of which must be elected.

Parliament possesses the ability to be dissolved at any time, to call elections. Most of the procedures of the Westminster Model have originated with the convention, practices and precedents of the UK Parliament, which are part of what is known as the British Constitution. However, convention, practices and procedures continue to play a significant role in these countries, as many constitutions do not specify important elements of procedure. For example, older constitutions in the Westminster Model, such as Australian and the Canadian constitutions, may not even mention the existence of the Cabinet and the titular head of the government, usually a Prime Minister, as these offices' existence and role were developed outside the primary constitutional context.

Criticisms of the Westminster Model

Critics often postulate that the Westminster Model breeds a variety of political cultures which determine its effectiveness in a truly democratic, accountable system of government. The critics also argue that the office of a prime minister in the Westminster Model often wields too much power. He or she effectively determines when "consensus" occurs in Cabinet. Cabinet members do not seem to have that degree of independence where they can actively disagree with government policy, even for productive means. Memories of *Boudria versus a Liberal Canadian Cabinet* come to mind. A Cabinet member such as Boudria may be forced to resign simply for opposing one aspect of the government's agenda, even though he or she may agree with the majority of the proposals. Westminster Model Cabinets also have to be large, mostly for political reasons. Cabinet, the chief organ of power and influence in the government, sometimes creates resentment in members of Parliament considered to be "back benchers". Although party discipline ensures that no-confidence votes are very rare, this also eliminates the usefulness of such votes as an active way of holding an incumbent government accountable. Sometimes then, implementing important policies and approving legislation such as the Canadian government's *Treasury Board Accountability Framework* and its *Federal Accountability Act* become highly improbable and at times well-nigh impossible.

THE CONSOLIDATED REVENUE FUND (CRF)

The Consolidated Revenue Fund (CRF), an aggregate of all public monies on deposit with government departments and agencies in the government of Canada, was created initially by the *British North America Act, 1867.* Funds are deposited either by the Canada Revenue Agency which collects taxes and custom duties or other departments and agencies, the latter of whom may charge user fees. The Minister of Public Works and Government Services Canada (PWGSC) or the Receiver General for Canada, **manages** the CRF and the Minister of Finance **controls** the CRF. A decision maker, employed by the government of Canada, in which position he or she temporarily or permanently holds, the latter to which has been delegated the commensurate authority, can exercise this authority under relevant sections of the *Financial Administration Act (FAA)*, ostensibly to request the Receiver General for Canada to spend funds from the CRF.

The Reader Should Remember: That before any action is taken affecting the program activities and/or operations of any government department or agency; authority must first be delegated and properly authorized. Approval alone is not authorization. The Treasury Board may approve, usually "in principle", but only Parliament can authorize. The level of delegated authority may be derived from the Annual Appropriation Acts, the Financial Administration Act or any other legislation voted by Parliament which ultimately controls the functions of a particular government organization. After the authorized events have taken place, it is then the responsibility of some employed decision maker to implement GAAP to record the increases and decreases associated with the assets, liabilities, expenses, revenues and owners' equity associated with the said events.

PART II

The Theories Associated
with GAPSAP

Part II, comprising chapters two to five, describes mainly the theories associated with GAPSAP. Chapter Two recounts the history of accounting and introduces the reader to the definition of GAAP. Chapter Three outlines those organizations and individuals which make a direct and indirect impact on accounting, delegation of authority and financial management in the government of Canada. Chapter Four defines classification and coding. Chapter Five provides a comprehensive view of budgetary control and the associated levels at which it is implemented.

2

The History of Accounting and the Definition of GAAP

OBJECTIVES OF CHAPTER TWO

The objective of this chapter is to:

- Provide the reader and course or workshop participant with a brief insight into the history and evolution of accounting; and

- Assist the reader and course or workshop participant to better understand initially how to apply GAAP and GAPSAP.

INTRODUCTION

After the advent and proliferation of charging, collecting and spending user fees in government departments and agencies, one of the major principles involved determining the cost of operations associated with collecting fees. In this way, the decision maker could discover whether any profit, loss or break-even resulted from the various transactions. To meet this and other related needs, the *Canadian Institute of Chartered Accountants (CICA),* selected private sector experts and the *Canadian Academic Accounting Association* worked together to formulate related accounting and auditing principles for public sector organizations. After this series of meetings, the *Public Sector Accounting and Auditing Board (PSAAB)* was created.

This chapter comprises the history and evolution of accounting, the principles of accounting as expounded by the *CICA,* the *Certified General Accountants of Canada (CGA)*, the *Society of Management Accountants of Canada (CMA)*, the *Public Sector Accounting and Auditing Board (PSAAB),* the *Treasury Board of Canada Accounting Standards (TBAS)*, and the Treasury Board of Canada's *Comptrollership* and *Financial Information Strategy (FIS)* Manuals: particularly their use, relevance and importance.

HISTORY AND EVOLUTION OF ACCOUNTING

Introduction

Unlike most other modern professions, accounting has a history of over 500 years, usually discussed in terms of one seminal event: the invention and dissemination of the double entry bookkeeping process. However, a view of accounting history that begins with Luca Pacioli's contribution seems to bypass a long evaluation of ancient and medieval accounting systems. A more fundamental question a financial pundit may well ask:

> "Why care about the history of accountancy at all?"

Certainly, a glimpse back into this period helps illuminate the past, which generally presents a sort of winding, limited path that makes for an entertaining story. Moreover, perhaps the most compelling reasons remain attempts by professional accountants and other interested parties to explain the phenomenal growth which accountancy has enjoyed internationally since the English Monarch granted Royal Charters to the *Society of Accountants* in Edinburgh more than 150 years ago.

In 1904, eighty (80) years after the emergence of a final accounting profession, about 6,000 practitioners carried the title of 'chartered accountant'. In 1957, there were only 38,690 chartered and incorporated accountants—Scottish, English and Irish. The *ACA* in England and Wales alone has a membership of 120,000 worldwide. This group excludes the many professionals in allied institutes in Barbados, Bermuda, Canada, New Zealand, Ireland, Australia, Scotland, South Africa, Trinidad & Tobago and other Commonwealth locations, along with *the American Institute of Certified Public Accountants (AICPA)* and the *International Federation of Accountants*: thus comparing a vast, worldwide method of professional accounting dominated by mammoth world-wide accounting firms.

In his work *"Ancient Accounting: Dawn of Man Through Luca Pacioli"*, A. C. Littleton, in his attempt to explain why double-entry bookkeeping developed in 14th century Italy extends to ancient Greece, lays out "seven key ingredients" that comprise the accounting profession's creation:

Private property: The power to change ownership since bookkeeping remains mainly about recording facts concerning property and property rights.

Capital: Wealth productivity employed, because, otherwise, commerce would be trivial and credit would probably not exist.

Commerce: The interchange of goods and services on a widespread level, since putting local trading in a small volume would tend to create the sort of press of business needed to spur the creation of an organized system thus replacing the existing ledger pages of record keeping.

Credit: The present use of future goods or services, because, there would have been little impetus to record transactions completed on the spot.

Writing: A mechanism for keeping a permanent record in a common language, given the limits of human memory.

Money: The "common denominator" for exchange, since there is probably no need for bookkeeping except when it reduces transactions to a set of monetary values.

Arithmetic: A means of computing the details of a particular deal.

Many of these factors did exist in ancient times. However, until the middle Ages, they were not found together in a firm manner with the necessary strength to push man to invent the double-entry concept. Writing, for example, remains as old as civilization itself, but arithmetic, defined as the systematic manipulation of numerical symbols, was really not a tool possessed by the ancients. Rather, the persistent use of Roman numerals in financial transactions long after the introduction of Arabic numerals appears to have hindered the earlier creation of double-entry systems.

Nevertheless, problems encountered by the ancients with record keeping, capital and verification of financial transactions were not entirely different from our current ones. Governments, in particular, had strong incentives to keep careful records of receipts and disbursements, especially those concerning taxes. Also, in any society where individuals accumulated wealth, there was a desire by the rich to perform audits on the honesty and skill of those slaves and employees entrusted with asset management.

But the last of the above-mentioned antecedents to double entry bookkeeping made the job of the ancient accountant extraordinarily difficult. In societies were nearly everybody was illiterate, writing materials costly, remuneration difficult and money systems inconsistent, a transaction needed to be extremely important to justify the making of an accounting record.

Accounting in Mesopotamia: circa 3,500 BC

Eons ago, before the appearance of dollars and cents, the Assyrian, Chaldean, Babylonian and Sumerian civilizations flourished in the Mesopotamia Valley. They produced some of the oldest known records of commerce. Babylonian became the language of business and politics throughout the Near East. More than one banking firm existed in Mesopotamia, supplying standard measures of gold and silver and extending credit on some transactions.

During this era, which lasted until 500 B.C., Sumeria was the country whose rulers held most of the land and animals in trust for their gods, giving impetus to their record keeping efforts. Moreover, the developing legal codes penalized features such as making memorials of transactions. The renowned *Code of Hammurabi,* handed down by the first dynasty of Babylonia (2285 – 2242 B. C.), for example, required that an agent selling goods for a merchant give the merchant a price quotation or at its face value, thus invalidating a questioned or questionable agreement. Therefore it is believed that most transactions were recorded and subscribed by some trading parties during this period.

The duties of the Mesopotamian equivalent of today's accountant, the scribe, appear to be similar but more extensive.

Scotland: the birthplace of modern western professional accounting

In is not unfitting when one comes to deal with modern professional accounting in the west, that Scotland should occupy the place of priority. In

Scotland the nomenclature *"Chartered Accountant"* originated. There one may also find one of the oldest existing societies of public accountants in western civilization. One must not be unmindful of the claims of Italy, to which country one is definitely indebted for so much in connection with the profession, but however important a position accountants occupied in Italy during the seventeenth and eighteenth centuries, their old Guilds and Colleges became either dominant or paradoxically extinct. In tracing the growth of the accounting profession in Scotland as elsewhere, one meets with many difficulties. In Edinburgh it was for a long time associated with the profession of law, so that we frequently find the designation of *writer* applied in one place to the same individual who in another is a designated accountant. Several members of the *Society of Writers to the Signet,* the leading *Solicitors' Society in Scotland,* practiced as accountants. Moreover, until comparatively recent times, much of the accountant's work was done in solicitors' offices. Again, to a certain extent in Edinburgh, but to a greater extent in the more commercial city of Glasgow, the designation of accountant was, in early times, a compendium of the kind of work which a Glaswegian accountant of the early part of the last century professed to undertake. The following is the list of duties James McClelland attached to a circular, dated 12th March, 1824, in which he announced that he had commenced business on his business on his account, to whit:

Factor and trustee on sequestered estates;

Trustee or factor for trustees of creditors acting under trust;

Factor for trustees acting for the heirs of persons deceased;

For a gentleman residing in the country, for the managing of his estate or other property;

Agent for houses in England and Scotland connected with enterprises in Glasgow;

The winding up of dissolved partnership concerns and adjusting partners' accounts;

Keeping and balancing all account books of merchants, manufacturers, shopkeepers, etc.

Examining and adjusting all disputed accounts and account books;

Making up statements reports and memoranda on account books or disputed and claims for the day brought before arbitrators and/or counsel;

Looking after and recognizing debts and dividends from bankrupt estates; and

All other departments and persons who practice the profession of accountancy.

On the 6th July, 1854, the *Institute of Accountants in Glasgow,* petitioned Her Majesty, Queen Victoria for its grant of a Royal Charter. The Petition, signed by 49 accountants set forth that:

The profession of an accountant had long existed in Scotland as a distinct profession of great respectability;

Originally then a member of these practicing gentlemen was fit for just that;

For many years back their members had been rapidly increasing and the profession in Glasgow then embraced mathematicians as well as other respectable bodies of persons;

The business of an accountant required, for proper practice, fit, consistent and named attainments;

The profession was not confined to the department of the actuary, which worked mainly for bankrupt individuals or companies;

It comprehended all methods connected with arithmetical calculation;

Accountants were often frequently employed by lack of law and the Courts in their investigation of the profession which while, to a greater or lesser extent, points of law that more or less apply;

They acted under which such remitted very much as the Masters in Chancery were understood in the *Act of England*; and

It was obvious that the due performance of a profession such as this liberal education was essential...

The Aberdeen Institute and *The Edinburgh Society* were incorporated later. It naturally took some time before the name became familiar to the public or even appeared in the mouths of the members themselves. However, ere long, the title *accountant* acquired a definite significance throughout Scotland, and in 1880 the same designation was adopted by *The English Institute.* Incorporated in that very year, it soon became a recognized word wherever English was spoken.

Professional World Wide Accounting Travel

In 1880, the newly formed *Institute of Chartered Accountants in England and Wales* solidified all the accounting examinations in Britain, Holland and Scotland. In addition to the 587 members initially enrolled, 606 more were soon admitted as new members. Standards of conduct and examinations for admission to membership were drawn up, and members began using the professional designation *"FCA"*, *Fellow Chartered Accountant*, by a fixed pattern as a proprietor in practice, and *"ACA"*, Associate Chartered Accountant, to signify a qualified member of an accountant's staff, or a member not in practice. By the late 1800s, large amounts of British capital were flowing towards the rapidly growing industries in the United States. Scottish and English accountants traveled to the U. S. to audit these investments, and a number of them stayed on and set up practice in America. Several American accounting firms, including the now defunct Arthur Anderson, can trace their origins to one or more of those visiting Scottish or English firms of *Chartered Accountants.*

City directories for the year 1850, listed 44 accountants in public practice in New York, 4 in Philadelphia and 1 in Chicago. By 1886, there were 115 listed in New York, 87 in Philadelphia and 31 in Chicago. Groups of accountants joined together to form professional societies in cities across America. In 1887, the country's first national accounting society was formed: *The American Association of Public Accountants*, the forerunner of the *American Institute of Certified Public Accountants (AICPA).*

Into the Twentieth Century and Beyond

The United States, though prosperous, was still an infant nation when the *AICPA* was formed. The civil wars ended with the United States still predominantly a farming-based economy. It was only the year before that the Apache Chief Geronimo had surrendered to the federal authorities. The ensuing decades saw enormous growth as industry began to overtake agriculture in financial importance. This period of growth also seemed to generate its share of financial scandals. Over-capitalization and stock speculation caused financial panics in 1873 and 1893. Stories of watered railroad stocks appeared in the headlines, along with concerns about growing monopolies in several industries. Labour unions developed in response to apparent corporate exploitation of workers. Eventually, *The Interstate Commerce Commission (ICC)* established a uniform system of accounting, the first instance of accounting used as an instrument of federal legislation.

The British at the time used the balance sheet in an effort to monitor management's use of shareholders' monies. American balance sheets were drafted mainly with bankers in mind and bankers of that era seemed to care more for a company's liquidity than its earning power.

By the turn of the century, there were at least four statements in use: summarizing changes in cash, in current assets, in working capital and in overall financial activities. During the 1940s, the accounting profession increasingly used the funds statement to measure the actual flow of monies, rather than determine the sum of working capital changes between sheet dates. The funds statement became increasingly a staple for the financial statement. In 1971, the *AICPA* began requiring this statement's inclusion in stockholders' annual reports. Nowadays, with more than 300,000 members, the *AICPA* remains the premier national professional accounting association for certified public accountants in the United States. Their website, replete with useful resources, includes the latest American accounting news, along with organization-specific materials.

SELECTED PROFESSIONAL ACCOUNTING DESIGNATIONS ISSUED IN THE UNITED KINGDOM

INSTITUTE OF CHARTERED ACCOUNTANTS OF ENGLAND AND WALES

The *ACA* designation, offered by *The Institute of Chartered Accountants of England and Wales,* is recognized as the premier financial business qualification. Intriguingly, the initials *ACA* are also advertised by the Institute as being "**A C**ut **A**bove".

ASSOCIATION OF CHARTERED CORPORATE ACCOUNTANTS

The *ACCA* is the global body for professional accountants. The association offers business-relevant, first-choice qualifications to people of application ability and ambition around the world who seek a rewarding career in accountancy, finance and management. The *ACCA* purports to use its expertise and expertise to work with governments, donor agencies and professional bodies to develop accountancy.

CHARTERED INSTITUTE OF MANAGEMENT ACCOUNTANTS

CIMA is a leading membership body that offers an internationally recognized professional qualification in management accounting. The designation focuses on accounting for business. As an organization, *CIMA* is committed to constant improvement and their reputation as a professional and regulatory body seems to have never been stronger in its corporate life. *CIMA* claims to be increasingly the first choice for students and employers in the U. K.

SELECTED PROFESSIONAL ACCOUNTING DESIGNATIONS OFFERED IN CANADA

CANADIAN INSTITUTE OF CHARTERED ACCOUNTANTS

The *CICA* is the umbrella body for chartered accountancy in Bermuda and Canada. Membership of the *CICA* totals 70,000 *Chartered Accountants (CAs)* and 8,500 students. The *CICA*, first established 1902, was called the *Dominion of Chartered Accountants (DACA)*. Milestones in the history of the *CICA* include: (1) 1922: First Canadian woman received the *CA* designation; (2) 1927: A common uniform qualifying examination was first proposed by the *DACA,* supported by all provinces, except Quebec; (3) 1939: A standardized uniform qualifying examination was extended to Quebec; (6) 1968: The *CICA Handbook*, incorporating Canadian accounting standards was first produced; (7) 1977: The *CICA* became a founding member of the *International Federation of Accountants;* (8) 2004: A proposed merger between the *CICA* and the *Society of Management Accountants of Canada (SMA)* failed through lack of membership support.

CERTIFIED GENERAL ACCOUNTANTS OF CANADA

Founded in 1908, the *CGA* is a self-regulating, professional association of 68,000 students and *CGAs. CGAs* work throughout the world in industry, commerce, finance, government, public practice and other areas where accounting and financial management are required. *CGA* clients range from major corporations and industries to entrepreneurs. Their expertise is valued in the private sector, government and corporate world.

SOCIETY OF MANAGEMENT ACCOUNTANTS OF CANADA

CMAs represent the leading strategic financial management professionals who claim to integrate accounting expertise and advanced management skills thus achieving business success.

GENERALLY ACCEPTED ACCOUNTING PRINCIPLES (GAAP)

To prepare a firm's financial statements, certain basic accounting principles need to be generally recognized and understood before individual transactions can be analyzed. These principles, generally recognized by *The International Federation of Accountants (IFAC)*, include *going concern, historical cost, matching, consistency, materiality, conservatism and substance over form*. The *going concern* principle is applied expecting that a firm, department or agency will continue to operate for the foreseeable future with no intention to curtail its operation. With the *historical cost* principle, determining a measurement base on which an item is to be recognized in financial statements remains one of the most difficult problems in accounting. A number of bases exist on which an amount of a single item may be measured; e. g. replacement cost, net realized value [the net amount that would be received from selling an asset], present value of future cash flows, market value, original cost [plus or amortization, appreciation, capital cost allowance or depreciation wherever appropriate]. The *matching principle* requires that revenue and expenses be accrued; that they be recognized as they are earned or incurred, or when they have an impact on an appropriation, not just when cash is paid out or received. There should be *consistency* of accounting treatment of like items within each accounting period to the next. *Materiality*, which describes the significance of financial statement to users, still remains a matter of judgment under particular circumstances. An item, or an aggregate of items, is considered 'material' if the probability exists that its omission of misstatement would influence or change a decision. With *conservatism,* expenses are usually over estimated and revenues mostly underestimated. With *substance over form*, financial statements should present the economic substance of transactions and events although their legal form may suggest a different treatment.

The Reader Should Remember: an ancient nation and famous individuals such as Mesopotamia, William the Conqueror and Luca Pacioli; the influence of Scotland on the nomenclature 'chartered accountant'; modern institutions such as The Canadian Institute of Chartered Accountants, The Institute of Chartered Accountants of England and Wales, The American Institute of Certified Public Accountants; and the current GAAP comprising such principles as the *going concern, historical cost, matching, consistency, materiality, conservatism and substance over form.*

3

Pivotal Individuals and Organizations that Maintain a Direct and Indirect yet Significant Impact on Accounting, Delegation of Authority and Financial Management Activities in the Government of Canada

OBJECTIVE OF CHAPTER THREE

The objective of chapter three is to provide the reader and the course or workshop participant with a small snapshot of those government organizations and individuals which have a direct and indirect yet significant impact on accounting, the exercise of delegated authority and financial management in the government of Canada.

INTRODUCTION

This chapter comprises those individuals and organizations in government, plus those mentioned previously in this text, which have a direct and indirect yet significant impact on the proper exercise of or, rather unfortunately sometimes, the abuse of delegated authority. These diametrically opposed, yet important functions are invariably implemented by those governmental individuals, operations and organizations that generate accounting, delegation of authority and financial management activities while they themselves may or may not adhere to GAPSAP. These individuals and organizations, the majority of them central agencies, include: The Sovereign of the United Kingdom and the Governor General of Canada; The House of Commons and The Senate; The Treasury Board of Canada; The Treasury Board Secretariat; The Office of the Comptroller General; The Minister of Finance; The Minister of Public Works and Government Services Canada or The Receiver General for Canada; The Auditor General for Canada; The Bank of Canada; The Public Service of Canada and The Public Service Commission.

HER MAJESTY, ELIZABETH II, QUEEN OF ENGLAND AND HER EXCELLENCY, MICHAELLE JEAN, THE GOVERNOR GENERAL OF CANADA

The government of Canada functions under a constitutional monarchy, the reigning UK monarch being Her Majesty, Queen Elizabeth II of England. In addition, *The British North America (Constitution) Act, 1982* drives important financial functions such as the fiscal workings of the Consolidated Revenue Fund (CRF), which in turn may be defined by the said *Constitution Act, 1982* as an "...aggregate of all public monies on deposit under control of the Minister of Finance and managed by the Receiver General for Canada..."

Whenever the Sovereign arrives in Canada on one of her or his official visits, she or he usually sits with the Senate and its appointed members, not among the elected "commoners" of the Lower House or House of Commons. Sometimes, depending on the time of her or his visit and the need for Parliament to vote "Supply", she or he may read the relevant Budget, which could be *the Main Estimates* or *the Supplementary Estimates.*

With the Sovereign absent, the then Governor General, the appointed incumbent being Her Excellency, Michaelle Jean, functions in the Sovereign's stead. This fiscal need for a Governor General has been tested at least four times in a Canadian parliament: when the government of the day was defeated either on a no-confidence vote or failed to succeed in having a Budget approved by the Lower House. In some instances no "Supply" was made available to carry on the day to day operations of the government. To fund vital governmental operations, the sitting Governor General usually executed her or his constitutional authority, at times signing a "special warrant."

THE ELECTED HOUSE OF COMMONS AND THE APPOINTED SENATE

After each federal election, 201 members (at a recent count) are elected to the House of Commons. The sitting Governor General or reigning Monarch then invites the leader of the ruling party which has won the election to form the government. These individuals, along with their Senate Colleagues, perform such important fiscal functions as voting *The Annual Appropriation Act,* and sitting members from both the ruling party and Her Majesty's Official Opposition who form a Public Accounts Committee with its chairperson usually being a member of the opposition. This Appropriation Bill only lasts for 12 months, its authority lapsing on March 31 of each year. Public servants usually remark that "…funds lapse…." That phrase is a bit of misnomer. Funds do not lapse. Public monies remain in the CRF. What lapses is the *authority* to spend funds out of the CRF, since the legal right to spend which was provided by *The Annual Appropriation Act* no longer exists. This remains crucial to the day to day operations in government. Individual decision makers occupying positions with the delegated authority can only authorize the purchase of goods and services received on or before March 31. Therefore, for accurate and timely accounting, any economic activity, affecting appropriations, made after the close of the fiscal year in which it was voted and approved, must then be adjusted in aggregate form, and only by the Minister of Finance in the annual Public Accounts. This adjustment is reported as *"…Adjustment(s) to the Previous Year(s)…."* Decision makers must therefore not abuse their delegated authority. They should refrain from debiting or crediting items to allotments for previous years by individual responsibility centre.

Tools and Resources for Parliamentarians' Use

As part of the Treasury Board Secretariat's efforts to improve reporting to Parliament, the government's Reporting Cycle shows the timing, events and reports related to providing financial and non-financial planning and performance information to Parliament. The documents produced within the cycle support the government's efforts to effectively plan and evaluate its performance, and Parliament's budgetary, appropriation and accountability functions.

THE SOLICITOR GENERAL

The Solicitor General, the Minister in charge of these organizations, helps to apply Canada's legislation to Canadians and visitors to Canada alike: The Royal Canadian Mounted Police; The Correctional Service of Canada, the federal prison service which incarcerates individuals who have been sentenced by the Courts to one year plus one day; The National Parole Board; and The Canadian Security Intelligence Service. In addition, the Minister of Justice or Federal Attorney General maintains responsibility for lawyers, judges and the law courts.

THE TREASURY BOARD OF CANADA

The Treasury Board of Canada, the oldest Canadian Cabinet Committee on record, derives its authority to exist and its legal rights to function from the *Financial Administration Act.* The Board, the only permanent Cabinet Committee in the government of Canada, comprises four elected and two appointed officials.

Of the six officials, four exist by virtue of their office in Cabinet, the remaining two are appointed at the Prime Minister's pleasure. Since the Prime Minister, with the awesome powers granted to him or her by the Westminster Model of government used in Canada, may not only appoint all Cabinet ministers, it can be ultimately said that the Prime Minister virtually appoints all six members of the Board. The four (4) board members, by virtue of their office, are: The President of the Treasury Board; The Comptroller General who serves also as the Secretary of the Treasury Board; The Minister of Finance; and the Receiver General for Canada who is also the Minister of PWGSC (whose department is the only Common Service Agency in the government of Canada). In addition, whenever Parliament is in session, the Treasury Board of Canada meets every Thursday.

THE TREASURY BOARD SECRETARIAT

This public service organization, the administrative arm of the Treasury Board, which in recent times has rationalized its size by including the former members of the new defunct Office of the Comptroller General, comprises mainly civil servants---in contrast to the Board which is made up of elected and/or appointed officials.

It is important that the reader makes this distinction. Canadian public servants are prone to using the name "Treasury Board" when referring to its Secretariat, and vice versa. The Secretariat essentially does what the Board tells it to do. On the other hand, despite legislation such as *The Annual Appropriation Act* and the *Financial Administration Act,* some politicians tend to be a law unto themselves.

This band of appointed public servants usually comprises 'experts' in all the program areas which obtain in the government. To name a few: accounting, finance, economics, statistics, human resources on all other program areas cover this rather vast, complex, varied and sometimes complicated set of government functions. Depending on the size of the department or agency being represented, one or more experts may be assigned to it. For example, departments as complex as PWGSC, Foreign Affairs, PWGSC and DND may have three or sometimes as many as six Treasury Board Secretariat experts assigned to each of them at any one time.

THE OFFICE OF THE COMPTROLLER GENERAL

As was stated before, this portfolio, downsized considerably, has been now reduced to a bare bones type of operation which includes only the Comptroller-General and his or her staff. As mentioned in the previous paragraph, some employees of the former Office of the Comptroller General have been reassigned to that of the Treasury Board Secretariat, while others have been "let go" by way of attrition.

The Comptroller General also holds the portfolio of that of the Secretary of the Treasury Board as stated previously, by virtue of his or her office. Every year, departments and agencies report on their organization's performance to this position. This report, discussed in this text in a later chapter, is known as the *Departmental Performance Report (DPR).* With its twin report, the *Report on Plans and Priorities,* this duo of which comprises *Part III of the Estimates,* as departments or agencies budget for their expected results and later report on their actual annual performance. The results of the previous fiscal year's performance appear in detail in the *DPR.*

THE MINISTER OF FINANCE

Under the terms of the *British North America (Constitution) Act, 1982,* the Minister of Finance *controls* the CRF. He or she, his or her Deputy Minister and his or her trusty band of appointed public servants, ensure there is always enough money in the CRF---usually through levying of taxes, collected by the Canada Revenue Agency or by borrowing from Canadians or elsewhere---to be further voted out and *managed* by the Receiver General for Canada under the legislative terms and authorities granted by the *Annual Appropriation Act* and the *Financial Administration Act.*

Incidentally, the CRF may be defined, under the terms of the *Constitution Act, 1982,* as "...the aggregate of public monies held on deposit by the Receiver General for Canada..."

THE RECEIVER GENERAL FOR CANADA AND THE MINISTER OF PUBLIC WORKS AND GOVERNMENT SERVICES CANADA

The individual appointed to this ministerial portfolio by the Prime Minister usually ends up wearing two hats, as it were, those of Receiver General for Canada; and The Minister of PWGSC.

The department operates as two separate but paradoxically interlinked organizations which carry out their functions concurrently. The Receiver General for Canada, under the *aegis* of the *Constitution Act, 1982*, **manages** the CRF.

PWGSC is a **common service agency.** This organization provides mandatory and non-mandatory services to all government departments and agencies. Its subordinate organizations such as Cheque Redemption & Control and Central Pay support the Receiver General for Canada and PWGSC. In addition, when an individual makes a payment to the government of Canada, the instrument is usually made: "...payable to the Receiver General for Canada..." The Receiver General for Canada (RG) also operates the following "bank" or control accounts which include: RG Deposit Control; RG Payment Control; RG Payroll Control; IS Debit Control; IS Credit Control; and RG Foreign Currency Control.

The Public Service of Canada

The Public Service of Canada comprises public servants employed by organizations that makeup the federal government. Authority for hiring and firing has been delegated to this Service by the Treasury Board. However, in recent times, Public Service Reform, creating a measure of flexibility in this process, has delegated a significant percentage of this flexibility to individual responsibility centre managers.

The Public Service Commission (psc)

The Public Service Commission (PSC) has been delegated certain important functions by the Treasury Board of Canada such as the hiring and firing of federal public servants; and the training of federal public servants.

Also, under public service reform, in recent times the PSC has re-delegated some of these powers for hiring and firing to individual managers. With the PSC's new challenge of flexibility, the commission maintains the important concept of transparency in its hiring practices.

The Auditor General for Canada

Under the terms of the *Auditor General's Act*, the Auditor General for Canada maintains his or her legal right to exist and remains responsible for the independent oversight or corporate governance, review, program evaluation and audit of all the accounting, financial and operational information recorded in the financial records of government departments and agencies. These audits, including the comprehensive or value for money, are generally conducted on an interim and final basis.

The Bank of Canada

The Bank of Canada, a famous and resounding institution, remains the final organization for the receipt and disbursement of public monies for all departments and agencies. A unique relationship exists fiscally between the RG, The Bank, the commercial banks and Cheque Redemption and Control.

One of the oldest financial institutions in Canada, the Bank of Canada was created under the legal authority of the *Bank of Canada Act*. A central clearing house between the RG, the government of Canada's official "banker", and the commercial financial institutions, cheques, other financial instrument deposits and issuances are first cleared through the commercial financial institutions such as the Royal Bank of Canada. They are also entered in the financial records of the RG such as the CFMRS, Cheque Redemption and Control (referred to by PWGSC employees as "Matane"), the individual financial systems of departments and agencies and finally through the Bank of Canada. Theoretically, whatever balances appear in the CRF, the RG's records, departmental financial systems, financial institutions, and accounts for the government of Canada all combined should reconcile to the balances shown at The Bank of Canada.

The Reader Should Remember: the government agencies which function such as Parliament, the Governor General, the Treasury Board, the Treasury Board Secretariat, the Minister of Finance, the Comptroller General, the Receiver General for Canada, PWGSC, Cheque and Redemption Control, The Bank of Canada, and the Office of the Auditor General.

Classification and Coding

OBJECTIVE OF CHAPTER FOUR

The objective of this chapter is to introduce to the reader and the course or workshop participant to the importance of the pivotal function of classifying transactions in plans, budgets, actual operations, forecasts and reports.

INTRODUCTION

The classification system intends to provide information for multiple users and uses both within and outside government departments and agencies. The classification of accounts provides the framework to identify aggregate information, supply details and summaries of and report financial transactions for planning, resource allocation, accounting, audit, evaluation, review, and statistics.

The Treasury Board of Canada's policy on classification requires transactions to be identified according to authority, financial reporting, purpose, responsibility and object. The coding, used in the government of Canada, is designed to provide a uniform structure that meets the following requirements:

This policy applies to all organizations considered to be departments within the meaning of Section 9 (1) of the *Financial Administration Act.*

The classification system forms part of the accounting system and, together with the budgetary process, provides government decision-makers at various levels with the information necessary to make their decisions and carry out their policy and control functions.

The classification of accounts for the government of Canada is dictated by the requirements to: provide information in a summarized form required for the Accounts of Canada; meet central agency and other requirements for uniform classifications of data on a government wide basis; and provide summarized and detailed information at the department or agency level.

To ensure effective control and disclosure of information, a department's classification of accounts should make provision for recording assets and liabilities, even though the latter may not be recorded in the Accounts of Canada, nor appear in the Statement of Assets and Liabilities of the government of Canada.

The Treasury Board Secretariat is responsible for policy development, advice, interpretation, and implementation assistance, including the appropriate training or information sessions for each department or agency, and for promulgating any changes required to the Chart of Accounts for the government of Canada. This includes the annual amendments to the Master List of Objects and the Master List of Programs and Activities which are now included in Chapters 6 and 8 of the Chart of Accounts Volume.

The word "coding" is one of the most widespread in modern computer science. What means the concept of "coding"? "Coding" may be perceived as the operation of identifying the symbols or the symbol groups on one code to the symbols or the symbol groups of another code. The necessity of "coding" arises first of from the need to adapt the form of message to the given "communication channel" or to some device intended for transformation, conversion or storage of information.

Coding theory has a long history. Number systems intended for number representation were the first codes. The next very old direction of coding theory is cryptography or secret coding. This one originated in the Egyptian science dating back almost 4,000 years, to the time when Egyptians used the hieroglyphic code for inscriptions on tombs. Development of modern coding theory was improved by the progress of communication systems. Shannon's information theory, based on the entropy concept, is the mathematical justification of the effective code theory. The Morse, Shannon-Fano and Haffman codes are examples of effective codes. The RG is responsible for recording transactions received from departments and agencies in the CFMRS, processing them according to the uniform classification method prescribed by statute or by the Treasury Board of Canada, and providing reports to various users in Parliament, central agencies and departments. To accomplish this, the RG provides Parliament, departments and agencies with any supporting operational instructions such as RG Directives, Bulletins and other guidance related to the classification and coding system.

Departments must ensure that their departmental coding links to the appropriate accounts and codes contained in the Government-wide Chart of Accounts (COA) and that their financial transactions are complete and accurate. At each month end, departmental financial transactions will be summarized (based on government-wide codes) and departments will send their trial balances to the Central Financial Management and Reporting System (CFMRS.)

The internal audit group of each department includes the reviews of classification and coding in its internal audit plans. The Government Operational Services Sector (GOSS) of PWGSC will monitor the quality of government-wide classification and coding.

The Treasury Board Secretariat monitors the overall maintenance of the data in the Central Agency Information System Relational Data Base. However, the primary responsibility for the application of this policy rests with each department or agency's Senior Full-Time Financial Officer.

POLICY ON CLASSIFICATION

The policy on classification is issued by the Treasury Board of Canada under the authority of Section 9 (1) of the *Financial Administration Act.* The Treasury Board Secretariat's responsibility includes the policy on classification of financial transactions and extends to cover the structure for the accounts and codes established in Government-wide Chart of Accounts (COA).

The Treasury Board policy on classification which requires transactions to be indentified according to *authority, financial reporting, purpose and responsibility,* provides a uniform structure that meets the following requirements: to provide the government wide information required for the CFMRS summarized trial balance, which is used to prepare the government's monthly summary financial statements and the annual Public Accounts of Canada; and to meet central agency and other requirements for uniform classifications of data on a government-wide basis.

The *financial reporting account* classification identifies the General Ledger government of Canada. This classification is needed to maintain the government-wide General Ledger and is used to prepare the government's financial statements. This field is also used to identify the treasury control accounts.

The *authority classification* ensures that the financial transactions of the government of Canada are accounted for by authorities (that is, allotments, appropriations and/or votes) that are established for each department and agency by Parliament. This authority classification is structured to address the multiple authority requirements.

The *purpose* or *business/service line code* or *program/activity classification* is used to account for the use of resources to promote overall government program objectives. It is results-oriented and deals with the policy sectors, programs and activities of the government of Canada. This code is commonly referred to as the government-wide activity code (GWAC).

The *object classification* identifies the types of resources acquired or disbursed through transactions with a third party or other government departments (OGDs). Examples are: the type of goods and services acquired or grants and contributions; the source of revenue; and the increases or decreases to financial claims and obligations.

The *transaction type* is used to identify transactions which are either internal to the government or transactions that are external (that is, related to parties outside the government of Canada accounting entity).

The Receiver General for Canada is responsible for the day to day management of the government-wide COA which includes: establishing, deleting or modifying accounts or codes and publishing updates.

PWGSC GOVERNMENT WIDE CODING BLOCK

To effect these classifications, a standard method of coding, applying numbers to each classification, has been formulated by PWGSC. A limit of 22 digits, alpha or numeric, has been assigned to the total CODING BLOCK. There are currently afoot, as happens often with these kinds of bureaucratic situations, plans to revise the size and structure of the coding block.

PWGSC consistently revises the functions of the coding block to accommodate the constant changing nature of the government of Canada. Normally, the block appears sequentially as presented below. With computers, a number of combinations, permutations, and variations may occur.

<u>LIMIT OF TWENTY-TWO (22) DIGITS</u>

DEPT/AGENCY	FRA	ACTIVITY (GWAC)	AUTHORITY	OBJECT (ECON)	TRANSACTION TYPE
000	00000	00000	0000	0000	0

Management Resources and Results Structure (mrrs)

The Treasury Board of Canada has developed a Management Resources and Results Structure (MRRS) requiring departments to define how they plan and manage diverse programs and related activities, allocate resources and achieve and report on results. The MRRS serves integrated purposes and offers multiple benefits such as Departmental MRRS to provide vital information; it aims to help departments and central agencies; and generates a source of current departmental information. As outlined in the MMRS policy statement, a departmental MRRS must have three elements: a *Program Activity Architecture (PAA);* clearly defined and measurable Strategic Outcomes; and a description of the current Governance Structure. Departments are responsible for: drilling down to the lowest level within a PAA, identifying and describing their programs; providing clear program titles and descriptions for all programs identified in a PAA; and identifying strategic outcome and program activity levels changes to comply with PAA requirements outlined in the MRRS instructions and in advance of ARLU 2008-2009.

For example, the Department of National Defence's MRRS includes a PAA with three programs: (1): Generate and sustain relevant, responsive and effective combat capable, integrated forces; (2): Conduct operations; and (3): Contribute to Canadian Government, society and international community in accordance with Canadian interests and values. Each program profiles three levels of activity (sub-activity, and sub-sub activity). These activities are causally linked to produce a predominant output for each program. Each program output contributes to or leads to a strategic outcome.

An added construct 'Executive and Corporate Services' provides a holding box to list all organizational entities that are not directly related to programs, with the associated resources redistributed across the three programs on a pro rated formula.

The PAA structure sits above and is separate from the organizational and financial structure as represented by the 'level one' organizations, their org IDs and the associated financial tracking system consisting of fund centres and cost centres linked to each level one organization, plus the separately tracked Work Breakdown System (WBS accounts). An interface links the org IDs or fund centres or cost centres with the PAA at the sub-sub activity level.

Anual Reference Level Update (arlu)

The Annual Reference Level Update (ARLU) is an annual process where three-year forecasts are revised and agreed upon by departments and the Treasury Board Secretariat.

A Reference Level is the current dollar balance of funding available to an organization (typically a department or agency) for each year as approved by the Treasury Board and/or authorized in statutory estimates related to the statutes of Canada. It is the aggregate of all approved funding levels for the organization and may include some of the following: program, operating, capital, non-budgetary expenditures, grants, contributions and revenues credited to the vote.

The ARLU also updates the forecast of expenditures for approved programs to provide a base for developing the Main Estimates and the government's expenditure plan as outlined in the Budget. ARLU information is collected via the EMIS.

Expenditure Management Information System (emis)

The EMIS, an integrated and secure budget system, supports the Treasury Board of Canada Secretariat (TBS) to fulfill its expenditure management role. Operated by the TBS' *Expenditure Management Sector (EMS),* the EMIS has been used effectively by the TBS' Expenditure Information Division (EID). The strategic outcome of this sector is to strengthen expenditure and financial management. Aligned with the sector, EID's strategic outcome is to provide enhanced financial, management and performance information. EID also supports this outcome as a service provider to EMS, and to the TBS at large, through providing financial, management and performance information; and the tools and technology to collect, store and analyze this information. As implementing the EMIS' strategy progresses, EID proposes to deliver Results and Expenditures in two dimensions: Planned and Actual.

Expenditure Management System (EMS) renewal ensures that all government programs are effective, efficient, focused on results, provide value for taxpayers' money and are aligned with current priorities and responsibilities.

Similar EMIS Initiatives Practiced Elsewhere

The TBS pays very close attention to other integrated Budget Office projects in Australia, New Zealand and the United Kingdom, as well as state governments in the United States, for lessons learned and best practices. These governments elsewhere are trying to improve the recording, monitoring and reporting of expenditures. Often the impetus behind such initiatives is the government's to create more accountability and openness.

OBJECT CODE DETAILS

The object classification or code, stated before, shows the TYPE of Asset, Liability, Expense or Revenue reported in a particular transaction. Similar in some vague way to the Financial Reporting Account classification, this coding is usually focused and detailed by the types of expense as follows: standard object, reporting object, class object, economic object and line object.

The economic object ends up being the most important object classification and coding process. This is because of the manner in which it functions, and the fiscal way in which its results are used government-wide.

Thus, more than one line object equals a reporting object;
and more than one reporting object equals a standard object.

The numbers or codes for standard objects are the same the government over for each department or agency. However, below that level any group or groupings of digits may be used. In addition, computers employ tables and files to add to or reduce the level of complexity or complication found in the numbering system(s).

MORE ON THE FINANCIAL REPORTING ACCOUNT (FRA)

Somewhat similar in use to the object classification, the FRA classification and coding represents basically the main elements of the accounting equation: government department's financial system and the private sector accounting system when being used.

The Financial Reporting Accounts (FRAs) included in departmental Central Management Reporting System (CFMRS) monthly trial balances contain the data needed by the Receiver General (RG) to prepare the financial statements on a monthly and annual basis. Monthly government-wide financial statements are included in the *Monthly Statement of Financial Operations (MFSO)*, which is used by the Department of Finance to produce results in the *Monthly Fiscal Monitor.* The government's annual financial statements are audited by the Auditor General for Canada and are included in the *Public Accounts of Canada* that is tabled, each fall, in Parliament. These statements are also included on a consolidated basis in the *Annual Financial Report of the Government of Canada*, which is published by the Minister of Finance.

The financial reporting account (FRA) structure is designed to identify accounting transactions as follows while linked to objects of expenditure and cash control or reconciliation accounts:

Assets:	class type of object
Liabilities:	obligation type of object
Expenses:	expenses type of object
Revenues:	source type of object

Cash reconciliation control accounts: similar to bank accounts.

In addition to the practical examples provided by participants during the lecture dealing with this chapter, here is a working example:

An imaginary government department, called Department XYZ: The Standard Development Agency, has designed its coding block as follows:

Dept./Agency	Financial Rptg A/C	Purpose	Authority	Object	Transaction Type
000	00000	00000	0000	0000	0

XYZ purchased from an external source a vehicle for the use of its RC Manager in Yellowknife. The entries that follow may be as follows:

Dr: 356 16275 5675 43000 4568 1 $ 60,000

Cr: 758 23003 7842 43000 7851 1 $ 60,000

The financial clerk needed to access the department's coding manual published with its financial manual to determine the codes associated with the various classifications. Note that the entire coding block is within the regulation 22 digits.

OTHER UNIQUE USES OF THE CODING BLOCK

Quite often, a department or agency's coding block is designed at the behest of its complex computerized departmental financial system (DFS). This DFS may use a condensed or imposed coding or the system may use a complicated set of interrelated tables and files. For example, a department may use this series in its coding as follows:

000000	000	000000
Dept. /Agency	GWAC	Combined Code

The department's computerized system encrypts and decrypts the last six digits of the coding block to determine a number of other necessary elements in the coding block, mainly the line object and FRA.

The Reader Should Remember: What classification means and why it exists. What and why coding exists. How these two functions differ or are similar to each other. That the main classification types are: department/agency; financial reporting account; authority; activity; object; and transaction type. In addition, the economic object is paramount. That classification and coding is an essential and significant link between planning, budgeting, reporting, control and the PWGSC government-wide coding.

5

Budgetary Control at All Levels

OBJECTIVE OF CHAPTER FIVE

The objective of this chapter is to provide the reader and course or workshop participant with a brief insight into the details of the various levels of budgetary control that obtain in the government of Canada.

INTRODUCTION

A *budget* is a quantitative expression of a plan of action. It states what the business plans to achieve in the next one or two years. In government organizations, some objectives of budgeting could be to: provide assurance to the public that funds are spent and used for the purposes authorized by the legislature; ensure that tax and non tax revenues are collected, resources allocated and expenses disbursed in an efficient and economic manner; and hold both in terms of outcomes achieved and value for money. (See *Federal Accountability Act,* 2006)

Budgets may be formulated for the organization as a whole or for any subunit normally being an area of responsibility within an organization. If budgets are formulated for various subunits, however, then they would normally be brought together in a *Master Budget.* This would summarize the objectives of all the subunits, for example: sales, production, personnel, finance, etc. Budgets are very useful in the following areas: planning and co-ordination, communicating and motivation, evaluating performance and control.

According to legal and parliamentary practice, funds may not be expended without legislative authority. In controlling expenses, Parliament reviews and authorizes the annual budget or *The Main Estimates,* for the forthcoming fiscal year.

The *Annual Appropriation Act* is voted by Parliament as it authorizes annual appropriations in *The Main Estimates.* Section 31 of the *Financial Administration Act* provides the Treasury Board of Canada with the authority regarding the form and content of the budget. The *Federal Accountability Act* provides for conflict on interest rules, restrictions on election financing and measures respecting administrative transparency, oversight and accountability. Development of the budget and fiscal plan is an integral part of financial management, since it determines the resources needed to fulfill the objectives of departmental programs and forms the basis for operational control and accountability.

Accountability defines the relationships between those in power and those affected by the use of that power.

A holistic view of these relationships is required to develop an understanding that is respectful of the diversity of parties involved. Funding targets are established by the Treasury Board of Canada to assist departments in developing annual reference levels. Departments identify annual reference levels for their programs and rank them in priority order as part of their initial review. *Annual Reference Level Update (ARLU)* proposals are reviewed by various administrative levels and finally approved by the Treasury of Canada.

Once annual budgets have been approved, voted, authorized and implemented, budgetary control is required to ensure that resources are properly used, and that actual revenues and expenses do not differ significantly from budget and forecasts. Ministers, deputy heads, senior managers and program managers across government must fulfill their responsibilities while managing budgets, consistent with legislative requirements and the Treasury Board of Canada.

Budgetary control is usually put into practice on a responsibility centre basis, as departments can be large and complex and cannot be centrally managed without the delegation of authority and management control throughout the department. Managers also need to account for their actions in relation to plans and to take corrective action to stay within budget.

THE THREE BASIC LEVELS OF BUDGETARY CONTROL

At the three basic budgetary levels in the government of Canada, control is exercised: by Parliament; by The Treasury Board of Canada, whose members also sit in Parliament; and by each department or agency whose Minister may also sit in Parliament.

At these three strategic, managerial and operational levels, the following actions result: at the Parliamentary level there is produced the Fiscal Plan; at the Treasury Board level, departments and agencies prepare the Annual Reference Level Update (ARLU); and at the department level, Part III of The Estimates is prepared.

In addition, the legislation by which authority is executed and control given includes principally: by Parliament, via the *Annual Appropriation Act* and the *Federal Accountability Act;* by the Treasury of Canada and departments and agencies, via the *Financial Administration Act;* and by individual department or agency acts.

Parliamentary Level of Budgetary Conrol – Level I

At the highest level in the government in Canada, authority may be derived from those who exercise the same under the *Annual Appropriations Act.* Various aspects of this Act are voted by the members of Parliament an average of four (4) times per year. These periods of time when Parliament meets are linked paradoxically to when the members of Parliament are on vacation. The periods of time when Parliament is in session and legislation is being voted, including some laws which relate to how the government's operations are funded, are known as *Periods of Supply.* The months when Parliamentarians usually take holidays are March, June and December of each year. Therefore, the three *Periods of Supply* occur between: December and March; March and June; and June and December.

Preparing and voting the *Fiscal Plan,* which in return relates to the highest level of strategic actions the government can take, occurs at the time when the Budget is presented to the House of Commons, usually sometime in February by the then Minister of Finance, the latter of whom traditionally wears a new pair of shoes when he or she reads the Budget. Should the Sovereign be visiting Canada, he or she reads the Budget to the members of the Upper House or the Senate.

New monies are voted or monies are transferred from one Program or Department to another, reported and voted or in summary form during the presentation of *Part I of the Estimates.* The summarized version may also be viewed in *Part II of the Estimates* by Department, Program and Standard Object of Expenditure. Different parts of The Estimates are voted by Parliament during these Supply Periods:

Supply Period	Approx. Month	Estimates' Part
December to March	February	Part I: Total Government in Summary
	December	Supplementary Estimates – Part "A"
	March	Interim Supply---Parts II & III
March to June	June	Full Supply---Parts II & III
	March	Supplementary Estimates – Part "B"
June to December	See Above	See Above

Part I of the Estimates represents the total Government Expenditure in Summary form by Strategic Change and by Department or Agency or Program or Activity.

Part II of the Estimates represents each department in summary form by Program and Standard Object of Expenditure.

Part III of the Estimates represents each department in detail by Program, Branch & Standard Object of Expenditure. A recently developed Part III comprises two reports: *The Reports on Plans and Priorities (RPP)* – prepared by March, 31, and finally voted on June; and the *Departmental Performance Report (DPR)* ---prepared and presented by each department or agency to the Treasury Board Secretariat by the following October.

While providing *Interim Supply,* Parliament appropriates 3/12ths of the government's total planned spending. While providing *Full Supply,* Parliament appropriates 9/12ths of the government's total planned spending. Often both voted Interim and Full Supply are not adequate or such items as Carry-Forwards and Re-profiling need to be also voted by Parliament. Traditionally then,

Parliament votes two *Supplementary Estimates: "A" and "B".* However, in times of dire emergency, such as the Iraq and Afghanistan conflicts, Parliament has been known to vote *Supplementary Estimates "C",* or even *"D"* or *"E",* depending on the pressing need(s) at that time.

Treasury Board Level of Budgetary Control – Level II

This section comprises *ARLU* versus *Appropriation (Vote);* significance of votes versus appropriation; legal and political significance of the division of appropriations into allotments; re-allocation of votes and allotments; numbering of votes; and frozen allotments.

In August of each year or thereabouts a *Call Letter* is sent out from the Treasury Board Secretariat to all department and agency *Senior Full Time Financial Officers.* This call letter includes instructions on how to prepare *Annual Reference Level Updates (ARLUs) and The Estimates.* The Treasury Board of Canada usually requires and requests a deadline of around October for each departmental or agency official responsible for preparing the necessary Central Agency Reports.

A *Reference Level* represents a sort of standard position in percentage activity and/or related dollars at which a program, branch, responsibility centre or individual is remunerated for the operations carried out on behalf of the department or agency. It is also the current dollar balance of funding available to an organization and may include some or all of the following: program, operating, capital, non-budgetary expenditures, grants and revenues credited to the vote.

The ARLU updates the forecast of expenditures for approved programs to provide a base for developing the Main Estimates and the government's expenditure plan as outlined in the budget.

For example, one's salary level may be considered a *reference level.* There exist four distinct changes or adjustments that may be made to a reference level: a temporary increase; or a permanent increase; or a temporary decrease; or a permanent decrease.

An example of a temporary increase would be that of the actual dollars paid an employee as he or she is compensated for a temporary increase in the level of labour activity which he or she performs. The permanent increase in this instance may occur through a permanent increase in the employee's daily or hourly rate of pay. One could therefore conclude that the average RC manager would wish to have the Treasury Board of Canada approve for his organization a permanent increase to the reference level(s).

An ARLU Adjustments summary page may appear in part like this:

Department or Agency XYZ

Current Adjustments				Legend	
Del. Adjustments	Type	Year	Total	Status	Action
Budgetary Adjustments	[Adjustment Details by Program Activity]				
	[Adjustment Totals by Department]				
		2007/08	$3,000,000		
Opening Balance		2008/09	$1,200,000		
		2009/10	$1,200,000		
		2007/08	$ 0		
# 20000 – Pending	Policy	2008/09	$ 0		
		2009/10	$ 0		

In previous years, a similar yet dissimilar function of funding requirements was known as the Multi-Year Operational Plan (MYOP). However, it must be noted that the *ARLU has **not** replaced the MYOP.* There only appear to be similarities in the two almost completely dissimilar budgeting and planning functions.

Parliament *votes,* and therefore *authorizes* appropriations. The Treasury Board of Canada, *approves* allotments, sometimes "in principle", but *DOES NOT AUTHORIZE appropriations.* Funds, though approved, are *not available* for spending until voted and authorized by Parliament. This aspect of funding is *paramount* and a pivotal point to be always noted when exercising delegated authority. The exercise of delegated authority *must* be always done in the proper manner by all decision makers in the government of Canada, regardless of their level of responsibility or authority in each organization.

An *allotment* is not an appropriation. It is a sub-division of an appropriation. This division is allocated to each department/agency within the authorities delegated under *The Financial Administration Act.* Ironically, though decision-makers need Parliament to vote the *Annual Appropriation Act*, the main working level of control exerted by the Treasury Board of Canada is generally by allotment.

Comparatively speaking then, appropriation and allotments may be presented as follows:

By Parliament Voting Appropriations	By Treasury Board Approving Allotments
(Using Annual Appropriations Act)	(Using Financial Administration Act)
Salary and Other O & M Appropriation	Operating Budget Allotment
	---Salary and Wages Sub-Allotment
	---Other O & M Sub-Allotment
Capital Appropriation	Minor Capital Sub-Allotment
	Major or Controlled Capital Allotment
Grants and Contributions Appropriation	Grants and Contributions Allotment
Statutory Appropriation	Special Allotment, Frozen Allotment

Significance of the Types of Votes to Parliamentarians and Public Servants

The types of votes assigned by Parliament are significant to a larger extent to parliamentarians and to a lesser extent to federal public servants.

When a program within a department or program has been voted capital and/or grants and contributions greater than or equal to $ 5 million, Parliament, not the department or program, necessarily, needs a separate vote.

Should the amount voted in both of the two budgeted elements be less than $ 5 million, the same amount is included within the Program Vote, sometimes known as a "catch-all" vote. Should either of the amounts voted for the above mentioned budgeted elements be more than $ 5 million, the amount which is less than $ 5 million is included in the Operating Expenditures Vote.

Public servants, though the amounts approved are done eventually by allotment, tend to keep the same vote names and numbers usually assigned for Parliamentary use, sometimes causing a slight confusion.

Small "P" Political Significance of Allotments within Operating Budgets

Under its Operating Budget Policy, introduced in 1993, the Treasury Board of Canada seems to apply small "p" politics, its method(s) of approval of funding, and defaults finally to flexibility in the decision making ability of each R.C. Manager in the approval of allotments. In addition, the remaining allocation of funds depends on legislation, say, statutory or special allotments, frozen allotments, political decisions such as those made with grants and contributions, and its own control, such as Controlled Capital allotments.

Some Simple Re-Allocations

The Treasury Board of Canada also usually leaves certain votes or appropriations such as grants and contributions and special votes to contain the same amounts when approving allotments.

However, capital votes or appropriations are sub-divided into minor and major or controlled capital allotments. Minor capital cut off amounts differ from department to department. This figure results from subtracting the total of major or controlled capital from the total capital vote or appropriation.

Numbering of Votes or Appropriations

Votes or appropriations are numbered in the following numerical sequence: 1, 5, 10, 15, 20, 25, 30, 35, etc. Votes or appropriations with the letter "L" preceding their numbers represent loans. Votes or appropriations with the letter "S" preceding their numbers denote Special or Statutory.

Frozen Allotments

Frozen allotments may comprise two main types: Allotments that have actually been frozen by the Treasury Board of Canada during the Central Agency's quest to control government spending, usually towards the end of the fiscal year; and Funds which have been advanced to a department/agency by the Treasury Board of Canada in the hope that the same department or agency would be able when called upon to repay the debt. Sometimes this advance is made on behalf of a third party and may be accounted for as a specified purpose account.

The Reader Should Remember: a Master Budget comprises several components, the expense component being the largest in the government of Canada; that three levels of budgeting exist with Parliament, the Treasury Board of Canada and each department; that vote and appropriations are the same; but that allotments are sub-divisions of a vote or appropriation. He or she should also remember the significance of exercising delegated authority as it relates to accountability and the final result.

Budgetary Control at the Departmental Level

OBJECTIVES OF CHAPTER SIX

The objectives of this chapter are to: make the reader, course or workshop participant fully aware as possible of the level of importance of the attached practical application of budgetary control at the working level in departments and agencies; and provide as saliently as possible, working examples of imaginary day-to-day government examples.

INTRODUCTION

This chapter comprises a theoretical and practical demonstration of how budgetary control functions from day to day at the working level in government operations. The main piece of legislation that controls this function remains the *Financial Administration Act.* The *Financial Administration Act* (FAA) is the cornerstone of the legal framework for general financial management and accountability of public sector organizations and Crown Corporations. These Sections of the Act, also most appropriate to this function, assists in maintaining the budgetary level of control at the departmental level: Section

19—Authority to spend revenues; Section31—Allotment control; Section 32—Commitment control, not "commitment accounting" as suggested by some government financial manuals and experienced public servants working in the finance function; Section 33---Payment authority; and Section 34---Spending authority.

In 2002-03, the government implemented full accrual accounting in order to prepare the Finance Minister's budget and the summary financial statements of the government of Canada included in the Public Accounts of Canada. However, the Main Estimates, or the appropriations, continued to be based on a 'near-cash' accrual basis of accounting. Accrual accounting recognizes transactions when the underlying economic event occurs, that is, it recognizes revenue when earned rather than when cash is received, and expenses when incurred rather than when paid for. Accrual accounting provides a more comprehensive picture of the government's financial situation and a more accurate reflection of the financial impacts of economic events and government decisions during the year.

At this juncture one should remember that one may spend public monies to acquire some good or service without disbursing a single dime of cash until later. Or one may alternatively, spend the monies simultaneously or even before or after one receives the good or service. The greater percentage of goods and service bought or sold are not exchanged the same time as the actual cash is disbursed or received. This brand of "out of sync" business situation remains at the heart of a vital accountancy concept entitled *"Accrual Accounting"*.

Historical cost accounting has this major challenge of the *matching principle* under accrual accounting. Under historical cost accounting, it is necessary to match expenses with revenue to determine earnings. The challenge performs this function in a manner that provides information to decision-makers concerning the firm's future economic prospects.

Therefore, the accountant has to calculate *accruals*, or, as it were, match expenses with revenues. Some examples of items accrued are: amortizing or depreciating assets; calculating future income tax liability; the approach used in oil and gas accounting; and prepaying items such as insurance and rent.

BRIEF REVIEW OF ALLOTMENT CONTROL

[SEE SECTION 31 OF FINANCIAL ADMINISTRATION ACT]

The Treasury Board of Canada approves the division of appropriations, which Parliament may have voted earlier, into five (5) allotments. A direct relationship exists between these allotments and assigning objects of expenditure. Actually, various allotments may comprise a number of these objects. In addition, allotments are controlled on a day-to-day basis at the operating level in each department or agency by Sections 32, 33 and 34 of the *Financial Administration Act.*

EXPENDITURE CONTROL

Introduction

Sections 32, 33 and 34 of *The Financial Administration Act* include the legislation of the four main steps in expenditure control in the government of Canada. These four steps are: expenditure initiation, commitment control (not commitment accounting), Section 32; spending authority; Section 34; and payment authority, Section 33.

Expenditure Initiation

After Parliament has authorized or voted appropriations or votes, the Treasury Board of Canada divides these particular amounts into allotments. Each department or agency, in turn sub-divides these amounts either manually or electronically by Responsibility Centre (RC) at the highest possible organizational level. Each RC Manager and other positions in the department or agency may have been delegated the relevant authority by their respective Deputy Head or Minister. This *expenditure initiation* authority provides each position held by a decision maker with the delegated authority to commence proceedings, usually the purchase of goods and services, on behalf of the department or agency. The decision maker must not, however, achieve personal benefit. Normally, this initial step in the expenditure control process acts as a catalyst for issuing some official document such as a purchase or work order. This document details the action to be taken on the good(s) to be purchased or the service(s) to be performed.

COMMITMENT CONTROL OR EXERCISING DELEGATED AUTHORITY UNDER SECTION 32 OF THE FINANCIAL ADMINISTRATION ACT

After authorizing the start of the purchase of goods and/or services, the decision maker should also have been delegated the authority to spend the required money from some kind of budget. Section 32 of *The Financial Administration Act* states that there should be sufficient unencumbered funds left in the allotment to settle the invoices the customer is sure to present when the services provided or item purchased proves to be the satisfaction of the person who has made the commitment in the first place. Section 32 requires that these funds be "set aside". No economic event has taken place in this instance so there is nothing for which the RC Manager, his subordinate, accountant or finance officer to "account". The computer system or a manual system is used to "put a hedge around" the necessary future necessary funds.

Usually a control number of sorts is assigned to the set aside funds so that an audit trail of sorts can be kept of this legal activity. In the more developed commitment **control** systems, a myriad of various types of commitments are defined and maintained. These include *bulk, hard, multi-year* and *soft* commitments, to name a few. Suffice it to say, the only one that is legally recognized by some fundamental government organizations such as the Treasury Board of Canada, is the type of "hard" commitment. In that instance, a legally binding document should exist. This document may include a purchase order or signed contract between a public servant and the government of Canada. For example, when "hard" commitments are made, the Treasury Board of Canada usually thinks twice or more before it would freeze the objects of expenditure or allotments involved.

However, as one middle level manager at PWGSC was reputed to have said more than once:

> "…Commitments should not be made to be a tempest in a teapot or to be used as a primary source of cash or operational budgetary control, but just to set aside funds to preserve their legal implications…"

Spending Authority, granted under Section 34 of the Financial Administration Act

The third step in the expenditure control process, *spending authority,* supports exercising the delegated authority that may have been provided under Section 34 of *The Financial Administration Act* to a position held on the delegation document or chart of a government department or agency.

In essence, Section 34 states that the government must receive or be perceived to have received a good or provided a service before the individual in the position with the delegated authority "signs off" or authorizes the purchase and /or receipt of the afore-to-mentioned good or service under Section 34 of *The Financial Administration Act.*

With this Section 34 *FAA* authority also comes the need to determine under the relevant Section of the *FAA* whether the terms of the contract between the provider of the good or service and Her Majesty the Queen have been met, or whether the contractual obligations of an employment contract between the government of Canada and the employee(s) who needs to be both remunerated, have been fulfilled. Therefore, one should remember that there are basically two types of contract that usually exist in the government:

> A contract *for* services with Her Majesty the Queen uses an independent contractor); but a contract *of* services forms a master servant relationship between an employee, usually a public servant, and the employer, the government of Canada.

N. B. *Existing independence* fundamentally separates these two types of contract. As long as there remains any hint of a master-servant relationship or control by one party to the contract over the other, independence is lost.

At the end of each fiscal year, goods and/or services must be received or performed on or before March 31. In this instance, a government organization may receive goods either FOB (free on board) supply point, or FOB, destination. This receiving action determines whether funding is released from an appropriation or vote or allotment or not. The timing of the action also remains legally crucial, since each *Appropriation Act* is voted for only one fiscal year. The associated costs of received goods or services must be removed from an appropriation, vote or allotment in the fiscal year(s) for which they have not been voted. Only the Minister of Finance has the legal, financial and accounting authority to account in total for the entire government for "Items Occurring in the Previous Year(s)". It is abundantly clear then, that a decision maker, who occupies a position, either temporarily or permanently, to which the commensurate authority has been delegated, should NEVER attempt to charge the costs of the economic activity of items purchased on the government's behalf in the previous year(s) or to be purchased in the subsequent year(s) to the current year's vote, appropriation or allotment. If this happens, the generally accepted principle of '*matching*' is being contravened, either blatantly or in error.

Payment Authority, granted under Section 33 of the Financial Administration Act

As long as another employee in the position with the delegated authority to approve the spending of funds for goods or services under Section 34 of *The Financial Administration Act* (Spending Authority), in reality, only the Receiver General for Canada has the ultimate authority under Section 33 of *The Financial Administration Act* to pay funds out of the CRF.

This authority, may, however, be also delegated to positions filled by individuals who are usually temporary or permanent finance officers. These individuals may then write cheque requisitions directing the Receiver General for Canada to prepare and release cheques to customers of the government of Canada. Alternatively, if the department or agency is maintaining one or more departmental bank accounts, cheques may be cut by the said department or agency. This method of payment is akin to petty or imprest cash, and functions along the same basic principles.

Finally, when the cheque is cut and delivered, the crucial step which ensures that the client receives the payment deserved falls into place.

Selected Receiver General Directives about properly implementing Sections 19, 32, 33 and 34 of the Financial Administration Act

It is not advisable for a federal government organization to collect user fees without the commensurate authority to respend such revenues. [See Section 19 of the *Financial Administration Act*].

Section 33 authority should never be exercised before Section 34 when settling an invoice or other means used for claiming a payment from the government.

Sections 32 and 33 authority may be exercised together by the same position holder on the same document.

It is highly unlikely that someone in a position without the delegated

Section 34 authority would attempt to exercise Section 32 authority without being delegated a commensurate Section 34 authority.

Section 34 authority should never be exercised to gain a personal benefit from the transaction.

Sections 33 and 34 authority should never be exercised together by the same position holder on the same document.

Section 19, etal. of the Financial Administration Act – Authority to spend collected non-tax revenues

Under the terms of *The Constitution Act 1982*, ALL revenues collected, tax and non-tax alike, collected in the federal government as long as they are public funds must be placed on deposit with the CRF.

To remove funds from the CRF, one must have the legal authority. If these are tax revenues, one must use either the authority voted under *The Annual Appropriation Act* or delegated under Section 33 of *The Financial Administration Act*. If the public funds are non-tax revenues, one must use the authority delegated under Section 19 of *The Financial Administration Act*. However, as we shall see later, legal authority to switch revenues from non-respendable to respendable, can also be derived from the authority delegated under the power of other Acts of Parliament.

This comes into serious effect quite often nowadays, as RC managers seem on a quest to collect more and more user fees. Some managers also assume that because they have collected such, they have the authority to spend willy-nilly, sometimes to the economic benefit of their RCs.

Conclusively then, only three general ways exist by which a decision maker may respend through bypassing the legal default which occurs as funds received are immediately credited to the CRF: by the use of a revolving fund; by way of a net voting or vote netting authority; and by using one of the five (5) types of specified purpose accounts which have been approved by the Treasury Board of Canada.

A Revolving Fund

A *revolving fund* is a funding technique, not a government organization, as is often popularly referred to by some public servants. Similar to a line of credit an individual or company may hold with a commercial bank, a revolving fund provides the government organization, through an Act of Parliament, the legal right to borrow monies from the Treasury Board of Canada up to an agreed upon dollar limit and at a previously agreed upon rate of interest. Should the revenues generated from the operation of this fund exceed the expenses incurred, up to 25% of the resulting surplus may be retained by the organization operating the fund. Any excess will remain in the CRF. For example, the Passport Office maintains the oldest revolving fund on record in the government. Authorized in 1969, the fund's limit remains at $ 4,000,000.

Net Voting or Vote Netting

This funding technique works like a two edged sword. Imagine a government organization needs $ 40,000,000 of funding. Parliament may have voted or authorized an appropriation of $ 30,000,000. The organization is then left with the remaining $ 10,000,000 to be raised by collecting user fees.

Any fees collected over the Treasury Board approved limit of $ 10,000,000, representing 25% of the excess of revenues over expenses is allowed to be spent with prior Treasury Board approval, this ostensibly increasing the total expenses the organization may have for that fiscal year.

However, should the same organization collect less fees than the approved the $ 10,000,000, it is highly unlikely that the Treasury Board would approve and recommend to Parliament that the latter vote or authorize additional funding, in essence, restricting total annual expenses of the said organization to what Parliament voted or approved earlier plus whatever has been collected in user fees. Hence, this type of funding is referred to as a "two-edged sword".

A Practical Imaginary Example of a Specified Purpose Account

The Treasury Board of Canada in its *Financial Information Strategy* manual describes the approval of five (5) types of specified purpose accounts. This example provides information on one of these types, where the department or agency maintains a deferred account to record transactions with an outside third party with whom the government organization is conducting business, usually over a multi-year period. The third party, usually a non-governmental organization (NGO), may be a provincial, territorial or municipal government pays, say, $ 5,000,000, representing cash advances on the anticipated cost of expected operations. In the books of this government organization, the following T-accounts may exist:

R G Deposit Control Account	Deferred Revenue---NGO X
---	---
5,000,000 |	| 5,000,000

On the payment of $ 1,000,000 in commensurate expenses by the government organization on behalf of NGO-X, the entry in the same T-accounts may reflect the following:

RG Deposit Control A/C	RG Payment Control A/C	Deferred Revenue---NGO X
------------------------------	------------------------------	----------------------------------
5,000,000 |	| 1,000,000	1,000,000 | 5,000,000

There may also be found corresponding detailed memorandum expense accounts kept by the government department for later report generation to NGO-X, as follows:

Debits for say,	Salaries expense	$ 400,000
	Other expense	250,000
	Capital expense	350,000

Public Monies

Public monies are funds received by a government organization and are on deposit for the government of Canada or Her Majesty the Queen in the CRF. Therefore, the funds on a deposit at a CANEX with the Department of Defence or for an inmate who is incarcerated in a federal correctional institution of Correctional Services Canada may not be constituted as "public monies". With public monies come that necessity of care, probity, protection and prudence that go with ensuring that the assets belonging to the government of Canada remain safeguarded, similar to the importance of exercising properly and not abusing delegated authority.

Types of Payment Methods Used by Departments and Agencies

A number of payment methods, identified in official financial reports and other types of accounting transactions by their *"Source Numbers"*, can be identified. These include cash, petty cash, imprest cash, cheques issued to customers (Source Numbers 133, 134), payroll cheques (Source 144), Departmental Bank Accounts (DBAs), money orders, postal orders, debit card payments, credit card payments, other electronic funds transfers, journal vouchers (Source 050), inter-department settlements (Source 060) and debits and credits for secondments of employee to other departments and agencies. (Source 049). The more difficult of the source number financial information to be reconciled between a department or agency's financial system and PWGSC's, CFMRS, are usually Sources 049 and 060.

The Reader Should Remember: That after Parliament has voted the Annual Appropriation Act authorizing that public monies be spent the CRF, at the day-to-day level in departments and agencies, steps including initiation of actions, commitments, spending, contracting and payment authorities are delegated by each Minister via his or her Deputy Head to positions in these organizations. Non-tax revenues also stay in the CRF where they have been originally credited unless a department or agency has been delegated the legal authority by way of a revolving fund, net voting, or utilizes the process of a specified purpose account, the latter having been approved earlier by the Treasury Board of Canada. Most important of all, the direct significance of the proper exercise of delegated authority on day to day transactions must never be abused, forgotten, missed or misunderstood by RC managers in government organizations.

7

Delegation of Authority

OBJECTIVE OF CHAPTER SEVEN

The objective of this chapter is to present how the reader, class or workshop participant may best exercise delegated authority.

INTRODUCTION

Exercising delegated authority remains the nucleus of organization and financial management in government departments and agencies. **Delegation** is the handing of a task to a superior or a subordinate. It is the assignment of authority and responsibility to another person to carry out specific activities.

CONCEPTS OF THE *PRINCIPAL-AGENT* THEORY AND DELEGATING AUTHORITY

Principal-Agent Theory conceives of delegation as involving a 'principal' for a particular policy area, for example, to another individual organization---the 'agent'. It is generally thought of as more of a predictive theory. In addition, it incorporates a wide variety of forms. Generally speaking, there are two primary areas of focus.

There is that which is concerned with 'agency' losses. This loss roughly corresponds to the extent that decisions or policy outcomes arrived at by the agent differ from the goals of the principal. The difference leads in turn to theories that concern minimizing agency loss while maintaining the benefits of delegation. Such theories tend to emphasize using ex ante and ex post controls which may help to ensure compliance. Every principal-agent approach stresses that principals and agents always have separate interests. Therefore as such, a beneficial delegation will always result in some element principal or agency loss.

Because of the focus on 'informational asymmetries', the agent may possess an advantage based on expertise. This expertise may be in the particular area in which his or her other position has been delegated authority. For example, the expertise in maintaining certain aids to navigation usually exists in greater measure with sub-contractors on the *Lake of the Woods* and the *Detroit River.* Both the Canadian and the United States Coast Guards are aware of this. Now, it must be remembered that authority in the government of Canada is delegated to positions which individuals with employment contracts hold either permanently or temporarily. As such, the independent contracts between sub-contractors and Her Majesty the Queen determine the terms and condition of buoy maintenance. At the same time, both Coast Guards are aware that these private firms with whom they have contracted may end up possessing most of the maintenance experience. This could put the firms or agents in an advantageous position relative to the governments or principals. The private sector firms could use this informational advantage in future contract negotiations.

DECISION-MAKING PRINCIPLES AFFECTING DELEGATION OF AUTHORITY

Four (4) principles not only promote the efficiency, economy, effectiveness and quality of the results of decisions made but also affect delegation of authority.

The *Minister* of a department or agency delegates her or his authorities to the *Deputy Head*, who in turn delegates her or his authorities to **positions** held permanently or temporarily by public servants at varying organizational and responsibility levels in her or his department or agency.

Delegatus non potest delegare. Authority which has been delegated cannot be re-delegated. To circumvent this principle of British common law, permission is therefore required either directly from the Deputy Head or from an individual permanently or temporarily occupying a senior or supervisory position. It is also a fundamental principle of adminisraive law.

There must be some sort of *delegation instrument* which is maintained regularly by the departments' or agencies' senior full time financial officer.

A *specimen signature card,* such as used by commercial financial institutions, completes the delegation process. On each card, kept on file for each person with delegated authority, administrative areas and levels, amounts of delegated authority, signatures of him or her to whose position authority has been delegated, and the signatures of her or him recommending the particular delegation are usually found.

DELEGATIONS BY A MINISTER OR DEPUTY HEAD

The Minister delegates his or her authorities to his or her Deputy Head. The deputy head then in turn re-delegates these authorities to positions held permanently or temporarily by public servants.

The department's or agency's delegation instrument lists these positions, and limits to amounts delegated and the organizational levels. Each department's or agency's senior full time financial officer must create and later update this instrument and keep copies of all specimen signature cards. PWGSC also keeps duplicates of specimen signature cards. Delegation of authority charts, specimen signature cards and letters requesting and approving re-delegation comprise the department's or agency's delegation instrument.

DELEGATUS NON POTEST DELEGARE

According to an old British common law principle, handed down to the Canadian authorities, similar to those operating in most versions of the West Westminster Model, one may not re-delegate an authority which has been already delegated by someone else, unless the original delegator expressly authorizes it. All authorities in a department or agency have been already delegated to positions by its deputy head. Therefore, the logical action for that individual holding that position to which authority(ies) has (have) been delegated would be absurd. He or she would need to find her or himself at the office of the deputy head, then request, receive or be denied the authority for such a re-delegation. This previously suggested action is not only patently absurd but impractical. As such, a reasonable short cut is usually taken. In large and complex government department such as the Department of National Defence, to anticipate the constant organizational change, a prospective delegator may always request the written permission of her or his immediate supervisor to effect this re-delegation of authority. In other departments and agencies, it is usually OK to find someone in any position senior to the one being occupied by the person asking permission to re-delegate. The prospective re-delegator can only hope that the person asked for permission will give the necessary written approval and authority.

AUTHORITIES DELEGATED SPECIFICALLY ON TREASURY BOARD SUBMISSIONS

The following authorities, usually found in their left-hand columns, are some selected financial proposals in most Treasury Board Submissions: adjustments to funding; accommodation premium; temporary access to Treasury Board Vote 5; permanent access to Treasury Board Vote 5; approval of a named grant and contributions or class contributions for certain organizations; approval of a class grant; approval of an increase to an existing grant or class grant; temporary frozen allotments; increases to vote netted or net voted revenues; adjustments to the Program Activity Architecture (PAA); debt write-off authority; debt forgiveness authority; remission of debt authority; and approval for project authority.

Adjustments to Funding

Adjustments to increase funding are required when an organization is seeking an increase to current year and/or future-year funding. Should an organization seek funding related to personnel, then the decision-makers must include an Employment Benefit Plan (EPB) amount, usually 2 percent of personnel costs in the funding authority request and also state that such funding is being sought in the authority paragraph. There is no need to refer to PWGSC accommodation charges, around 13% of personnel costs, if they do not apply. [See definitions below] However if they do, then that should be stated in the authority paragraph and a separate approval, as shown below, should be prepared.

Authority is required when an organization has been directed by the Treasury Board of Canada Secretariat to permanently reduce spending on a specific initiative that has an impact on future years. An example of when one would seek this type of authority could be as a result of a spending restraint initiative.

Accommodation Premium

This authority is required in order to cover the 13 per cent accommodation premium levied by PWGSC on new salary resources.

Temporary Access to Treasury Board Vote 5

This authority is required when an organization is seeking temporary access to Vote 5 or government contingencies. Temporary access to TB Vote 5 is used primarily when an organization has insufficient spending authority to cover existing requirements and the funding is urgently required prior to the next supply period.

Permanent Access to Treasury Board Vote 5

These authorities are for all named grants or those contributions or class contributions in certain organizations that, according to their vote wording, require parliamentary approval. One must have one's grant or those contributions, if applicable, listed in The Estimates in order to make such an applicable grant or contribution payment.

Approval of a Named Grant or Contribution or Class Contribution for Certain Organizations

These authorities are for all named grants or those contributions and class contributions in certain organizations that, according to their vote wording, require parliamentary approval. One must have one's grant or those contributions, if applicable, listed in The Estimates in order make such an applicable grant or contribution payment.

Approval of an Increase to an Existing Named Grant or a Class Grant

These two authorities are required for an increase to a named grant or a class grant. The increase to the named grant or the class grant needs to be printed in The Estimates or be already listed in The Estimates to make this type of grant payment.

Approval of Terms and Conditions for a Contribution or Class Contribution Agreements

This authority is required for all new, renewed, or amended contribution or class contribution agreements.

Temporary Frozen Allotments

This authority is required when an organization has been directed by the Treasury Board of Canada Secretariat to withhold spending on a specific initiative until the organization has met one or more conditions.

Permanent Frozen Allotments

This authority is required when an organization has been directed by the Treasury Board of Secretariat to permanently withhold spending on a specific initiative that has an impact on the current fiscal year or the next fiscal year if requested after the Annual Reference Level Update closes.

Specified Purpose Allotments

This authority is required when an organization has been directed by the Treasury Board of Canada Secretariat to create a specified purpose allotment. The authority is used to separate a portion of an organization's voted appropriation for an initiative or item. A specified purpose allotment is established when the Treasury Board wishes to impose special spending controls.

Transfers Between Votes, both Internal and External

This authority is required when an organization wants to do internal vote transfers or to transfer funds to another organization. Transfer of funds within the same vote does not require this authority. These types of transfers are reflected through The Regular Supplementary Estimates and Annual Reference Level Update processes.

Increases to Vote Netted or Net Voted Revenues

This authority is required when an organization wishes to increase previously approved vote netted or net voted revenue amounts.

Adjustments to the Program Activity Architecture

This authority is required when an organization wants to adjust its Program Activity Architecture (PAA) at the strategic outcome or program activity level.

Debt Write Off Authority

This authority is required when an organization wants to write off a debt due to the Crown. *Budgetary* or *non-budgetary* loans and any associated interest on these loans can be written off under Section 25 of the *Financial Administration Act.* In the case of non-budgetary loans, the amount written off must be charged to a budgetary appropriation.

Remission of Debt Authority

This authority is required when an organization wants to remit a debt due to the Crown. Any *budgetary* loans and any associated interest on those budgetary loans can be remitted under Section 23 of the *Financial Administration Act. Non-budgetary loans* can also be remitted.

Approval for Project Authority

This authority is to seek both preliminary project approval authority as well as spending authority from Treasury Board when required, usually before the project definition phase starts. While the GST becomes a part of the project cost and expenditure authority, funds in this regard do not flow to the project manager but are usually listed separately.

CHART 7A   SPECIMEN DELEGATION OF AUTHORITY INSTRUMENT OR CHART

Position	Initiation of Expenditure Section 32 FAA	Spending Authority Section 34 FAA	Payment Authority Section 33 FAA	Authority to Hire and Fire	Other	Comments
Director General	Full*	Full	Full	Full	Full	Full
Financial Manager	Full	Full	Full	Full	Full	Full
Human Resource Manager	Full	Full	Full	Full	Full	Full
Material Manager	Full	Full	Full	Full	Full	Full

_____MINISTER   _____DEPUTY HEAD

*Full designates the ability to spend the entire approved or authorized budget with a single action of the exercise of delegated authority.

CHART B   SPECIMEN SIGNATURE CARD

Group AA	Function	Amount	Level
Step 1 Section 32 FAA	Initiation of Authority	_____	_____
Step2	Commitment Control	_____	_____
Step 3 Section 34 FAA	Spending Authority	_____	_____
Step 4 Section 33 FAA	Payment Authority	_____	_____
Group BB	Hiring and Firing; Purchase Order; Purchase Requisition; Asset Acquisition; Other	_____	_____

_____

Approved by

_____20XX

_____

Signature

_____20XX

The Reader Should Remember: the details of how authorities are delegated. Terms such as delegatus non potest delegare are vital. Documents such as the *Specimen Signature Card* and the organization's *Delegation of Authority Chart or Instrument* play pivotal roles. The main principle lies within the power of each government minister to delegate to her or his deputy head and then to positions held permanently or temporarily public servants. In addition, authority for contracting is also delegated by both PWGSC and The Treasury Board of Canada. Authority is always delegated to positions not to individuals themselves.

PART III

The Practice of Implementing Generally Accepted Accounting Principles (GAAP)

The Theory of Accounting

OBJECTIVE OF CHAPTER EIGHT

The objective of this chapter is to introduce the reader and the course or workshop participant to the general working theory of accounting.

INTRODUCTION

Every element of society, from the individual to an entire industry or government organization, needs to make decisions on how to allocate its resources.

"...Accounting is that process which aids these decisions by recording, classifying, summarizing, and reporting business transactions and interpreting their effects on the affairs of the business entity..."

Most accounting and bookkeeping students have heard the term "double-entry bookkeeping." Five tenets essentially support the way the whole system works: The first thing that happens in business life which calls for accounting records is that someone makes out a business document which relates to a transaction between the one business and some other business. The document may be an item such as a cheque, credit note, invoice, journal voucher, petty cash voucher or receipt. Secondly, these documents may then be recorded in some more permanent journal or book. Alternatively, the documents themselves may be retained as a permanent record, either in some file or binder. Thirdly, entries are then made from these permanent records into some sort of main book. This may be a bound book, a loose-leaf book, mechanical, electric or electronic files stored in the memory of the computer. Fourthly, one then does some sort of balancing act with the relevant figures to prove that those entries are essentially correct. Finally, after the balancing act one prepares a set of reports for use by decision-makers so the latter can take proper actions.

FUNDAMENTALS OF ACCOUNTING AND INTRODUCING WORKING EXAMPLES

Accounting comprises three basic elements: **assets**, **liabilities**, and **owners' equity.** So that one may quickly understand what these elements mean and how they are inter-related, one may consider them from the point of view of two types of businesses: an imaginary small accounting practice, a sole proprietorship, Samuel L. Bell, Chartered Accountant, and the Passport Office, a Special Operating Agency whose parent department is the Department of Foreign Affairs and International Trade (DFAIT). These two types of businesses differ, the former from the private sector and the latter is a public sector firm. However, the fundamental principles which guide their accounting policies and practices remain almost identical. Both the Chartered Accounting firm and the Passport Office maintain a set of clients who in turn usually pay cash "on the barrel head", some of it in advance, some later for the services which the two businesses provide.

ASSETS

Anything of value that a business *owns* is an asset. Among the most common assets any business owns are: cash, accounts receivable, furniture, inventory, and office equipment. The Passport Office, for example, at the end of one particular period had: cash, totaling $ 16,400.00: accounts receivable amounting to $ 1,000.00; furniture valued at $ 3,000.00; inventory supplies of $ 500.00 and office equipment purchased for $ 40,000.00. The total assets of the Passport Office were $ 60,900.00. Samuel L. Bell, Chartered Accountant, at the end of the same fiscal period had cash of $ 7,000.00; furniture costing $ 3,700.00; and office equipment costing $ 4,300.00. Samuel L. Bell, Chartered Accountant's total assets were $ 15,000.00. Each of these assets represents a number of individual items. The item 'cash', for example, refers not only to currency and coins but also to cheques, money orders, direct debit and credit entries for sales made to customers. In addition, cash includes the amount that a business has in transit and on deposit in a chequing or a savings account at a financial institution. The 'computer equipment' represents such items as personal computers and other peripheral equipment such as printers and scanners.

The term 'equipment' used here covers typewriters, calculators, photocopying machines, cash registers and the like. In any accounting practice or other business venture, related assets must be grouped into categories such as these, rather than be itemized separately.

In all public and privately owned organizations maintaining and reporting their financial information, there remain, of course, other kinds of assets such as raw materials, tools, machinery, vehicles and land. However, not all assets comprise these tangible items. For example, both the Passport Office and the accountancy practice of Samuel L. Bell, Chartered Accountant show accounts receivable. This type of asset represents the unpaid amounts owed to the Passport Office and Samuel L. Bell, Chartered Accountant who purchased passports, other immigration documents and accounting services and have not paid for them with cash. In accounting, an accounts receivable is an asset mainly because it represents a claim against the customer's property until he or she pays the amount owed to the company.

LIABILITIES

Any debt that a business **owes** is a liability. The business which owes the debt, similar to the Passport Office and Samuel L. Bell, Chartered Accountant in our working examples, is the debtor. Assigning the value of the funds to the firm(s) to whom the debt(s) is (are) owed, as in our example, Grand & Toy and the Queen's Printer, creates the creditor(s). For example, when a business or individual borrows money from a bank, a liability is created for the amount of the loan. Or if the business buys equipment, goods or services without paying for them immediately, promising to pay for the purchase at some future date, the liability is created for the amount of the money owed to the customer who would have received the goods or services. In our two working examples, the Passport Office and Samuel L. Bell, Chartered Accountant are the debtors, and the Queen's Printer and Grand and Toy are the creditors respectively. The Queen's Printer is owed $ 10,000 for printing services and Grand and Toy

$ 6,000 for office supplies. Therefore the Passport Office has a liability of $ 10,000 and Samuel L. Bell, Chartered Accountant that of $ 6,000.

In accounting terminology, liabilities are usually identified by the word 'payable'. The money the Passport Office owes the Queen's Printer and that Samuel L. Bell, Chartered Accountant owes Grand and Toy is called 'accounts payable'. A written promise to pay a bank a certain amount in the future is called a 'loan payable' or 'bank loan'. A similar promise in writing that pledges property as security for the payment of the debt is called a 'mortgage payable'. Of all the various types of liabilities that a business may have, accounts payable are by far the most common encountered. Among individual borrowers it could be a loan payable or a mortgage payable.

OWNERS' EQUITY OR INVESTMENT IN CANADA

Every business, such as Samuel L. Bell, Chartered Accountant, has one or more owners—one in the case of a single proprietorship, such as a single accounting practitioner, for example, Samuel L. Bell, Chartered Accountant, or more than one in the case of a partnership, such as a large accountancy firm like De Loitte & Touche or a big corporation such as MacMillan Bloedell. The financial interest an owner has in a business is called the owners' equity. Other terms, such as capital, proprietorship, net worth or present worth may also be used to refer to the financial interest of an owner. This may be referred to as 'Investment in Canada' in Canadian government organizations such as the Passport Office. The preferred term in non-government organizations (NGOs) in Canada is 'owners' equity'.

During the remainder of this text, for the reader's ease of understanding, Samuel L. Bell, Chartered Accountant continues to be the main practical example. Bell's equity in this accounting firm at any given time equals the difference between the assets of the business and the claim of others against those assets. This relationship will be expressed as the equation: **assets minus liabilities equal owners' equity**. In addition the equation is described further in another section.

THE ACCOUNTING EQUATION

The accounting equation builds upon three fundamental elements defined above: assets, liabilities and owners' equity. *Assets*, on one hand, represent what the business *owns*. *Liabilities* and *owners' equity* represent the **total claim** against those assets. Therefore, *Assets equal Liabilities plus Owners' Equity*. By means of this equation, we can determine Samuel L. Bell, Chartered Accountant's equity in his business. The assets of this business total $ 15,000. Since the liabilities are $ 6,000, Samuel L. Bell, Chartered Accountant's equity must be $ 9,000. Or let us examine an even easier, more familiar example. Let us say, that Monsieur Serge Dupont *owns* a house in the Gatineau, Quebec. The house has a market value of $ 400,000. However, Serge also *owes* the local branch of a Quebecois bank, the Caisse Populaire, $ 350,000 for a mortgage on the same house. Therefore Monsieur Dupont's owners' equity in the house equals $ 50,000.

Thus, we can see, in our chosen working example below, the following details which represent Samuel L. Bell, Chartered Accountant, and Sole Proprietor:

Assets				=	**Liabilities**	+ **Owners' Equity**
Cash +	Acc. Rec. +	Furniture +	Off. Eqpt.	=	Acc. Pay.	+ Samuel L. Bell
7,000+	300 +	3,700 +	4,000	=	6,000	+ 9,000
	15,000			=		**15,000**

As summarized below as it is detailed before, this relationship between assets on the one hand and the liabilities and owners' equity on the other is expressed by the **accounting equation:**

Asset   =   Liabilities + Owners' Equity

As the above equation demonstrates, the *two sides* of the accounting equation *must always be equal* because the rights to all the business' assets are owned by a single person or more than one person. Remember also that the creditors have a temporary claim against the assets of a business. Until the liabilities have been paid, the owner also has a claim against the remaining assets of the firm. If no liabilities exist, by default, the owners' equity equals the total assets.

Balance Sheet

A *balance sheet* is a piece of paper, invented by Simon Stevin of Bruges in 1536, which shows the assets of a business listed on one side, and the liabilities and owners' equity listed on the other. In other words, a balance sheet is a simple formal presentation of the fundamental elements that comprise the accounting equation. This presentation provides an itemized list of the assets, liabilities, and owners' equity of a business as at a specific time or date. The primary purpose of the *balance sheet* is to present this information in an orderly fashion for the use of owners, creditors and others interested in the financial standing of a business. This bit of foolscap has been sometimes called a snapshot of a business at a precise given moment in time. Similarly, a single line of financial coding represents an even smaller snapshot of a particular financial transaction in a government entity at a precise moment in time.

Analyzing a Balance Sheet

The form of a balance sheet follows the accounting equation: *assets equal liabilities plus owners' equity*. In most countries outside the United Kingdom, assets are shown on the left side of a balance sheet, and the liabilities and owners' equity on its right. In Britain, the reverse obtains. The word 'balance' emphasizes the fact that the total of the figures on the left, whatever they represent, MUST always equal the total of the figures on the right. The balance sheet prepared for Samuel L. Bell, Chartered Accountant shows the assets, liabilities and owners' equity as at the close of the business day on September 30, 2XX8.

Samuel L. Bell, Chartered Accountant

Balance Sheet

As at September 30, 2XX8

Assets		Liabilities and Owners' Equity	
Cash	$ 7,000	Accounts Payable:	
Accounts Receivable:		Grand and Toy	$ 6,000
Pierre Boucher	1,000	Owners' Equity:	
Furniture And Fixtures	3,000	Samuel L. Bell, Capital	9,000
Office Equipment	4,000		
TOTALS	**$ 15,000**	**TOTALS**	**$ 15,000**

A balance sheet shows the kinds of assets and the recorded value of each type of asset, and the total amount of assets. The claims against these assets come from two sources: liabilities and owners' equity. Therefore, a balance sheet also shows the kind and amount of each asset as well as the total of the liabilities and owners' equity.

The format of a balance sheet differs from that of the accounting equation in four (4) different ways: 1.The balance sheet contains a heading that answers these questions: Who? [The name of the business]. What? [The name of the statement]. The date is extremely important because the figures show the financial position on that particular day. 2. Accounts receivable are shown as a total control balance, or itemized by each debtor. 3. Accounts payable are also shown as a control balance, or itemized by each creditor. 4. The word 'capital' is used with the owner's name in the equity section of a balance sheet. 'Owners' equity is a general term used to indicate the *total financial interest* of an owner, whereas 'capital' is the term specifically used to indicate the *total investment* of an owner. Thus, in the owners' equity section of the balance sheet in our practical example, the phrase 'Samuel L. Capital' is used to indicated Samuel L. Bell's total investment in the firm.

Accounting examiners often test the candidates' understanding of the balance sheet by asking them to calculate some basic figures from a balance sheet. Unfortunately, terms can have more than one meaning, and some ambiguity may surface as a result. Terms used by examiners include: *capital employed, fixed assets, monetary assets, non-monetary assets and working capital.* The definitions of these terms appear below:

Financial assets are assets that derive value because of a contractual claim. Stocks, bonds, bank deposits, and the like are all examples of financial assets.

Non-financial assets are assets with a physical value such as land, property or some type of object.

Fixed assets, or **non current assets** also known as property, plant and equipment is a term used in accountancy for assets and property which cannot easily be converted into cash. This can be compared with current assets such as cash or bank accounts, which are described as liquid assets. In most cases, only tangible assets are referred to as fixed. Fixed assets normally include such items as land, buildings, motor vehicles, furniture, office equipment, computers, fixtures and fittings, and plant and machinery. These often receive a favourable tax treatment, such as a capital cost or depreciation allowance, over short term assets.

Capital employed may be described, amongst other terms used, as the total of the assets in the business.

Capital owned means the capital owned at the balance sheet date by the owner. It is defined as the balance sheet total less the external liabilities. It is sometimes called the net worth of the business to its owner. In public sector outfits it may be described as the Investment in Canada or reduction to Accumulated Debt.

Liquid assets have one or more of the following features: They can be sold either: (1) rapidly, (2) with minimal loss of value or, (3) anytime within market hours.

Liquid capital, or **fluid capital**, is a readily convertible asset, such as money or other bearer economic instruments, as opposed to a long term asset like real estate. Liquid capital may be held by individuals, companies or governments.

Working capital is the amount of capital that is available to meet the day to day expenses of running the business. Money from the sale of fixed assets may not be readily available and some of the current assets are combined [Section 32 of *The Financial Administration Act* of the government of Canada] to pay current liabilities as they become due. Therefore working capital = current assets – liabilities. At Samuel L. Bell, Chartered Accountant, the working capital of that accounting firm stands at: 7,300 – 6,000 = 1,300. According to the *Public Accounts of Canada for the fiscal year 2006-2007*, the current liabilities of the government of Canada exceeded the amount of its current assets, showing, unfortunately, a negative working capital situation for the government of Canada.

Monetary assets are those assets whose amount is fixed by contract or otherwise as to the number of dollars to be received, regardless of changes in the general price level. Cash and accounts receivable are examples of monetary assets.

Non-monetary assets are those assets whose amount is not fixed by contract or otherwise as to the number of dollars to be received, regardless of changes in the general price level. Inventory, land and equipment are examples of non-monetary assets.

Current assets comprise a balance sheet account that represents the value of all assets that are reasonably expected to be converted into cash within one year in the normal course of business. Current assets include cash, accounts receivable, inventory, marketable securities, prepaid expenses and other liquid assets that can be readily converted to cash. In personal finance, current assets are all assets a person can readily convert to cash to pay outstanding debts and cover liabilities without having to sell fixed assets. In the United Kingdom, current assets are also known as 'current accounts'.

Preparing a Balance Sheet

Generally, a balance sheet is prepared by the accountant and audited by the auditor. The statement can be written in ink, typed or printed. No matter how the balance sheet is prepared, it must contain the proper data, must be accurate and must be neatly presented. Accountants follow certain guidelines when preparing a balance sheet.

Heading

Enter the heading: WHO, WHAT and WHEN at the top of the balance sheet. Centre each of these items on a separate line.

Assets Section

Centre the assets on the first line of the left side of the balance sheet. Then list each asset, beginning with cash, along the left margin. Begin each word of an asset type with a capital. Record the value of each asset type in the money column next to the asset type. Next, list each asset type in the order of how easily it can be converted into cash. For example, at the start of the listing would be cash. At the end of the listing would be some type of asset that is not easily converted to cash, say a lot of land. Most accountants prefer to list the type of assets in a certain order known as the liquidity order.

Hardly any problems may be associated with assigning a dollar value to cash and accounts receivable. Both of these two types of assets may be used to pay debts and other expenses of the business. Of course, a short time exists before the amounts due from customers will be converted into currency or cash; but nevertheless the value of the currency assigned to each customer's debt is in reality 'cash'. Other types of assets, however, such as land, buildings, furniture, equipment, etc., are not usually acquired for the purpose of immediate conversion into cash. An indirect conversion exists as the assets are used to generate business for the enterprise which itself may or may not be converted into cash. For Samuel L. Bell, Chartered Accountant, assets like the computer, addressing, duplicating and photocopying machines and others, represent economic resources that will be used to produce revenues or probably converted later into cash, through the sale of services. A generally accepted principle in the accounting profession in recording the 'value' of these assets can be stated as follows:

> *It is a generally recognized accounting principle that a balance sheet does not purport to show either the present value of assets to the enterprise or values that might be realized in liquidation. The accepted bases for assets are the cost at the date of their acquisition.*

Until these debts have been paid, each creditor has a temporary claim, for example, on the assets of Samuel L. Bell, Chartered Accountant, the debtor. This principle simply means that accountants prefer to record such assets on the basis of the currency that has been used to acquire these economic resources. The currency amounts listed do not necessarily indicate the prices at which the asset could be sold. 'Market value' is a very important function in the statement. In the language of business, therefore, the 'value' of an asset may simply mean the historical cost of that asset, and not necessarily the present value or worth of that asset. For example, when stating the currency amounts associated with inventories, *The Canadian Institute of Chartered of Accountants Handbook* states that this type of asset should be recorded at 'lower of cost, that is, historical, or market value'.

Liabilities Section

Centre the title 'liabilities' on the first line of the right side of the balance sheet. Then list each liability, beginning with accounts payable, at the centre margin. Begin each word with a capital letter. Other types of liabilities may include loans payable and mortgage payable. Record the amount of each type of liability in the money columns on the right side. There may be one account payable, one loan payable and one mortgage payable, or several accounts payable, several loans payable or several mortgages payable. Just like the assets, liabilities are usually placed in a particular order. Since liabilities represent debts to be paid, most accountants prefer them in the order they must be paid or in a reverse sort of order of liquidity. Those that need to be paid within the current year are placed before those to be settled over a longer period of time. For example, if the business has a bank loan due within ten days, then this loan payable would be listed before a set of accounts payable to individuals of firms. Debts to be paid over a longer period of time, also classified as long term liabilities, such as a mortgage payable, would be listed at the bottom of the liabilities section. Again, in the United Kingdom, these items are shown in the reverse order.

Owners' Equity Section (also known as Investment in Canada)

Skip a line after the liability section, and then centre the title for the owners' equity section. This section of the balance sheet varies slightly according to the type of organization on which it is reporting. In a single proprietorship such as Samuel L. Bell, Chartered Accountant, the name of owner appears in the owners' equity section. If Bell and Williams, Chartered Accountants, were a partnership and owned equally by Samuel L. Bell and Francis J. Williams, the financial interest of each owner would be shown. If the business were a corporation with hundreds or thousands of owners, it would be impractical to list all the names, addresses and equity of each shareholder on the balance sheet. Therefore, as one account for a profit organization it may be called Owners' Equity. Should the firm be owned and operated by the government of Canada, this summary account could be then called Investment in Canada.

The Reader Should Remember: the accounting equation: *assets = liabilities + owners' equity;* the definition of an asset, a liability, an expense, a revenue; what is a balance sheet; how to analyze a balance sheet; and the generally recognized accounting principle about what a balance sheet does and does not do. The accounting equation *should* balance after every transaction.

Analyzing Business Transactions

OBJECTIVE OF CHAPTER NINE

The objective of this chapter is to introduce the reader, course or workshop participant to the theories, policies and practices involving business transactions.

INTRODUCTION

Each financial activity in which a business engages is an economic event that affects the fundamentals in the accounting equation. For instance, if a business buys materials, receives money from or pays money to its customers, one or more of the fundamental elements change. These economic events which affect the fundamental elements are called *transactions*. Before an accountant, accounting clerk, administrative officer, bookkeeper or finance clerk can record a transaction, he or she must first analyze and determine the possible and probable effect(s) upon the fundamental elements.

Balance Sheet Transactions

To illustrate the kinds of effects these transactions may have on the fundamental elements, one must first analyze a few transactions for Samuel L. Bell, Chartered Accountant, during the month of October, 2XX8. As of September 30, 2XX8 let us assume that the accounting equation for the firm looked like this:

Assets					=	Liabilities	+	Owners' Equity
		Accounts		Office		Accounts		Samuel L. Bell,
Cash	+	Receivable	+ Furniture	+ Equipment	=	Payable	+	Capital
7,000	+	300	+ 3,700	+ 4,000	=	6,000	+	9,000
Totals:		**15,000**				**15,000**		

Any transactions in which Samuel L. Bell, Chartered Accountant engages after September 30, 2XX8 will affect the fundamental elements in this accounting equation.

Asset Transactions

This sub-section comprises some practical examples of buying assets for cash; buying assets on credit; returning assets bought on credit; and the impact on the owners' equity account balance.

Buying Assets for Cash

When cash is paid for an asset, only one fundamental element is affected: the following example we may visualize this transaction:

TRANSACTION

On October 1, 2XX8 Samuel L. Bell, Chartered Accountant buys a computer from Dell Computers for $ 1,000 and tenders a cheque for payment.

ANALYSIS

The office equipment asset account increases by 1,000. The cash asset account decreases by 1,000 because the business now has less money. Therefore, the impact on the fundamental elements follows:

Cash +	Accounts Receivable	+ Furniture	Office + Equipment	Accounts = Payable	Samuel L. Bell, + Capital
7,000 +	300	+ 3,700	+ 4,000	= 6,000	+ 9,000
-1,000			+ 1,000		
6,000 +	300	+ 3,700	+ 5,000	= 6,000	+ 9,000
		15,000			**15,000**

At this point, it is probably prudent to introduce those control or bank accounts used in both the departmental financial statements of Canadian government departments and agencies and the common service agency, PWGSC or The Receiver General for Canada. They are also referred to as cash reconciliation control accounts:

Cash payment control; cash deposit control; payroll control account; interdepartmental settlement (I. S.) debit control; interdepartmental settlement (I. S.) credit control; cash payment control in U. S. dollars; cash payment control in other foreign currencies; cash payment control departmental bank account (DBA); zero balance account (ZBA); non-treasury control – Department of Finance; program payment control; and other control assigned on February 1, 2001.

Buying Assets on Credit

When assets are brought on 'credit', the assets are received by the firm at the time of purchase but are not paid for until some future date. Buying an asset on credit creates a liability called 'accounts payable'. This kind of transaction affects two fundamental elements of the accounting equation: assets and liabilities. Both increase. In some organizations in the government of Canada, those who have not fully complied with the concept of full accrual accounting, a kind of liability is created at the end of the fiscal year. This liability is known as payable at year end (PAYE). The situation in which a PAYE is created requires that: the item of good or service purchased is received on or before March 31; there is proof that such an item has been received; and the customer has NOT submitted an invoice for payment. In the following examples we see a presentation of accounts payable.

TRANSACTION

October 2, 2XX6: Samuel L. Bell, Chartered Accountant buys additional furniture for $ 5,000 on credit from Sears Canada Limited.

ANALYSIS

The asset account: furniture increases by $ 5,000 because the business acquired more furniture. The liability account: accounts payable increases by $ 5,000 because the business owes more money. That which follows also shows the impact on the accounting equation:

ASSETS				=	LIABILITIES	+ OWNERS' EQUITY
Cash	+ Accounts Receivable	+ Furniture	Office Equipment =		Accounts Payable	Samuel L. Bell, + Capital
6,000 +	300	+ 3,700	+ 5,000	=	6,000	+ 9,000
		5,000			5,000	
6,000 +	300	+ 8,700	+ 5,000	=	11,000	+ 9,000
	20,000				**20,000**	

Returning Assets Bought on Credit

When a business returns assets bought on credit as yet not paid for, two fundamental elements of the accounting equation are affected: assets and liabilities: both decrease.

TRANSACTION

October 3, 2XX8: Samuel L. Bell, Chartered Accountant returns $ 1,000 of computer equipment from Dell Computers which were damaged.

ANALYSIS

The asset office equipment decreases by $ 1,000 because the business now has less equipment. The liability accounts payable decreases by $ 1,000 because the firm now owes less money to its creditors, who in turn have a smaller claim on Samuel L. Bell, Chartered Accountant's assets. That which follows again shows the impact on the accounting equation:

Owners' Equity Section

Skip a line the liability section, and be sure to centre the title for the owners' equity section. This section of the balance sheet or statement of financial position varies slightly according to the type of business organization being reported on. In a single proprietorship such as Samuel L. Bell, Chartered Accountant, the name of the owner, Samuel L. Bell, appears in the owners' equity section. If Samuel L. Bell changes to a partnership owned equally by Samuel L. Bell and Francis J. Williams, both practicing chartered accountants, the financial interest of both would be shown. If the business were a federal government 'not-for-profit' organization, the amount in the owners' equity section may be entitled 'Investment in Canada'. The example below shows the effect on various accounts, the fundamental elements and the accounting equation:

ASSETS						= LIABILITIES	+ OWNERS' EQUITY	
Cash	+ Accounts Receivable	+ Furniture	+ Office Equipment	=		Accounts Payable	+	Samuel L. Bell, Capital
6,000 +	300	+ 8,700	+ 5,000	=		11,000	+	9,000
			(1,000)			(1,000)		
6,000 +	300	+ 8,700	+ 4,000	=		10,000	+	9,000
	19,000					**19,000**		

Collection of an Account Receivable

When a customer of a business pays his or her debt in whole or in part, only one fundamental element of the accounting equation is affected: assets. The asset cash increases, and the asset accounts receivable decreases by an equal amount.

TRANSACTION

October 3: Samuel L. Bell, Chartered Accountant, receives a cheque for $ 200 from Jean-Paul Baptiste in payment of his debt with the accounting firm.

ANALYSIS

The asset cash increases by $ 200 because the business now owns more money. The asset accounts receivable decreases by $ 200 because the customer no longer owes any money to the business. Again, the reader can view a practical demonstration of how these changes affect individual accounts, the fundamental elements, and not least of all, the accounting equation:

ASSETS				= LIABILITIES	+ OWNERS' EQUITY
	Accounts		Office	Accounts	Samuel L. Bell,
Cash +	Receivable +	Furniture +	Equipment =	Payable +	Capital
6,000 +	300 +	8,700 +	4,000 =	10,000 +	9,000
200	(200)				
6,200	100 +	8,700 +	4,000 =	10,000 +	9,000
		19,000			**19,000**

LIABILITY TRANSACTIONS

This subsection comprises: increasing owners' investment, paying liabilities; and decreasing owners' investment.

Increasing Owners' Investment

When the owner increases his investment in the business, two fundamental elements of the accounting equation are affected – assets and owners' equity. Both elements increase.

TRANSACTION

October 5: Samuel L. Bell decides that the accounting firm, Samuel L. Bell, Chartered Accountant, needs more cash to pay for additional computer equipment and furniture which he plans to buy. He therefore withdraws $ 5,000 from his personal bank account and deposits it into the firm's chequing account.

ANALYSIS

The asset cash increases by $ 5,000 because the business now has more money. The owners' equity Samuel L. Bell, capital increases by $ 5,000 because the owner has now increased his investment in the business. The effects on the individual accounts, the fundamental elements and the accounting equation are shown below:

ASSETS				= LIABILITIES	+ OWNERS' EQUITY
	Accounts		Office	Accounts	Samuel L. Bell,
Cash +	Receivable +	Furniture +	Equipment	= Payable	+ Capital
6,200 +	100	8,700	4,000	= 10,000	+ 9,000
5,000					5,000
11,200 +	100	8,700	4,000	= 10,000	14,000
		24,000			**24,000**

Paying Liabilities

When a business settles a liability in whole or in part, two fundamental elements of the accounting equation are affected: assets and liabilities. Both decrease.

TRANSACTION

October 4: Samuel L. Bell, Chartered Accountant writes a cheque for $ 2,000 to Dell Computers. This payment is to be applied against the total amount Samuel L. Bell, Chartered Accountant owes Dell Computers.

ANALYSIS

The account cash decreases by $ 2,000 because the business now has less money. The liability account accounts payable decreases by $ 2,000 because the business now owes less money to its creditors.

ASSETS				= LIABLITIES	+ OWNERS' EQUITY		
Cash +	Accounts Receivable +	Furniture +	Office Equipment =	Accounts Payable +	Samuel L. Bell, Capital
11,200 +	100 +	8,700 +	4,000 =	10,000 +	14,000
(2,000)				(2,000)	
9,200 +	100 +	8,700 +	4,000	8,000 +	14,000
		22,000			**22,000**

Decreasing Owners' Investment

When the owner withdraws assets from the business, two fundamental elements of the accounting equation are affected: assets and owners' equity. Both fundamental elements decrease.

TRANSACTION

October 6: Samuel L. Bell withdraws $ 1,200 from Samuel L. Bell, Chartered Accountant's chequing account and deposits the funds in his personal savings account.

ANALYSIS

The asset cash decreases by the $ 1,200 because the business now has less cash. The owners' equity account, Samuel L. Bell, Capital decreases by $ 1,200 because the owner has now decreased his investment in the business.

ASSETS				= LIABILITIES +	OWNERS' EQUITY	
	Accounts			Office	Accounts	Samuel L. Bell,
Cash +	Receivable +	Furniture	+	Equipment =	Payable +	Capital
9,200+	100 +	8,700	+	4,000 =	8,000 +	14,000
(1,200)						(1,200)
8,000	100 +	8,700	+	4,000 =	8,000 +	12,800
		20,800				**20,800**

The transactions that have been analyzed in this topic illustrate the three principles that apply to the analysis for all these types of transactions: Each transaction must have an impact on at least two items: The transactions must not be "in kind" but be expressed in terms of money. After all of, and each of the impacts also, the accounting equation must remain in balance.

REVENUE AND EXPENSE TRANSACTIONS

An owner operates a business for two main reasons: (1) To have an impact on the environment, socially and physically, and (2) To make a profit, usually a financial one, and to hereby increase his or her equity in the business. According to the second reason, a profit therefore results when revenues derived from the sale of goods and/or services exceed the expenses incurred to earn the same revenues. This, incidentally, is known as the "matching principle". The economic events which determine whether a business will profit are known as "revenue transactions" and "expense transactions". It should be also remembered that though the second reason is to generate profit, a loss may also result.

When a business organization sells goods or services, it either obtains cash or maintains an account receivable with its customers. As a result of these sales, the left side accounting equation increases by an identical amount because the claims against the assets must always be equal to the total of the assets themselves. Since liabilities are not always affected by these transactions, it remains that the owners' equity is affected. Owners' equity is therefore then increased, by the same amount, resulting from an excess of revenues over expenses.

Now, if the same amount of cash received or the accounts receivable created is less than the amount of the value of the corresponding sale, the difference may result in a decrease in owners' equity, because the business suffered a loss from the transaction. One can then conclude that profits resulting from revenue transactions increase owners' equity, and losses resulting from revenue transactions decrease owners' equity.

To illustrate how revenue transactions can alter owners' equity, we will analyze a few cash and credit sales by Samuel L. Bell, Chartered Accountant during October. Note that revenue is listed *separately* under owners' equity to distinguish this amount from Capital, the owners' equity in the business.

Receiving Revenues from Cash Sales

When the government or a commercial private sector business sells goods or services for cash, two fundamental elements of the accounting equation are affected---assets and revenue realization under owners' equity.

TRANSACTION

October 31: Samuel L. Bell, Chartered Accountant has received $ 1,500 in cash as revenue from the sale of services, also valued at $ 1,500 in October.

ANALYSIS

The asset cash increases by $ 1,500 because the business now has more money. Owners' equity benefits by $ 1,500 because of increases in revenue.

ASSETS				=	LIABILITIES	+	OWNERS' EQUITY
Cash +	Accounts Receivable +	Furniture +	Office Equipment =		Accounts Payable	+	Samuel L. Bell, Capital
8,000 +	100 +	8,700 +	4,000 =		8,000	+	12,800
1,500							1,500
9,500 +	100 +	8,700 +	4,000 =		8,000	+	14,300
		22,300					**22,300**

As a result of the transaction, Samuel L. Chartered Accountant now has additional cash of $ 1,500. Thus the left side of the accounting equation now equals the right side. The accounting equation remains in balance.

Receiving Revenue from Credit Sales

When a public or private sector business sells on credit, two fundamental elements are basically affected – assets and revenue realizations under owners' equity. Both fundamental elements increase.

TRANSACTION

October 31: Samuel L. Bell, Chartered Accountant sells services on credit both to Jonathan Swift for $ 1,000 and Marie Curie Blanchette for $ 500.

ANALYSIS

The asset accounts receivable increases by $ 1,500 because the debtors now have agreed to pay the business at some future date. The owners' equity increases by $ 1,500 because of the increase in the revenues.

ASSETS				=	LIABILITIES	+ OWNERS' EQUITY
	Accounts		Office		Accounts	Samuel L. Bell,
Cash +	Receivable +	Furniture +	Equipment =		Payable	+ Capital
9,500 +	100	+ 8,700	+ 4,000	=	8,000	+ 14,300
	1,500				Net income	1,500
9,500 +	1,600	+ 8,700	+ 4,000	=	8,000	+ 15,800
	23,800					23,800

As a result of the sale on credit, the left side of the accounting equation increases because the asset accounts receivable increases. The right side of the equation increases by the same amount because the total claims against assets must equal the total of the assets themselves. Since liabilities are not affected, it is the revenue realized under the owners' equity that increases. The accounting equation remains in balance.

Expense Transactions

In order to operate a business effectively, it must receive revenues. From these revenues, money has to be spent on items that assist the earning process, such as salaries, advertising and telephones. These costs, when matched against current revenues, are called expenses. The matching of revenues and expenses, an important generally accepted accounting principle, determines whether a business operates at profit or at a loss.

In accountancy, the terms income and expense are sometimes used in preference to the terms profit and loss. Before federal government department and agencies became fully compliant to generally accepted accounting principles (GAAP), the terms income and expenditure were more popular than the terms now used by most important departments and agencies, revenue and expense. The arithmetic difference between revenue and expense is either a loss or a profit. When revenues exceed expenses, incomes result. Conversely, when expenses exceed revenues, losses result. One can easily picture a Venn diagram with two overlapping circles. When the two circles are equal in area, neither profits nor losses result. What is experienced is a break even situation. If either the revenues or the expenses are greater than the other, the area where the two circles intersect represents either profits or losses. This depends on which element is greater and its corresponding element lesser. To demonstrate how expenses can cause a decrease in owners' equity, let us examine a few expense transactions of Samuel L. Bell, Chartered Accountant for October.

Paying Expenses

When a business pays cash for an expense, the left side of the accounting equation decreases because the cash account has decreased. A similar decrease on the right side of the accounting equation under owners' equity balances the accounting equation. Since expenses are always deducted from [or charged to] revenues, or again as most accounting theorists say, always "represent charges against revenues", they cause a decrease in owners' equity.

TRANSACTION

October 31: Samuel L. Bell, Chartered Accountant pays expenses of $ 500 in salaries and $ 100 for utilizes.

ANALYSIS

The asset cash decreases by $ 600 ($ 500 + $ 100) because the business now has less money. The owners' equity decreases by $ 600 because the business has incurred two types of expenses.

ASSETS				= LIABILITIES +		OWNERS' EQUITY
	Accounts		Office	Accounts		Samuel L. Bell,
Cash +	Receivable +	Furniture +	Equipment	= Payable	+	Capital
9,500 +	1,600	+ 8,700 +	4,000	= 8,000	+	14,300
				Net income		1,500
(600)						(600)
8,900 +	1,600	+ 8,700 +	4,000	= 8,000	+	14,300
	23,200				**23,200**	

As shown above, Samuel L. Bell, Chartered Accountant had expenses of $ 600 matched against revenues of $ 1,500 during the same accounting period. As revenues were greater than expenses, a net income of $ 900 resulted. The final effect of matching revenues against expenses in the same accounting period produced a net increase of $ 900 to owners' equity. In the accounting equation above, this credit is shown under the heading of "net income".

However, the reader should note two significant points at this juncture: if expenses had been greater than revenues in this accounting period, a net loss could have resulted, thus decreasing owners' equity by a commensurate amount. The paramount importance of matching revenues against expenses in the same accounting period must never be overlooked. Some years ago, a manager at the Queen's Printer in Ottawa attempted to match revenues against expenses in *two different* accounting periods. Thus, a rather unusual accounting and financial boondoggle resulted, misunderstood by many public servants employed in the departments and agencies with which the Queen's Printer had been doing business.

FINANCIAL STATEMENTS

Introduction

Financial assets and liabilities are usually defined quite broadly by accountants. Thus, Section 3060 of the *CICA* defines a financial asset as: cash; a contractual right to exchange financial instruments with another party under conditions that are potentially favourable; an equity instrument of another entity. Similarly, a financial liability is any liability that is a contractual obligation: to deliver cash or another financial instruments with another party under conditions that are potentially unfavourable. Thus financial assets and liabilities include such items as accounts and notes receivable and payable, debt and equity securities held by the firm and bonds outstanding.

We think of financial reporting as a device through which accountants have adopted policies of full disclosure, to expand the set of information that is publicly available. Also, timeliness of reporting will reduce the liability of insiders to profit from their information advantage.

The information gathered after one analyzes the transactions of a public or private sector operated enterprise may eventually be summarized in two financial statements: the income statement or statements of operations and the balance sheet or statement of financial position.

These statements are presented to owners or managers so that the reader might analyze how successful or unsuccessful the business has been operating in the past and use this information to plan future operations.

Income Statement

The revenues, expenses and net income or loss for a period of time are formally presented in the income statement. This statement is also known as the profit and loss statement, the statement of income and expenses, the operating statement, according to the Treasury Board of Canada's standards, the statement of operations. This statement prepared for Samuel L. Bell, Chartered Accountant, reports the revenues, expenses and net income for the month of October:

Samuel L. Bell, Chartered Accountant

Income Statement

For The Month Ended October 31, 2XX7

Revenues:	Expenses:
Sales To: Jonathan Swift $ 1,000 Marie Curie $ 500 Total Revenues: $ 1,500 *Net Income For Month:* $ 900	Salaries $ 500 Utilities $ 100 *Total Expenses:* $ 600

The time covered by the income statement is known as the *accounting period* or the *fiscal period.* Every private or public sector operated organization prepares an income statement, usually on an annual basis. However, many firms issue income statements more frequently to keep their reported information up to date. Therefore, an accounting period may cover any length of time that a business has appropriated for its needs---for example, one month, three months, six months or a year.

Any consecutive twelve month period is called a fiscal year. For example, the fiscal year observed by departments and agencies in the government of Canada runs from April 1 to March 31. A twelve month period that begins January 1 and ends December 31 is known as a calendar year. In the government of Canada, an organization, Employment Insurance, operated on a calendar year. Its parent organization, Citizenship and Immigration, operated on a fiscal year. It would seem that Samuel L. Bell, Chartered Accountant, uses an accounting period of one month, as indicated in the heading of the firm's income statement. It is important to show the accounting period in an income statement so that the information being provided can be properly interpreted. Samuel L. Bell, Chartered Accountant earned its net income in one month. The significance of this amount could be vastly different if the accounting practice had taken six months or even a year to earn the same amount of money.

PREPARING AN INCOME STATEMENT

Introduction

There are a number of guidelines one needs to follow while preparing an income statement.

Heading

Enter the heading — WHO, WHAT, WHEN — at the top of the income statement. If an accounting period covers three months, for example, January, February and March, the date line would read: "For the quarter ended March 31…." If the accounting period covers a calendar year, the date line would read: "For the year ended December 31…" Should the accounting period cover a fiscal year, the date line would read: "For the fiscal year ended March 31…" As in the case of Samuel L. Bell, the date would state that which appears in the heading of the example cited for that sole proprietorship.

Revenues Section

Enter the Revenues (tax and non-tax in the case of the government of Canada) followed by a colon on the first line of the margin. Indent and list the sources of revenue beneath this title. Begin each word with a capital letter. When there is only one source of revenue (in the government of Canada these sources are always restricted to two), show the amount directly in the second money column. If there are several sources of revenue as can occur in private sector organizations, list the individual accounts in the first money column and the total amount in the second money column.

Expenses Section

On the line beneath the last entry in the income section or in a series of columns placed parallel to or by the side of the income section, enter the title "Expenses" followed by a colon. Indent and list the itemized expenses beneath the title. Expenses are usually referred to as "objects of expenditure" in the government of Canada. Begin each word with a capital letter. Follow the same preparation whether the items are listed as expenses or objects of expenditure. The individual amounts appear in the first money column. If there is only one source or element of expense, the amount would be entered directly in the second money column.

Net Income or Net Loss Section

Rule a single line across the money column under the total of expenses or objects of expenditure. Subtract the total expenses from the total revenues or vice versa and record the difference in the second money column on the next line. Identify the amount calculated as "net income" or "net loss". Then rule a line across the money columns to show the columns are complete.

BALANCE SHEET

The second statement prepared for the user is the balance sheet. The balance sheet shows the financial position "as at" a specific date. The balance sheet prepared for Samuel L. Bell, Chartered Accountant as at October 31 would reflect the following:

Samuel L. Bell, Chartered Accountant

Balance Sheet

As At October 31, 2XX7

Assets		Liabilities And Owners' Equity	
Cash	$ 8,900	Accounts Payable	$ 8,000
Accounts Receivable:		Total Liabilities	$ 8,000
Jonathan Swift	$1, 600	Owners' Equity:	
Total Receivables	1,600	Samuel L. Bell, Capital	$ 14,300
Furniture	8,700	Net Income	900
Office Equipment	4,000	Total Owners' Equity	$ 15,200
Total Assets	**$ 23,200**	**Total Liabilities & Onrs. Eqty.**	**$ 23,200**

The balance sheet shows that Samuel L. Bell, Chartered Accountant's equity as at October 31, 2XX7 was $ 15,200. This amount expresses the owner's investment [Capital of $ 14,300 plus a net income of $ 900 for October, 2XX7].

The Reader Must Remember: a balance sheet or statement of financial position presents the financial picture of the business as at a given date. An income statement or statement of operations shows the details of business transactions over a span of time. These two statements form the basic elements for managers, other decision makers, readers and others who are interested in the operational and financial status of the firm.

PART IV

Practical Application of Generally Accepted Accounting Principles (GAAP) as introduced earlier in Part III

Using Accounts

Objective of Chapter Ten

The objective of chapter ten is to show the reader, course and workshop participant how to use the accounts found in the accounting equation.

Introduction

Every financial transaction changes one or more of the two fundamental elements in the accounting equation. These changes, without exemption, must be recorded so that financial statements may be prepared. In chapter five, sample transactions were recorded in the form which each transaction has an effect on these fundamental elements. It would be impractical, however, to prepare a new accounting equation or balance sheet after each transaction. It is necessary, therefore, to keep an efficient set of records and the accounting system(s) to reflect these changes. The portion of this basic recording system is known as an *account*. Using accounts is a basic and fundamental accounting procedure of any accounting system.

ACCOUNTS

An *account* is a device used to record the changes to the two fundamental elements of the accounting equation [*assets = liabilities + owners' equity*]. In an accounting system, the form of the account varies with the system of data processing used. For example, a lot of small Canadian businesses use the software "Mind Your Own Business" (MYOB). The government of Canada's departments and agencies use such platforms as the Common Departmental Financial System (CDFS) and Systems, Application and Programming (SAP). The simplest form of account is a *T-account*. Although this type of account is scarcely used in an actual accounting system, it appears in this text for illustration purposes. Its simplicity should enable the reader to understand how to use the fundamental elements of accounting. As its name denotes, the T-account is in the form of the letter "T". The T-account has one side for recording increases and the opposite side for recording decreases. For example:

Left Side	Right Side
Increase or Decrease	Decrease or Increase

DEBITS AND CREDITS

In accounting theory, the left side of each account is known as the debit (Dr.) side, whereas the right side of each account is known as the credit (Cr.) side. Centred on the top of the account form is the account title and figure, representing the name and number of the particular item the account represents. An amount which is recorded on the left side an account is called a *debit*, and recording the debit is also known as *debiting the account*. An amount recorded on the right side of any account is called a *credit*, and recording the credit is also known as *crediting the account.*

It should be emphasized that the accounting terms debit and credit merely refer to the *sides* of each account. Many beginning accounting and bookkeeping students seem to believe that the term debit denotes something unfavourable or vice versa, and by the same token the term credit means something favourable or vice versa. This concept of morality associated with the words debit and credit is a complete and sometimes disturbing fallacy.

Because a T-account has two sides, it remains a convenient device for showing increases and decreases to the account. All amounts recorded on a particular side of an account are increases to be added, and all amounts on the opposite side of the same account are decreases to be subtracted. For example, whenever cash increases the amount is recorded on the debit or left side. Thus, when cash amounts of say $ 180 and $ 50 are received; each increase in cash is always shown on the debit or left side of the cash account. Conversely, whenever cash decreases, the amount is recorded on the credit or right side. Thus, when cash payments of say $ 40 and $ 60 are made, each decrease is shown by crediting the cash account.

The difference between the debits and the credits in an account is called the *account balance.* Each account balance is determined as follows: Total all debits. Total all credits. Subtract the smaller amount from the larger amount. In the above example, the balance of the cash account is found by totaling the debits ($ 180 + $ 50 = $ 230); totaling the credits ($ 40 + $ 60 = $100). Since the total of the debits is larger than the total of the credits, the account has a debit balance.

In other words, to make it a little bit more explicit, when doing accounting in the United Kingdom, one usually classifies accounts into three basic types: *real, personal and nominal.* Real accounts always represent something we can see, touch and move such as cash, inventories, buildings, furniture and computers. Personal accounts are those headed with a person, business or firm. These could include items such as accounts receivable, loans receivable, loans payable and mortgage payable. Then nominal accounts keep a record of those transactions for which we have nothing to show. These would include expense such as salaries, hydro, heat, gas and rent. On the other hand, nominal accounts may also comprise those that result in profits such as tax revenues or non-tax revenues.

By using this three-pronged classification, one may be able to establish *three basic ground rules* for debiting and crediting accounts. We debit real accounts when we purchase an asset, we credit real accounts when we sell an asset, depreciate it or amortize its value. With personal accounts, we debit the recipient of goods, services or money; we credit the giver of goods, services or money. With nominal accounts we debit losses and expenses and we credit profits and gains.

Finally, whatever method or approach one uses to determine a debit or credit, when faced with a transaction, one should always ask oneself three questions and apply the probable answers:

WHAT TWO ACCOUNTS ARE AFFECTED? Ensure you name those accounts.

WHAT TYPE OF ACCOUNTS ARE THEY? Classify them, whatever mode of classification you apply, whether in the private sector or the public sector.

WHICH ACCOUNT IS TO BE DEBITED OR CREDITED? If cash is one of the two accounts in the proposed entry, cash *always enters as a debit and leaves as a credit*. If you are certain whether to debit or credit, as happens with the cash account, the other side of the entry will be definitely the opposite.

BASIC PRINCIPLES FOR INCREASING OR DECREASING ACCOUNTS

In the previous paragraph the description of the method of recording increases and decreases in the cash account shows that cash increases when one records the amount on the debit side of the side account, and that cash decreases when one records the amount on the credit side.

To understand why accounts are increased on one particular side and decreased on the other, one must review the order in which the accounting equation is usually written: *assets = liabilities + owners' equity*. Note as stated previously that assets are placed on the left side, while liabilities, and also owners' equity, are placed on the right side of the equation. The only differences in placing the owners' equity on the left side occur in balance sheets reported in the United Kingdom or in the government of Canada's annual Public Accounts. With this positioning in mind, we can now apply THREE BASIC PRINCIPLES to all accounts: PRINCIPLE NUMBER ONE: An increase in an account is recorded on the side of it origin; that is, on the same side on which the account is placed in the accounting equation. PRINCIPLE NUMBER TWO: A decrease in an account is recorded on the opposing side of its origin, that is, on the opposite side to which the account is placed in the accounting equation. PRINCIPLE NUMBER THREE: The balance of an account will *NORMALLY* appear on the side of its origin; that is, on the same side as that on which it is shown in the accounting equation. A possible exception to this rule may be when a bank balance, usually shown as a debit, would be shown as a credit if the account were in an overdraft situation.

Asset Accounts

Assets originate on the left side of the accounting equation, and are therefore shown on the left side of the balance sheet. Therefore an asset account increases on the debit side or its side of origin, and decreases on the credit side or the opposing side of its origin. The balance of an asset account will therefore *normally* be shown as a debit balance.

Liability Accounts

Liabilities originate on the right side of the accounting equation and therefore, on the right side of the balance sheet. Therefore a liability increases on the side of its origin, the credit side, and decreases on the opposing side of its origin or debit side. The balance of a liability account will *normally* be a credit balance.

Owners' Equity Accounts

The owners' equity amount originates on the right side of the accounting equation and therefore is shown on the credit side of the balance sheet. Therefore, the owners' equity account increases on the side of its origin, the credit side and decreases on the opposing side of its origin, its debit side. The balance of the owners' equity account will *normally* show a credit balance.

Opening Accounts

The use of accounts to record increases and decreases in the two fundamental elements requires that an individual account be opened for each asset, liability and owners' equity account item. To illustrate how these accounts are opened, T-accounts will be set up for Samuel L. Bell, Chartered Accountant, and a balance sheet prepared as at that date.

Samuel L. Bell, Chartered Accountant
Balance Sheet
As At October 31, 2XX7

Assets		Liabilities And Owners' Equity		
Cash	$ 8,900	Accounts Payable		$ 8,000
Accounts Receivable:		Owners' Equity:		
Jonathan Swift	1,600	Samuel L. Bell, Capital	$ 14,300	
Furniture	8,700	Net Income	900	
Office Equipment	4,000	Total Owners' Equity		15,200
Total Assets	**$ 23,200**	**Total Lblts. And Ownrs. Eqty.**		**$ 23,200**

T-accounts appear in the books of Samuel L. Bell, Chartered Accountant:

Cash	Acc. Rec.: J. Swift	Furniture
Oct 31 8,900|	Oct 31 1,600|	Oct 31 8,700 |
Office Eqpt.	Acc. Pay. Queens' Printer	Net Income
Oct 31 4,000|	|Oct 31 8,000	|Oct 31 900
Samuel L. Bell, Capital		
Oct 31 | 14,300		

Opening Asset Accounts

Since assets appear on the left side of the accounting equation and the balance sheet, the asset balances are recorded on the left side of the T-accounts. The first balance listed on the balance sheet is cash, with a debit balance of $8,900; therefore the Cash account is debited with $ 8,900.

The second account listed on the balance sheet is accounts receivable. A separate account is opened for each debtor, so that the amount that each owes can be easily and quickly determined. The name of each debtor on the account title is preceded by the phrase "Acc. Rec." or "A. R.", which is the abbreviation for accounts receivable. This abbreviation is issued to keep the account title as short as possible. The debtor Jonathan Swift is debited with $ 1,600.

Opening Liability Accounts

Since liabilities appear on the right side of balance sheet the balances in the liability accounts are recorded on the credit side of the T-accounts. The first liability is accounts payable. A separate T-account is opened for each creditor so that the amount that is owed can be quickly calculated. The abbreviation "Acc. Pay." or "A. P." precedes the creditor's name to identify the account as an accounts payable. Samuel L. Bell, Chartered Accountant has one such account: The Queen's Printer, credited for $ 8,000.

Owners' Equity Accounts

The owners' equity account also appears on the right side of the balance sheet. Therefore, the owners' equity balance is recorded on the credit side of the T-account. With Samuel L. Bell, Chartered Accountant, the total owners' equity on October 31, 2XX7 is $ 15,200.

Ledger

A group of accounts similar to the eight first opened for Samuel L. Bell, Chartered Accountant is called a **ledger.** The ledger for Samuel L. Bell, Chartered Accountant on October 31, 2XX7 would contain all the accounts shown on an earlier page.

The accounts on the debit side of the accounts total $ 23,200. The accounts on the credit side also total $ 23,200. The debit balances are asset accounts and the credit balances are liability and owners' equity accounts. Since, in the accounting equation introduced earlier on, **assets = liabilities + owners' equity**, the total debit balances or assets in the ledger **must** always equal the total credit balances or liabilities plus owners' equity. However, it must be noted that in a loss situation, where expenses exceed revenues, the debit balances are not always assets; neither do the credit balances always represent owners' equity.

Formerly, the word "book" was used to describe the form in which the individual accounts were kept. Original ledgers were actually books. Today, with modern methods of mechanical and electronic data processing, accountants prefer to define and /or refer to the ledger as the files or electronic records in which all accounts are maintained.

RECORDING CHANGES IN ASSETS AND LIABILITES

Introduction

The previous topic explained how individual T-accounts are set up and how opening or beginning balances are entered. Once these opening balances are recorded, an accounting system **must** provide for electronic, mechanical or manual procedures to record the many daily business transactions that will affect the accounts filed in the ledger. In the language of business, the routine procedure of recording day by day, the currency results, both local and foreign, of foreign transactions are traditionally known as bookkeeping. All accounting systems begin with the bookkeeping activity of recording efficiently the many daily transactions that will increase some accounts and decrease others whether these changes occur on the left side or the right side.

The Nature of the Business Transaction

As explained in a previous chapter, a business transaction is simply a financial event that affects the two fundamental elements in accounting. Two basic characteristics of a business transaction need to be noted: One: Each transaction is an exchange or trade off of something for something else. For example, in a previous chapter you learned that, when cash is paid for acquiring say, a computer, the asset account office equipment increases and the asset account cash decreases. In other words, cash is exchanged for office equipment or the computer. This exchange or trade off means that there are at least two parties involved: one business is buying while the other business is selling the fixed assets: The currency amounts exchanged in the transaction are the same amount and stated as identical figures for both parties. In the transaction requiring a computer or office equipment for cash, the buyer will record the purchase of the computer. Then the buyer and the seller will record the financial result of the transaction in the same money amount, that is, there is a single figure that is identical for each transaction recorded in the buyer's books and the seller's books.

Reinforcing the Double Entry

The double aspect of each transaction introduces the theory behind the double entry principle of recording business transactions. This principle, first published by Luca Pacioli in 1494, is the oldest principle in accounting and remains generally accepted by the accounting profession today.

This double entry principle may be stated as follows: From the viewpoint of a business or government enterprise, each transaction is a trade off between two parties. Therefore, a record of the event requires that a statement of the amount of money describing the "thing" acquired *must* show equal debits and credits recorded for each transaction. Three fundamental rules help to analyze business transactions: (1) Each transaction affects at least two accounts. Clearly then, as sometimes practiced in the government of Canada's financial records, the "one sided" transaction is at a minimum anomalous, erroneous and ludicrous. (2) If only two accounts are affected by a transaction, then the debit entry in one account must be equal to the right side entry in the other account. (3) If more than two accounts, as can be seen in large government departments such as the Department of National Defence, then the total debits must be equal to the total credits. Once one has selected the amounts involved in the business transaction, one can apply two or more fundamental principles for increasing and decreasing accounts: An *increase* in an account is recorded on the side of its origin; that is, on the same side that the account *originates* in that fundamental equation (*assets = liabilities + owners' equity*) and on the balance sheet. A *decrease* in an account is recorded on the opposite side of origin; that is, on the same side opposite to that on which the account originates in accounting equation (*assets = liabilities + owners' equity*) and on the balance sheet.

To illustrate how these rules are applied in practice, November's transactions for Samuel L. Bell, Chartered Accountant in the individual T-accounts items have already been set up. The beginning balances are taken from the balance sheet as at October 31, 2XX7. Each of the November transactions will be analyzed to show: (1) which account increases and which account decreases; (2) which accounting principles apply to the recording of these changes; and (3) what the debits and the credits should be.

Changes in Assets Accounts

These transactions illustrate the principles for increasing and decreasing asset accounts: November 3, 2XX7: Samuel L. Bell, Chartered Accountant purchased for cash another computer for $ 2,000 and a photocopying machine for $ 500.

WHAT HAPPENED	ACCOUNTING PRINCIPLE	ACCOUNTING ENTRY
The asset Office Eqpt. increased by $ 2, 500	To increase an asset debit the account	Debit: Office Eqpt.: $ 2,500
The asset Cash decreased by $ 2,500	To decrease an asset credit the account	Credit: Cash: $ 2,500

T-accounts:

+	Cash	-		+	Office Equipment	-
Oct 31 8,900| Nov 3 2,500				Oct 31 4,000		
					Nov 3 2,500		

November 29: Samuel L. Bell, Chartered Accountant sold services on credit to Jonathan Swift for $ 500 and to Marie Curie for $ 400. Although the transaction involved two debits and one credit, the total of the debits must equal to the total of the credits.

WHAT HAPPENED	ACCOUNTING PRINCIPLE	ACCOUNTING ENTRY
The asset Acc. Rec. J. Swift increased by $ 500 and the asset Acc. Rec. M. Curie increased by $ 400	To increase an asset debit the account To increase a revenue account credit the account	Debit: Acc. Rec.:J. Swift $ 500 Acc. Rec.: M. Curie $ 400 Credit Sales: $ 900

T-accounts:

+ Acc. Rec. Jonathan Swift -	+ Acc. Rec. M. Cure - -	Credit Sales +
Oct 31 $ 1,000 |	Oct 31 Nil |	|
Nov 29$ 500 |	Nov 29 $ 400|	| 29 $ 900

Changes in Expense Accounts

Owners' equity decreases when an owner withdraws cash (an asset) for his personal use. It also decreases when expenses are incurred to operate the business.

November 29, 2XX7: Samuel L. Bell, Chartered Accountant paid expenses of $ 500 for rent, $ 1,500 for salaries, $ 200 for supplies and $ 1,300 for utilities. The total of the debts equals the credits.

WHAT HAPPENED	ACCOUNTING PRINCIPLE	ACCOUNTING ENTRY
The account cash decreased by $ 3,500	To decrease cash credit the account	Credit: Cash $ 3,500
The account rent increased by $ 500, the account salaries increased by $ 1,500, the account supplies by $ 200 and the account utilities by $ 1,300	To increase expense accounts	Debit: Rent $ 500 Salaries 1,500 Supplies 200 Utilities 1,300

T-accounts:

```
+       Cash        -        +   Rent Expense   -    +   Salaries  Expense  -
--------------------------        ----------------------------        -------------------------------
Oct 31 8,900| Nov 3  2,500        Nov 29  500 |         Nov 29 1,500|
            |
            |    29  3,500
```

```
+     Supplies Expense    -              +   Utilities Expense  -
-------------------------------------        ----------------------------------
Nov 29    200|                               Nov 29  1,300|
```

November 29, 2XX7: The Queen's Printer spent $ 500 on rent, $ 1,500 for salaries, $ 200 on supplies and $ 300 on utilities. The RC Manager exercised her delegated *Financial Administration Act* Section 34 spending authority. After the financial clerk exercised his delegated *Financial Administration Act* Section 33 authority, he sent a cheque requisition to the Public Works and Government Services Canada (PWGSC) to pay the authorized expense.

WHAT HAPPENED	FAA AUTHORITY	ACCOUNTING PRINCIPLE	ACCOUNTING ENTRY
Expenses approved	Section 34	None	None
PWGSC bank account	Section 33	To increase expense	Credit:
decreased by $ 2,500		accounts: Debit accts	Pymt. Cntrl. $ 2,500
Rent expense by $ 500		To decrease credit	Rent Exp $ 500
Salaries expense by		control account:	Sal. Exp $ 1,500
$ 1,500, Supplies		credit the account	Sup. Exp $ 200
expense $ 200 and			Utlts. Exp. $ 300
Utilities exp. by $ 300			

T-accounts:

```
+ PWGSC Pymnt. Cntrl. A/C -          +  Rent Expense  -      +   Salaries Exp. -
----------------------------------        -------------------------        -------------------------
Oct 31 nil   |  Nov 29 $ 2,500          Nov 29  $ 500|           Nov 29 $ 1,500 |
+    Supplies Expense    -              +   Utilities Expense   -
----------------------------------        -------------------------------------
Nov 29 $ 200|                            Nov 29 $ 300 |
```

WORKING HINTS

Making Corrections

When making accounting entries, one must never correct an error by erasing or by writing a correct figure over an incorrect one. When one makes a mistake one should draw a neat horizontal line through the entire figure or word and write the complete correction *above* it.

The Importance of Legible Handwriting

One of the most costly problems in business results from the lack of attention by most individuals to write clearly and legibly, especially in the writing of numbers. One large Canadian company in the private sector reported that its data processing unit lost a lot of time while processing branch sales reports because the input personnel could not enter handwritten numbers correctly. One might be surprised to learn that numbers are handwritten more often than they are printed or typewritten. There is only one acceptable business principle while judging one's handwriting:

"Can someone else read your written numbers correctly?"

Here are a few working hints that may improve the writing of numbers: (1) Do not hurry when writing numbers. Take time to form each number perfectly. (2) Write each number slanted slightly less than half the line space. You must leave enough space above the numbers to make a proper accounting correction. (3) Place a comma between each set of three digits. Try to always add the cents column.

The Reader Should Remember: how to use the various accounts; what the accounting equation is and what are its two elements; what is an asset; what is a liability; what is revenue; what is expense; what is owners' equity; what is an account; what are the three principle points to remember when making a transaction; the three basic principles to all accounts; how changes affect assets, liabilities and owners' equity individually and collectively; and the importance of having a legible handwriting.

Journalizing and Posting

OBJECTIVE OF CHAPTER ELEVEN

The objective of this chapter is to take the reader and the course or workshop participant through the theories and practices involving journalizing and posting.

INTRODUCTION

In the procedures described in a previous chapter, the debits and credits for each transaction were entered directly into accounts. When many transactions are involved, although as is the case in private and public sector organizations, however, the entering of debits and credits directly into accounts have several serious limitations: (1) It is difficult to locate a specific transaction because the record of that transaction exists only in the form of a debit or credit entry to another account. (2) It is difficult to compare the volume of transactions from day to day because sometimes no daily record of transactions is kept. (3) It is difficult to locate an error because the debits and credits for each transaction seldom appear together.

These limitations must be considered in organizations that use large computerized systems such as SAP, where the information is usually entered directly from the source document to a ledger, after the transaction (especially in the government of Canada) has been duly authorized. However, sometimes to avoid these difficulties, for instance, during the transfer of amounts between transactions, a special record called a *journal* is made before the debits and credits are transferred to the individual accounts. Thus the first step in the accounting cycle is the daily record of transactions, (either in a journal or via a blank rubber stamped form on which the accounts and related amounts to be debited and credited are written) a process known as *journalizing*. This second step in the cycle is to transfer the data in the journal or on the coded document to accounts in a ledger—a process known as *posting*.

THE JOURNAL

A *journal* is a daily record of the essential facts and figures of every transaction in which a business is engaged. A journal can be a bound book, a group of loose leaf sheets or a computer file. The word "journal" comes from the French word *jour* meaning "day". The journal remains then in essence, the bookkeeper's or accountant's book of transactions—in other words, his or her business diary. Since transactions are usually recorded in a journal in chronological order (that is, according to the date on which they occurred), it is not that difficult, when using a journal to trace the details of any transaction, while leaving a trail of records that can be audited.

The process of journalizing does not change the accounting principles associated with debiting and crediting to increase or decrease the two fundamental elements. The only difference between this procedure and the one described previously is that of a transaction sometimes recorded in a journal before it is posted in a ledger. Because the journal entry is often known as the "first record" of a transaction, a journal may also be called a book of original entry. Some books of original entry include the cash journal or a cash blotter; the general journal; the purchase journal; and the materials or materiel journal.

Journalizing Procedures

The accountant or bookkeeper often receives information concerning a transaction from a source document such as a cheque stub, an invoice, purchase or work order or sales slip. Before he or she records this information in a journal, he or she must first analyze the impacts of the transaction upon the fundamental elements, and then classify and code these changes according to specific accounts. The actual entry he or she then records should reflect her or his analysis, classification and coding. The entry must contain: the date; the titles and numbers of the accounts affected; the debit and credit amounts; and a brief explanation if required.

The following illustration shows how the accountant or bookkeeper in Samuel L. Bell, Chartered Accountant's employ would record a transaction for November 3, 2XX7. In this particular transaction, Samuel L. Bell, Chartered Accountant bought another personal computer for $ 3,000 and a photocopying machine for $ 5,000, both paid for by cash.

GENERAL JOURNAL

Folio (Page) Number: ____

ACCOUNT TITLE	Posting Reference	DEBIT	CREDIT
DATE NUMBER AND EXPLANATION 2XX7			
Nov 03 00xxx000 Office Equipment	13459	8,000	
000xx0 Cash	23231		8,000

Explanation: Samuel L. Bell, Chartered Accountant, bought a computer for $ 3,000 and a photocopying machine for $ 5,000, and paid for both items by cheque.

Here are some basic guidelines which an accountant or bookkeeper may follow while making a journal entry.

Date

Write the year in small figures at the top left hand cover of the divided date column. Abbreviate the month and enter it below the year. Record the day of the month for each transaction. However, do not repeat the month and year except at the top of each new page or when either the month or year changes.

Debit Entry

Record the debit account number and title in the next column on the same line as the date. Then enter the debit amount in the debit column.

Credit Entry

On the line below the debit entry, indent about two centimeters and record the credit number and the title. This indentation also presents the debit-credit process visually. Enter the credit amount in the credit column.

Explanation

On the line below the credit entry, begin again at the date margin and re-cord the explanation of the transaction. Since the debit and the credit account numbers and titles also reveal the reason, by default, for the entry, expla-nations are frequently omitted except for those transactions which may be unusual or complicated. When used, explanations should be short, lucid, clear and to the point.

Posting Reference

The posting reference (Post. Ref.) column is not used while journalizing. It is, however, used when posting items and amounts to the ledger.

THE LEDGER

The journal provides a complete record of the daily transactions of some of the detailed activities of a business. In some large private sector firms such as Abitibi Price or MacMillan Bloedel, or public sector organizations like Industry Canada or the Department of Foreign Affairs and International Trade (DFAIT), the book of original entry provides a complete record of all the daily transac-tions of the company. For example, if a customer called to find out how much he or she owed or was owed, the accountant or bookkeeper would have to check all the entries to find what the customer's current balance was. Suppose one of the senior executives in the particular company wanted to know how much cash the firm had on hand, it would take too long, be too hazardous and fraught with the possibility of human error to collate, calculate and report this information from the cash journal, as every cash entry would need to be checked. Therefore, by transforming all the debit and credit entries of all jour-nalized transactions on directly coded documents to individual accounts, all the entries pertaining to a single account may be located in one place. Thus, it be-comes relatively simple to determine the current balance in any one account.

Ledger Accounts

The accounts used to show all the increases and decreases in one place for each asset, contra, control, liability, and owners' equity are called ledger accounts. In the past, the ledger in which these accounts were actually kept in a bound hard cover book. From this ancient practice came the original definition of the ledger as the "book" of accounts. Some small businesses still use a bound ledger, but today the methods of recording vary according to the modern system of data processing being used by an organization, usually mechanical, electric or electronic. In some of the older manual or mechanical systems, the tendency was to use loose leaf binders in a filing cabinet, "tickler" or "B/F" files, or just a plain ledger of "in" and "out" trays. Moreover, within any of these types of files, the genre of loose leaf files have been known to offer greater flexibility, especially in remote locations where the availability of electrical power to drive electric, electronic or mechanical systems is sparse. In these flexible files, the ledger accounts may be rearranged if necessary, and the ledger sheets, cards or loose leaf files may be readily removed so that entries can be made by using manual aids. With most electronic data processing (EDP) systems, however, the information for ledger accounts may be kept on storage devices such as magnetic tape, floppy disk, magnetic disk, flash drives or CD ROMS. Today, the term "ledger" should be viewed as a group of accounts that is filed according to the system of data processing, usually electronic, and adopted by the various types of business.

Whereas the journal or source document could be referred to as the "original entry", the ledger is the secondary or final entry. The sheer bulk of daily cash entries, say in a large financial maintaining and reporting institution such as the Bank of Montreal or PWGSC's Cheque Redemption and Control Branch, is so enormous that it often becomes impractical to record the entries for cash to the ledger accounts as soon as the transaction occurs. Therefore, the transfer of information to and from the journal(s) or source document(s) and ledger(s) may be reserved for some later or more convenient period. In addition, subledgers for pooling and controlling items such as accounts receivable, deposits on hand, accounts payable, fixed assets, materials, materiel, finished goods and work in progress inventories may also be maintained. "Control" accounts in the firm's main ledger are sometimes used to total and balance those subledgers.

In accounting and bookkeeping, this process of transformation is known as "posting"; and the type of aid, whether a manual, electric or electronic device which makes the transfer may be known as a *posting machine.*

THE FORM OF LEDGER ACCOUNTS

For many years, the standard form of accounts was based on the T-account, a central line vertically dividing the standard account in two: a money column on the left side received the debit amount, and a similar money column on the right side received the credit amounts. The abbreviated T-account remains an excellent "tool" when entering and processing transactions. It is, however, rarely used in modern accountancy, accounting and bookkeeping practices. Today, with the sophisticated, efficient and effective systems of electronic data processing, the most common form of ledger account remains the *balanced ledger form*. This form is sometimes referred to as the "self-balancing ledger form" because the balance is calculated automatically by a computer program such as Free Balance, MYOB, CDFS, SAP or Oracle, immediately after any transaction is posted.

In a balanced ledger form, the account maintains a special column marked "balance" to show the current balance after each posting. One type of balanced ledger form, and one that will be used later on in this text, is the three column form shown in the following illustration.

ACCOUNT TITLE

Account Number_____

[Debit Side]		[Credit Side]
Account Title Posting Reference Debit	Credit	Balance
Date		

The balanced ledger form comprises the following columns starting at the left with a space for a date; an explanation of the transaction; a posting reference to the page or journal or other ledger in which the transaction is also recorded; and three money columns---the debit column, the credit column and finally, the balance column for the calculated running or current balance.

Note that the following of the first two money columns follow the basic definition of debit and credit when applied to an account; the debit money column is on the left side of the account; the credit money column is on the right side of the first column and therefore is on the right side of the account. The balance column is usually added to the money columns when a ledger account is opened, the actual title of the account is placed on the top of the form, directly above the date column, and the account number is inserted at the right side, directly above the balance column.

The number assigned to each account indicates the order in which the account is listed on a balance sheet and on an income statement. The numerical sequence also determines the order in which all accounts appear in a ledger. This numerical sequence, similar in concept to the duodecimal system found in the way a library numbers its books, is called a *chart of accounts.* The chart lists all the account titles and the numbers assigned to them. A typical three-digit type of chart appears below.

CHART OF ACCOUNTS

Account Names	Account Numbers
Asset accounts	101 through 199
Liability accounts	200 through 299
Owners' Equity accounts	300 through 399
Revenue accounts	400 through 499
Expense accounts	500 through 599

The first digit in any account number indicates the group in which the account belongs. For example, account numbers beginning with the digit 1 may designate asset accounts, those beginning with the digit 2 may designate liability accounts. The next two digits indicate the sequence of the numbers assigned to other accounts so that new accounts can be inserted within the sequence later on.

According to the section on record keeping in the *Contents of a Business Kit* issued by the *Canadian Institute of Chartered Accountants:*

> *The basic road map into any accounting system is the chart of accounts. It is this chart which helps to access the information which will be captured by your accounting system, needs to be dynamic and should grow as the size and needs of your business changes....To establish a good working chart of accounts, you will need to ask some questions....: Will your business have inventory to account for? If so, will it be purchased in final form or will there be production costs? Are fixed assets a significant portion of your business? Will you sell only one product or service or will there be several types of businesses? Will you have accounts receivable from customers which you will have to keep track of? Are you going to sell in only one location or will you do business in several cities or in several provinces? Are the products you sell subject to sales tax? Do you need to keep track of costs by department? What type of government regulations are you subject to?*

For example, at McGill University, their financial handbook describes the purpose of their chart of accounts was to provide an overview of the University's coding structure which facilitates financial management, control and reporting. The manual describes a chart of accounts as the coding elements used to budget, classify, code, record and report on financial transactions. It further goes on to say that every transaction must be properly coded to be a valid posting in a ledger.

The Receiver General for Canada describes its Government Wide Chart of Accounts as providing a framework for identifying, aggregating and reporting financial transactions to satisfy the government's corporate information requirements. The Chart of Accounts (COA) contains the accounts and codes to be used by departments in their monthly trial balances that are transmitted to the Central Financial Management Reporting System (CFMRS). Responsibility for the government-wide chart of accounts is shared between the Treasury Board Secretariat and the Receiver General for Canada. In this instance the Board's responsibility focuses primarily on the policy issues and the structure of the government wide coding block. The Receiver General for Canada maintains the accounts and codes as well as publishing the chart of accounts. Individual departments and agencies are responsible for ensuring that their departmental coding is linked to the appropriate accounts and codes contained in the government wide chart of accounts and that their financial transactions are complete and accurate.

A chart of accounts has been set up for our sample company, Samuel L. Bell, Chartered Accountant, as shown below.

Samuel L .Bell, Chartered Accountant
CHART OF ACCOUNTS

ASSETS	LIABILITIES AND OWNERS' EQUITY
101 Cash 102 Accounts Receivable: J. Swift 103 Accounts Receivable: M. Curie 104 Furniture 105 Office Equipment 501 Rent Expense 502 Salaries Expense 503 Utilities Expense 504 Supplies Expense	201 Accounts Payable: Grand and Toy 202 Accounts Payable: Queen's Printer 301 Samuel L. Bell, Capital 401 Sales

The system of "numbering" accounts makes it easy to locate an account quickly, because it identifies the account as an asset, contra, control, expense, liability or owners' equity account.

POSTING PROCEDURES

Information in the journal or source documents should be posted to the ledger at frequent intervals, so that the information in every account is kept up to date. The smaller the amount of entries made at one time, the easier it is for the entrant to find errors, and so keep the accounts in constant balance. According to their needs, some businesses post daily, some post once per week, others just once each month.

The procedure to be followed in posting from the journal or other source document(s) to the ledger accounts may be described by the steps outlined below. This type of entry is called an "opening entry" as it is the initial one in a new set of "books". The following are the eight initial steps needed to begin each posting: (1) Find the ledger account for the first debit listed in the journal entry. (2) Record the date in the "date" column. These two sets of dates must be the same. (3) Enter an explanation should one be needed for clarification. (4) Record the balance in the balance column. This number could also be zero. (5) In the "posting reference" column of the ledger, enter the reference number showing the source from which the original entry begins. (6) Record the debit or credit amounts in the relevant column. Double check the entry. (7) Double check the number posted in the "posting reference" column. (8) Locate the next account in the ledger. Repeat the posting process to the account(s) required.

The Reader Should Remember: the limitations of debit and credit; the definitions of a chart of accounts, government-wide Chart of Accounts, contra accounts, control accounts, a journal, journalizing, a ledger, posting, and the standard account numbering process.

12

Routine Checks of Arithmetical Accuracy

OBJECTIVE OF CHAPTER TWELVE

The objective of this chapter is to guide the reader, course or workshop participant through the steps which comprise the routines needed to check the arithmetical accuracy of transactions, their journalizing and their posting.

INTRODUCTION

In Chapter One the author pointed out that every business requires an accounting or bookkeeping system that provides management with useful information to make informed decisions while producing goods and services. To provide this useful information, this system must maintain accurate, prompt and up-to-date records for the company. The system will also need the completion of the latest recordings and postings based on the actual economic events which are being recorded as transactions. Up to this point the reader may have noted that each transaction must be correctly analyzed, recorded and posted to the correct ledger accounts. To record this great amount of numbers, management should insist that the system keeps reasonable checks and balances on its mathematical accuracy. These proofs may vary according to the size of the firm or the volume or intensity of the transactions involved. Some examples of routine procedures follow. Many businesses have adapted most if not all of them to check the mathematical accuracy of their accounting records.

Checking each Source Document for Arithmetical Accuracy

The process of accounting begins with a transaction that is recorded on some form of business paper called a *source document.* There are many different kinds of source documents used in accounting. Some examples are canceled cheques, cheque stubs, deposit slips, payroll time cards, purchase invoices, receipts and sales slips. Regardless of the kind of source document, an efficient accounting system usually employs many clerks who with the aid of adding machines or some other manual, electric or electronic mechanism with a printed and/or listed display, will check the mathematical accuracy of each source document before recording it within the journal(s)or within the ledger(s). Many of these documents, their definition, meaning and use will appear in later chapters of this text.

Checking the Journal, Ledger and/or the Ledger for Mathematical Accuracy

Two of the most costly errors that occur are either: the result of a different figure recorded in the journal and/or ledger from that found in the source document; or the presented total of the figures on a source document not being equal to that which was calculated.

Once the entry has been incorrectly made, it becomes very difficult to locate the error. Good accounting practice recommends that there should be double checks of the figures against the source document and total it with an accompanying posted listing, or any class of figures found in such a document. The double entry principle of an equal debit for each credit remains a visual checking system in itself. For each transaction recorded in the journal, ledger or source document, one must note the amount(s) placed in the debit column and that placed in the credit column. Many an accountant or bookkeeper supports the necessity for a routine check also. They too would recommend that columns be totaled *BEFORE* posting is done. They would also recommend that columns be totaled before a second page is attempted to be processed. In both instances, the use of an adding machine, preferably with a printed listing, may be used to complete the totaling.

CHECKING AN ACCOUNT BALANCE FOR MATHEMATICAL ACCURACY

The process of checking an account in a three-column balanced ledger form remains a single procedure. In a lot of instances this procedure is done with the assistance of an adding machine, preferably one with a printable listing. Again, please remember: The balance of an account normally appears on the side of its origin. That is on the identical side it is shown in the accounting equation [*assets = liabilities + owners' equity*] and on the balance sheet. So, therefore, the following may apply:

Class of account	Side of trial balance normally shown
Assets	Debit
Liabilities	Credit
Owners' Equity	Credit
Revenues	Credit
Expenses	Debit
Contra and Control	Debit and/or Credit

As a visual reminder, please note:

ASSETS	REVENUES
Increase: Plus	Decrease: Minus
EXPENSES	LIABILITIES
Plus	Minus
Increase: Plus	Increase: Minus
Decrease: Minus	Decrease: Plus
CONTRA and/or	CONTROL Accounts
Plus: and/	or Minus
Increase and Decrease:	Plus and/or Minus

TO MAKE SURE, NOTE THE EQUATION:
ASSETS = LIABILITIES + OWNERS' EQUITY

CHECKING THE LEDGER FOR MATHEMATICAL ACCURACY

When transactions are posted correctly in the correct amounts and to the correct accounts, the ledger should balance, all other variables being equal. A number of things occur with electronic entries made in electronic ledgers maintained by such systems as: AMS, CDFS, CFMRS, GMAX, SMA and SAP: (1) Error reports are produced after each entry or set of entries is made; and (2)

Error reports are produced by the system after the timing of the entry(ies) and also after the summation of ledger accounts, to test, for example, if all entries are being made correctly.

One of the better types of mathematical accuracy is achieved by preparing a summary of the balances of the ledger accounts. This summary, known as a *trial balance*, lists the titles of the accounts followed by the accompanying debit and credit balances in the numerical order in which each account appears in the ledger.

PREPARING A TRIAL BALANCE

The following entails the procedures for preparing the heading and body; ruling and testing; and taking a quick trial balance.

Heading

Centre the heading at the top of the trial balance. This heading answers three questions: (1) WHO [the name of the company]; (2) WHAT [the name of the form]; and (3) WHEN [the date].

Body

List all the accounts in numerical order, just as they appear in the ledger. Write the account in the first column, and the account balance in the appropriate debit or credit column.

Ruling and Testing

After the account balances have been entered, rule a single line across both money columns and total the figures in the columns. If you have applied the routine checks of mathematical accuracy, the total debit balances should equal the total credit balances. The trial balance is then completed by ruling a double line across both money columns and the column for the Account Number. The sample trial balance for Samuel L. Bell, Chartered Accountant at November 30, 2XX7 appears below the following page.

The trial balance serves three purposes: (1) It proves the equality of the total debits and credits in the ledger, thus providing a mathematical check on the accuracy of the posting procedure. If the total debits do not equal the total credits, then there is an error in one or more of the accounts in the ledger. (2)

The total balance may also be used as a basis for preparing the financial statements. (3) When posting several volumes of transactions in systems such as AMS, CDFS and SAP used by larger government departments as Correctional Services Canada and the Department of National Defence respectively, it is prudent to take trial balances after entering twenty or thirty transactions. This would make it easier to locate any errors or omissions which may have occurred during the posting and/or journalizing processes.

Samuel L. Chartered Accountant

Trial Balance

As at November 30, 2XX7

ACCOUNT TITLE	ACCOUNT NUMBER	DEBIT	CREDIT
Cash	101		
Acc. Rec.: Jonathan Swift	102		
Acc. Rec.: Marie Curie	103		
Furniture	104		
Office Equipment	105		
Acc. Pay.: Grand & Toy	201		
Acc. Pay.: Queen's Prntr.	202		
Samuel L. Bell, Capital	301		
Sales	401		
Rent Expense	501		
Salaries Expense	502		
Utilities Expense	503		
Supplies Expense	504		
TOTALS			

A trial balance may be prepared at any time. As mentioned above, for example, after a series of journal entries has been recorded, journalized and posted, the accountant or bookkeeper may consider it reasonable to check upon the maintenance of the debit and credit equality. Some accountants prefer to take a trial balance immediately after any posting is completed in the ledger. To the group, the ledger should always be in balance. Of course, the practicalities of carrying out such as an event in large organizations such as Abitibi Price, Bombardier, MacMillan Bloedel or Public Works and Government Services Canada are well nigh impossible. Generally, however, a trial balance is taken at the end of each month, and should be certainly taken before any attempts are made to prepare financial statements.

Taking a Quick Trial Balance

As mentioned above, in some organizations which have myriads of transactions such as the Royal Bank of Canada, the Department of National Defence or Nova Corporation, it is necessary for the accountants to take a quick trial balance. In situations like these, when a formal trial balance is not required, an accountant may use an adding machine with a printed listing to check the equality of the debits and credits found in the ledger. Therefore, for speed and accuracy, each account with a balance may be entered directly on the machine tape from the ledger. Or sometimes alternatively, a quick list of accounts may be recorded on tape as pluses and minuses from the up-to-date balances stated electronically in the data processing device. In the order in which these accounts appear in a physical hard copy ledger, each debit balance is first entered on the listing and shown visually on the listing as an addition. The credit balances in accounts then appear as minus entries in the listing. When the final account balance has been registered, the net balance appearing on the machine listing should be **zero**. If it is not zero, an error has been made and the listing may be used for a reference as the accountant double checks through original source documents, any journals employed at the time, and the ledger.

The Reader Should Remember: the content and functions of the accounting equation [*assets = liabilities + owners' equity*]; how to fix errors found in original transactions, journals and ledgers; and how to strike and use a quick trial balance.

13

The Financial Statements

OBJECTIVE OF CHAPTER THIRTEEN

The objective of this chapter is to provide the reader with the detailed steps necessary to be followed in preparing the basic financial statements such as the balance sheet and the income statement.

INTRODUCTION

In addition to proving the equality of debit and credit balances in the ledger accounts, the trial balance also serves to provide the data needed to prepare an income statement and a balance sheet. Accounts listed on the upper portion of the trial balance are those which usually appear on the balance sheet; therefore they are called balance sheet accounts. Accounts grouped in the lower portion of the trial balance are the ones that usually appear on the income statement; therefore they are called income statement accounts.

Income Statement

An income statement is prepared before a balance sheet because the net income or loss amount must be reported in the balance sheet. The source and amount of revenue and amount of expenses are obtained from the trial balance.

Classified Balance Sheet

The amount of each asset and liability may also be obtained from the trial balance. For the owners' equity, the balance of the capital account may also be obtained from the trial balance, but the net income or net loss may in addition be obtained from the income statement. The owners' equity of the balance sheet can now be completed.

In modern business accounting practice, an accountant would group assets and liabilities according to these generally accepted accounting principles: (a) Assets reported in the balance sheet should be classified at least into two groups: current assets and fixed assets. (b) Liabilities reported on a balance sheet should be classified as current and long term liabilities.

Current Assets

Current assets comprise cash and other assets that are expected to be converted into cash within one year of the balance sheet date. These types of assets are generally listed in order of their probable liquidity; that is, of their expected conversion into cash.

Fixed Assets

Fixed assets are those items whose expected usefulness to the business will extend over several years. These assets are usually listed in order of their permanence.

Current Liabilities

Current liabilities comprise all those debts of the firm which are payable within one year of the balance sheet date.

Long Term Liabilities

These items are debts of the firm which are not due within a year. One example is a mortgage payable. As per the *Notes to the Financial Statements of the Government of Canada* as found in the *Public Accounts 2002/2003*, this reporting entity of the government of Canada includes all departments, agencies, corporations and funds which are owned or controlled by the government and which are accountable to Parliament. The financial activities of all these entities are consolidated in these financial statements except for enterprise Crown corporations such as the Canada Mortgage and Housing Corporation (CMHC) and other government enterprises which are not dependent on the government for financing their activities. These corporations are reported under the modified equity basis of accounting. The government reports all revenues and expenses on an accrual basis. Tax revenues are accounted for in the period in which the revenue arose. Assets are valued at the lower of cost or net realizable value. Liabilities and financial obligations to outside organizations are recorded at the estimated amount ultimately payable. Both financial and non-financial assets are reported on the government of Canada's Statement of Financial Position. Non-financial assets are charged to expense through amortization or upon utilization. Non-financial assets are not taken into consideration when determining the net debt of the government, but rather are deducted from the net debt to determine the government's accumulated deficit.

Government non-tax revenues are derived from exchange transactions with third parties. Other revenues are recognized in the period to which they relate. Expenses for government operations are recorded when goods are received or services are rendered. Contingent liabilities and potential liabilities may become actual liabilities when one or more future events occur or fail to occur. Environmental liabilities reflect the estimated costs related to the management and remediation of environmentally contaminated sites.

ESSENTIAL CHARACTERISTICS OF A BUSINESS

According to Canadian law, owners of business corporations may be called shareholders. Through the purchase of the corporation's shares, the owners provide the company with share capital. In the balance sheet of a business corporation, one can expect to find under the total liabilities a section called Shareholders' Equity and the account Share Capital representing the amount of the investment the owner has in this company.

Under the policies laid out in the *PSAAB Handbook, the Treasury Board Standards* and the *CICA Handbook*, the owners' equity in most Canadian federal government enterprises is sometimes referred to as "Investment in Canada". A business corporation is permitted to borrow funds by using bonds. So does the government of Canada. Canada Savings Bonds are an excellent example. A bond is simply evidence of long term debt. Because bonds are issued with a repayment period of several years, one can expect to find a bonds payable account with the classification of long term liabilities in the balance sheet.

Under single proprietorships, such as Samuel L. Bell, Chartered Accountant and other businesses such as partnerships, the business corporation is required by law to pay an income tax to the government. Government organizations such as the Passport Office, the Queen's Printer and Consulting and Audit Canada are exempt from paying taxes.

The Reader Should Remember: the trial balance must be correct before financial statements are prepared. The definition and composition of the balance sheet and income statement is paramount. How the government of Canada reports its audited financial statements in the Public Accounts is also mentioned briefly. The essential characteristics of a business are also outlined more so from the point of view of Canadian legislation.

14

Closing the Ledger

OBJECTIVE OF CHAPTER FOURTEEN

The objective of this chapter is to present the reader and the course or workshop participant with a set of steps generally used in closing the general ledger at the end of the accounting period under consideration.

INTRODUCTION

The ledger is designed to accumulate data about transactions in specific accounts so that at the end of an accounting period the accountant or bookkeeper can easily prepare the income statement or balance sheet. Once these financial statements have been completed, the accountant must get the ledger ready for the next accounting period. This procedure is known as closing the ledger. It begins specifically with the closing of the income and expense accounts.

In the government of Canada, this process takes place at two main levels. At level number one, each department closes its own books, the meanwhile reconciling the PWGSC General Ledger and Control Accounts to their counterparts maintained in the CFMRS of PWGSC; and at level number two, PWGSC via its functions as the Receiver General of Canada, closes the upper level of the consolidated books of Canada, also preparing the Public Accounts of

Canada, reported annually in three sections: Part I of III; Part II of III; and Part III of III.

Closing the Revenue and Expense Account

When the ledger was opened, three kinds of owners' equity accounts were established: (1) A capital account to record owners' investment and withdrawals in the owners' equity: (2) A revenue account—to show revenues from sales: tax revenues [levied and collected by the Canada Revenue Agency]; non tax revenues such as user fees, also levied and collected by other government departments or agencies; and (3) Expense accounts that record the expenses recorded as a result of doing business [and also referred to as Objects of Expenditure in the government of Canada]. The last two kinds of accounts, the revenue and expense accounts, are established primarily as a record keeping convenience: they keep the revenue and expense separate from investments and withdrawals and thus simplify the preparation of the income statement at the end of the accounting period.

As revenue and expense accounts are intended to accumulate revenue and expense data for accounting periodically, they are known as temporary or nominal accounts. The balance sheet accounts, on the other hand, are designed to provide a continuous record of assets, liabilities and owners' equity. The balance sheet accounts are thus considered permanent or real accounts because they provide information from one accounting period to another, as long as the firm reported on remains a going concern.

At the end of the accounting period, after the income statement has been prepared, the balance of the temporary accounts *must* be reduced to zero. This is necessary so that the accounts can be used to accumulate the revenue and expense data for the next accounting period. In order to reduce these temporary account balances to zero, they need to be transferred to some other account, the *Revenue and Expense Summary*. This transfer process is known as *closing the accounts*.

COMPLETING THE ACCOUNTING CYCLE

Introduction

In an earlier section we used a revenue and expense summary to close the temporary income statement account of the ledger. Therefore, this revenue and expense summary account acts just as though it were a clearing house of sorts. By using closing entries, this clearing house receives the balances of the revenue and expense accounts in order to facilitate calculating the net income and net loss of the accounting period within the ledger. It should be also made abundantly clear that closing the ledger is a *means* to an end, but not an end in itself. The *BASIC PURPOSE* of this closing routine shows the identical information in the balance sheet as far as the owners' equity account is concerned. After the accountant or bookkeeper has completed this transfer, he or she closes the ledger for the old accounting period, making the books ready to receive the entries for the new period.

The Post Closing Trial Balance

Before the accountant or bookkeeper records transactions for a new accounting period, he or she must make a final check to ensure that the ledger remains in balance. As entries were made in the ledger since the trial balance was first struck, either to correct errors or to close the company's accounts, more mistakes may have occurred. Therefore the official must make another check by striking another trial balance; the latter is called a *post closing trial balance.* Thus this accounting maxim should be always followed for taking a trial balance again *after* any entries have been made in a ledger. The post closing trial balance, prepared just like a regular trial balance, only lists permanent accounts. These accounts which remain after the ledger has been closed are usually the balance sheet accounts.

The Accounting Cycle

The following steps, which comprise the accounting cycle, will now be reviewed, *Step 1:* **Journalize:** Analyze all source documents and enter those transactions which need to be entered into the journal(s). *Step 2:* **Post:** Transfer debits and credits from the source document(s) or journal(s) to the ledger accounts. *Step 3:* **Prepare a trial balance:** Prove the quality of the debits and credits into a ledger.

A Trial Balance may be defined as a list of balances on the accounts of a business at a given moment in time. It is usually prepared periodically to check the accuracy of transactions in accounting or bookkeeping.

Step 4: **Prepare basic financial statements:** Set up an income statement and a balance sheet. *Step 5:* **Prepare a closing trial balance:** Prove the equality of debits and credits after closing the ledger.

Visualize the Accounting Cycle

The accounting cycle may be visualized for two specific reasons: (1) To show how an individual transaction is set up. Transactions result in changes to an account and in a trial balance. (2) To show the inter-connection between the five steps outlined in the previous section.

The Reader Must Remember: the steps in closing the books; the reasons for closing the books; and the steps in the accounting cycle.

PART V

Accounting Procedures and Systems for Operating a Business

This part of the accounting text comprises chapters on banking activities; processing cash receipts and cash payments; payroll accounting; processing purchases of merchandise of supplies; processing sales on credit; and end of period adjustments. As per usual, this section of the text is written from a private and public sector perspective, with a special emphasis on the latter.

15

Banking Activities

OBJECTIVE OF CHAPTER FIFTEEN

The objective of this chapter is to provide details to the reader and the course or workshop participant on the banking activities found both in a private sector setting and that which obtains in government financial institutions.

INTRODUCTION

The preceding chapters have covered the journalizing and posting of transactions and receipt and payment of cash. There are, however, various other activities which relate to the handling of cash receipts and payments. What happens, for example, to the cash item after the transactions are journalized and posted? Where does the accountant or bookkeeper obtain the information for recording cash and other pertinent questions that may be determined by reviewing the banking activities of a business?

In accounting terminology, *cash* always comes in as a debit and leaves as a credit. This makes preparing both sides of an entry where cash is involved relatively simple. Now, since *cash always enters on the left and leaves on the right*, no matter what the economic activity being recorded, wherever cash is involved, the opposing side of the related accounting entry is really the only bit which needs to be analyzed deeply and carefully. Cash refers specifically to currency in the form of coins and paper; negotiable instruments such as cheques, bank drafts and money orders issued to and received from others; plus credit card and debit card slips deposited in the bank.

To control cash and to provide an efficient system of handling it, most businesses deposit **all** cash receipts in the bank by the end of the business day and then make all cash payments, except petty and imprest cash, by cheque, by bank draft, by credit card, by debit card or by electronic transfers. Commercial banking in Canada is carried on by a number of financial institutions, including: The Bank of Montreal, The Bank of Nova Scotia, The Canadian Imperial Bank of Commerce, The Royal Bank of Canada, The TD Canada Trust, Banque Canadienne Nationale (National Bank of Canada), Caisse Populaire, La Banque Provinciale du Canada (The Provincial Bank of Canada), The Mercantile Bank of Canada, and The Bank of British Columbia. These financial institutions are *chartered banks* because each bank is incorporated by an Act of Parliament to operate within the power of the *Bank Act.* The *Bank Act* which became the charter of each new bank outlines the rules for conducting the business of banking in Canada. This Act remains important because every ten years the government of Canada reviews banking in the country, deciding whether to renew or withdraw the charter granted to each bank.

One of the outstanding features of the commercial banking system is the number of branches that chartered banks provide, both in Canada and other countries such as the English speaking islands of the Caribbean. It should be also remembered that a chartered bank in Canada is a bank **of** branches not a bank *with* branches. The head office does not transact any business with the public, but it does control the activities of all branches by setting policy and requiring regular reports. Under the branch system, Canadian banking provides excellent service throughout Canada and even overseas. By performing many kinds of services for business and the country, especially in holding deposits and making loans, the chartered banks play a vital role in the progress of the Canadian economy.

In the government of Canada, the banking system includes: commercial banks, as mentioned in the previous paragraph; The Bank of Canada; The Superintendent of Financial Institutions; financial institutions and organizations under the aegis of The Receiver General for Canada (PWGSC); and The Ministry of Finance.

FINANCIAL INSTRUMENTS

In Canada, accounting for financial instruments is laid down by Section 3860 of the *CICA Handbook*, issued in 1995. Section 3860 deals primarily with the definition and disclosure of financial instruments. The section defines a financial instrument as:

> "...any contract that gives rise to both a financial asset of one party and a financial liability or equity instrument of another party..."

THE BANK OF CANADA

The Bank of Canada, formed in 1934 by a special act of Parliament, is Canada's central bank. It does not accept deposits from individuals, and it does not compete with chartered banks in commercial banking fields. The Bank of Canada, however, does play a most important role in Canada's banking system. One of the chief functions of the Bank is to act for the government as the control of the country's paper currency. Since January 1, 1945, the Bank of Canada has the sole right to issue paper money and coins for circulation in Canada. The dollar bills it issues are officially called Bank of Canada notes and are at present circulated in the following denominations: $ 5, $ 10, $ 20, $ 50, $ 100 and $ 1,000. In addition to paper currency, the government of Canada, through the operation of the Royal Canadian Mint with two main production plants in Ottawa, Ontario and Winnipeg, Manitoba, issues the following denominations of metal coins: $ 2, $ 1, 50 cents, 25 cents, 10 cents, 5 cents which are all cupronickel coins; and the one cent, which mixes tin, copper and zinc.

BANKING ORGANIZATIONS FOUND WITHIN THE RECEIVER GENERAL FOR CANADA

PWGSC, as stated earlier, is a common service agency, responsible for a number of functions, including cash and banking. The organizational units which perform the cash and banking routines in PWGSC include: Cash Management Unit; Cheque Redemption and Control, located in Matane, Quebec; Cheque Receipt and Production; and Banking which uses control accounts.

CASH MANAGEMENT

There is a basic policy concerning cash management in the government of Canada. Not only should all cash receipts be promptly deposited, more than likely at the close of each business day; but the importance of receiving cash should supersede the bank payment activities. The Treasury Board of Canada has issued a *"Manual on Cash Management."* The 1984 Report of the Auditor General for Canada to Parliament stated that cash flowing into and out of the government's bank account, the Consolidated Revenue Fund (CRF), totals approximately $ 500 billion yearly. The size of this cash flow makes good cash management a necessity in the government. The Auditor General has defined cash management as:

> *"...those activities relating to the billing, collection and deposit of moneys owed to the government, the payment of moneys and the use of government cash balances..."*

Cash was defined as:

> *"...those moneys flowing into and out of the CRF..."*

Cheque Redemption and Control Directorate

When cheques are issued by The Receiver General for Canada for payment, according to the tenets of the *British North America (Constitution) Act, 1867,* a record is maintained of all cheques issued and honoured, not only by the commercial banks and those specifically honoured cheques, but records are also kept in the Cheque Redemption and Control Branch (CRCB) of PWGSC. CRCB also assiduously maintains as accurate a record as is possible, including detailed information on all canceled cheques, especially the amounts paid out by the commercial banks and the names of the individual(s) presenting the instruments for payment.

Cheque Receipt, Production and Distribution

When cheques are received, since, as mentioned before, these items are considered as cash, the policies concerning cash management, as laid out by the Treasury Board of Canada have been followed. The issuance of cheques out of the CRF, controlled by the Receiver General for Canada, is under the Minister's authority granted through the *Supply and Services Act,* the *Appropriation Acts*, the *Financial Administration Act* and the *Constitution Act*

(1867) Act. This process may be further detailed under these cheque issue functions: cheques issued to companies; cheques issued to non-public servants; cheques issued to public servants; and cheques related to payroll.

Banking, Reconciliation or PWGSC Control Accounts

As mentioned earlier in this textbook, a number of pseudo bank accounts called control or reconciliation accounts are maintained in the financial systems operated or owned by individual government departments and agencies and the CFMRS operated and owned by The Receiver General for Canada. These accounts include Deposit Control accounts, Payment Control accounts, Payroll Control accounts, IS Debit Control accounts, IS Credit Control accounts, and Foreign Currency Control accounts. Departments and agencies balance and reconcile these accounts found in their financial systems to those found in the CFMRS.

Payment by cheque

A business opens a current account with the assurance of making cash deposits in a safe place and also to write cheques. When a current account is opened whoever is authorized to write cheques on the account must sign the specimen signature card(s) established for the account and kept on record at the particular financial institution. Any signature on this card must be kept on file so that the required signature(s) on the subsequent cheque(s) can at any time be compared with the signature(s) on the card(s).

The government maintains current accounts in each of the commercial banks in Canada giving Canadians instant access to the necessary funds. Cheques issued by the government are either payment for capital bought, supplies, services, or payroll expenses.

Drawing a Cheque

Under Canadian law, a cheque is defined as a:

> "...bill of exchange drawn on a bank, payable on demand..."

In common usage, a cheque is a written order given by a depositor directing his bank to deduct a specific sum of money from his or her bank account and to pay that amount to a person or company designated on the cheque. There are three parties to each cheque: the depositor is the *drawer* of the cheque; the bank on which the cheque is drawn is the *changer;* and the person or company to whose order the amount on the cheque is to be paid: the *payee*.

Cheques may be written in ink, printed or typed. A pencil must never be used. Regardless of the method used in preparing a cheque, certain aspects of the procedure are the same: (1) When using a standard cheque book, fill in the cheque stub so that it will not be overlooked. (2) Number cheques consecutively, if they have not been pre-numbered by the printer. (3) Never erase a cheque. (4) Never destroy "voided" cheques. (5) Write the date on which the cheque is being issued. (6) In the space provided after the name of the payee, write the amount of the cheque in figures. (7) Write the amounts in words. (8) A cheque may be filled in by anyone, but it must be signed only by the person authorized to do so.

CREDIT AND DEBIT CARDS

In more recent times, banks and businesses alike have been using credit and debit cards. Credit cards are issued mainly in Canada through financial institutions from one or more companies such as VISA, Master Card and American Express. These credit cards are used to contract large volumes of day to day business. In the government of Canada, which also uses credit cards, the Treasury Board of Canada has published policies and procedures in an effort to control the use of cards by public servants and independent contractors. It should be noted that agreements signed between individuals, credit cards and/or Her Majesty the Queen always legally take precedence over any kind of policy and procedural documents issued by the Treasury Board of Canada.

Debit cards, unlike credit cards, which immediately remove funds from the relevant account of the holder or authorizer, are rarely used in the government of Canada to effect purchases of goods and services.

OTHER BANKING ACTIVITIES

In Canada, cheques are used in the majority of daily business transactions. To handle the large volume of cheques processed each business day, the chartered banks must provide and maintain a mechanism for transferring cheques from one branch of a bank to the other and from one bank to another, thus satisfying the balances that remain in accounts. Amongst some 128 banking terms, the process of returning cheques and settling accounts is known as clearing. Two main types of clearing exist: (1) an internal clearing process that returns cheques drawn on branches of the same bank; and (2) an external clearing system to allow banks to make an exchange of cheques held by each bank and to settle differences in amounts exchanged.

Generally, all cheques are first sent to the bank's main branch or the bank's regional data centre. Here cheques are sorted and bundled for clearing. Cheques drawn on the same bank are returned to the branches, while cheques drawn on other banks are exchanged at one of the banks, which is designated the *clearing house*. Once the cheques are exchanged and settlements are approved, cheques are then returned to the bank's branches. The following diagram depicts the kind of cheque clearing which obtains within the government of Canada:

GOVERNMENT DEPARTMENT OR AGENCY
Authorization under Sections 33 and 34 of the Financial Administration Act

CRDC	PWGSC	CFMRS	COMMERCIAL BANK(S)	BANK OF CANADA
v	Sections 33 and 34 of FAA	v		
v	v	v	v	v
v	v	Double-Check	v	v
v	v	v	v	v
		v		

SUPPLIER or
CUSTOMER or
PENSIONER or
PUBLIC SERVANT

Other banking activities include voucher cheques, certified cheques, money orders, bank drafts, and credit and debit cards: already mentioned, lines of credit, petty cash, departmental bank accounts, 'not sufficient fund' activity and stop payments.

Voucher Cheques

Many businesses use a special cheque form called a *voucher cheque.* The financial institutions call it a *commercial cheque.* The common form of voucher cheque is perforated so that it can be separated into two parts: one part the cheque itself and the other, the voucher which details the payment.

Certified cheques

In certain business transactions involving large sums of money, such as the purchase of real estate or an automobile, the payee of the cheque may want to be sure that the cheque will be paid without delay when presented. To provide the payee with this certainty, the drawer obtains a *certified cheque.* A certified cheque carries the guarantee of the drawee, the bank, that sufficient funds are available to pay the cheque whenever it is presented.

Bank Money Orders and Bank Drafts

When safety and distance in transmitting funds are involved, a business person can provide from her or his bank a money order or bank draft.

Lines of Credit

Government departments and agencies overseas, usually in Offices of the High Commissioner for Canada, maintain lines of credit in order to facilitate the daily conduct of business. At a relatively recent count, Foreign Affairs and International Trade (DFAIT) maintained a total of approximately $ 5,000,000 as a departmental line of credit to serve individual missions overseas. Each mission is limited to a specific amount. Two derivations of the line of credit process comprise funding mechanisms, such as a revolving fund, operating under a separate piece of legislation; and a frozen allotment.

Petty Cash, Imprest Cash and Departmental Bank Accounts

Operating under the same basic principle of the holder of the funding mechanism drawing cheques of varying size from the Receiver General for Canada, the funds from the PWGSC issued cheque are either kept in a controlled cash drawer or a separate bank account called a departmental bank account (DBA). With DBAs, the department controlling this relatively small bank account writes cheques on the account. This type of mechanism is generally maintained by larger more complex departments and agencies such as CIDA, DFAIT, Agriculture and Agribusiness Canada and the Department of National Defence. The general steps used in this procedure for replenishing these types of funds follow: (1) Total the vouchers/DBA cheques for disbursement from the fund. (2) Prove the fund. (3) Draw a cheque to petty cash, imprest cash or the DBA for the amount of the total disbursements. (4) Attach the vouchers to the cheque and submit the cheque to the proper person for the signature. (5) After the cheque is signed, cancel the vouchers so they cannot be used again and then file them in a dated envelope. (6) Cash the cheque and place the money in the imprest pretty cash or deposit the cheque in the DBA's chequing account. The following diagram represents the petty cash, imprest cash or DBA process which these organizations follow:

Step 1	Establish Fund	Cheque Sent	
	v	v	
	v	CHEQUE	Cash and Enter
	v	v	v
Step 2	Make Disbursements	Petty or Imprest	Petty or Imprest
		Cash vouchers or >>Enter>>Cash Book or>>Journalize	
		DBA Cheques	DBA Cheque v
		Register	Post
Step 3	Replenish	CHEQUE >>>>>>>>>>>>> Cash and Enter	
		v	
		v	
		Cheque Sent	

NSF Cheques and Stop Payments

Should a holder of a chequing account with a financial institution write a cheque, when this instrument is presented for honouring by the holder's bank and there are not enough funds in the holder's account, the bank usually returns the cheque marked "NSF" or "Insufficient Funds", meanwhile charging the holder's account with a significant sum of money.

Occasionally, a cheque which has been issued may have been lost, stolen or sent to the wrong person or company. When this occurs the drawer of the cheque has a legal right to put a "Stop Payment" on the cheque, provided that it has not already been presented to her or his bank for payment and the amount has not been deducted from the holder's account.

Depositing Cash Receipts

To achieve and maintain control over cash, a business should pay, except for miniscule and petty amounts, all bills by cheque, credit card, debit card or electronic transfer, and thus keep a record of how cash is being spent. By the same token, a business should deposit *all* of its cash receipts in the bank at the end of each business day in order to have a clear record of taking cash and depositing it promptly. Cash items may also be prepared for payment of cash. These items may comprise coin, currency, cheques, bank drafts, money orders, and credit slips. Sorting of deposits and funds in cash drawers or boxes may be handled thus: (1) Coin according to denomination; (2) Currency according to denomination; (3) Cheques, debit and credit card slips according to bank and type of bank and credit card company. (4) Cheques, money orders or bank drafts, before they can be deposited must be *endorsed*. Endorsement should be made across the back of cheques, money orders and bank drafts. *Endorsement in blank* is the simplest way of endorsing a cheque. *Full endorsement* is safer. This is the case when the name of the party to whom the cheque is to be transferred is stated. The most appropriate endorsement, a *restrictive* one, is that which indicates the *purpose* for which the money is to be used. Then the bank is required to place its endorsement below the restrictive one.

Preparing a Deposit Slip

After the coin, currency, debit and credit slips have been sorted, and the cheques and other negotiable instruments have been duly endorsed, a deposit slip is filled out. This document shows all the details of the deposit. The duplicate deposit slip, provided by the bank teller, is very helpful in providing an audit trail---some specifically, that cash receipts have been deposited. The following are steps to take while preparing a deposit slip: (1) Write the current account, or savings account, number in the space provided. (2) Write the date on the date line. (3) Write the name and address of the depositor in the appropriate section. (4) Record the total pile of currency opposite the correct denomination, and extend the value. (5) Record the total amount of coins in the coin line.
(6)Total the currency and coin and record this sum opposite the cash total. (7) List each cheque in the cheque section and record this total. (8) List each kind of negotiable instrument in the other instrument section. (9) List each debit and credit card slip in the credit card section and total. (10) Total all totals to provide a grand total. (11) In the space provided for the depositor's initials, write yours.

Making the Deposit

When the deposit slip and the cash items are presented for deposit, the bank teller usually checks the coin and currency items first and all others next. When the depositor submits her or his cash items for deposit, the bank uses her or his deposit slip as a source document by which the amount is to be added to her or his account. Deposits made at the bank by a cashier or other person responsible for cash receipts should be accompanied by the appropriate level of physical security for the cashier's safety.

VERIFYING THE CASH BALANCE

If the balances do not agree and a trial balance shows that the ledger is in balance, chances are the error is in the cheque book. The most common kinds of cheque book error include: (1) adding or subtracting figures incorrectly on the cheque stub; (2) carrying the wrong amount forward from one sheet to another in the cash journal; (3) failing to record a deposit or recording the same deposit twice; (4) failing to fill out a stub when a cheque is drawn and journalized; and (5) failing to deposit cash receipts for some reason.

THE BANK STATEMENT

Once per month the bank usually sends the depositor a statement, which is the list of all additions to and transactions from her or his account. The bank statement usually shows the following: (1) balances at the end of the previous period; (2) deposits added during the month or accounting period; (3) cheques and other charges subtracted during the month; and (4) the balance of the account for each line of transactions is also recorded.

The balance in the bank statement does not necessarily equal that in the cheque book. The difference is not always an error by either the bank or the depositor. The reasons for this may the result of: (1) outstanding cheques that have been drawn and subtracted from the depositor's cheque book, but not yet presented to the bank for payment; (2) deposits in transit, that have been made and added to the depositor's cheque book, but have not been listed on the monthly bank statement; (3) dishonoured cheques, when money cannot be collected on a presented cheque; (4) bank charges made by the bank which would not normally appear in the depositor's records; (5) service charges, imposed by the bank for many of the special services it provides; and (6) errors in calculation which usually occur on both sides: the bank's and the depositor's.

Bank Exchange Charges

Basically, most cheques drawn on banks are subject to *exchange*, a charge made by the bank to help offset the expense in clearing the cheque(s) from out of town. The payee (not the drawer) must pay the exchange charges. However, not all out of town cheques are subject to exchange.

Reconciling the Bank Statement

This procedure involves determining the factors which may be causing the difference(s) between the bank statement's balance and that of the depositor. The procedure for preparing this reconciliation: (1) Prepare the heading for the bank reconciliation statement. (2) Take the balance that is shown on the bank statement and record it on the reconciliation statement. (3) Compare the amount of the deposits linked on the bank statement with the amounts of the deposits listed on the cheque stubs. (4) On the reconciliation statement, list all deposits currently in transit. (5) Compare canceled cheques and special debit memoranda enclosed with the bank statement and those listed by the bank. (6) Arrange the canceled cheques in numerical order. (7) Compare each cheque (canceled and voided) with the cheque book stubs. (8) On the reconciliation statement, list all the numbers and amounts of cheques that have not been checked off on the stub. (9) Subtract the total amount of cheques outstanding from the sub-total calculated. (10) Record on the second section of the reconciliation statement the current balance found in the cheque book. (11) List any discrepancy item(s) held as an error in the depositor's records. (12) Total the bank charges and the corrected errors. Subtract this amount from the cheque book balance recorded on the reconciliation statement. This is the adjusted cheque book balance which should be identical to the adjusted bank balance. (13) Finally, make corrections and adjusting entries after completing the bank reconciliation. In the government of Canada, the control or bank balances recorded in each department or agency's financial system must also be reconciled to the amounts shown (recorded) by the CFMRS.

The CFMRS and each department or agency's financial system should each record every cheque cut by PWGSC on behalf of the department or agency. The debit of each entry is recorded in detail by each departmental system. Correspondingly, the CFMRS records a summary of all such debit entries.

Safeguarding funds

Every business runs the risk of robbery, embezzlement and fraud. Some methods used to protect against such losses include: (1) taking out insurance against burglary and robbery; (2) depositing cash receipts in the bank one or more times each day; (3) using a night depository for after hour deposits; (4) employing an armed-guard service to take funds to the bank; (5) placing funds to be deposited in a safe; (6) requiring identification when cashing cheques; and (7) making use of pre-numbered receipts as evidence of cash transactions.

The Reader Should Remember: the specifics of cash management in general, but even more so those cash management details peculiar to the government of Canada, and the organizations in government which are involved with cash management.

Processing Cash Receipts

OBJECTIVE OF CHAPTER SIXTEEN

The objective of this chapter is to portray to the reader and the course or workshop participant the steps to be followed when processing cash receipts.

INTRODUCTION

An accounting system includes not only financial procedures in *processing data* but also a sequential approach to be used in the accounting cycle. These sequential steps follow: (1) Journalizing; (2) Posting; (3) Preparing the trial balance; (4) Preparing the financial statements; (5) Closing the books; and (6) Preparing a post closing trial balance.

An accounting cycle is also used to prepare data before it is processed. This phase may be also called *input.* There follows a diagram of the rudimentary steps in any system:

One of these processes is called *cash control*. Cash control may be divided into two broad steps: (1) Control of cash receipts; and (2) Control of cash payments. This chapter details the control of cash receipts.

A SYSTEM FOR THE CONTROL OF CASH RECEIPTS

In very small business enterprises, the owner often maintains all the accounting records him or herself. In a major business, however, it is well nigh impossible for just one individual to perform such a task. Therefore, additional staff must be added to assist.

The 1984 Report of the Auditor General of Canada to Parliament also stated that billing and collection practices directly affect how quickly the related funds are received and deposited. For example, on July 31, 1983 one department had accounts receivable of $ 3.8 million of which $ 2.5 million (86%) were more than 90 days old. Government departments and agencies should ensure that they deposit receipts as quickly as possible.

Establishing Cash Controls in an Accounting System

All accounting systems must contain adequate controls to ensure accuracy, honesty, efficiency and speed. As the business becomes larger and larger, there are five special journals, amongst others, that may be used:

Special	Use
Cash receipts	Receipt of cash from sources
Cash payments	All payments of cash
Purchases	Purchases for cash or on credit for all merchandise
Sales	Sales of merchandise or service for cash or on credit
Payroll	Chronological record of all company remuneration

In addition, a general journal is sometimes used to record all transactions that do not belong in any of the special journals.

PRINCIPLES FOR THE CONTROL OF CASH RECEIPTS

Cash is involved in more transactions than any other asset---current and fixed. However, cash is the asset which remains most susceptible to mishandling and theft. As a result, every good business needs an effective accounting system which not only provides accurate records of cash receipts but also minimizes the opportunities for theft and mishandling. The following basic principles are intended to help control cash receipts effectively. (1) Create source documents showing: how much cash was received: the date on which it was received; why cash was received; and sometimes who made the payment. Common source documents include cash register tapes; pre-numbered sales slips; and pre-numbered remittance slips. (2) Divide the responsibility. The most important principle of cash control is to separate the function of handling from the function of recording the cash receipts and their subsequent deposit in the bank. (3) Deposit all cash receipts intact.

THE CASH RECEIPTS JOURNAL

Every business enters into transactions which involve the receipt of cash. The number of transactions and the amount of cash involved may vary, depending upon the type and sort of business.

Journalizing Cash Receipts

When transactions involving cash receipts are recorded in a journal, the cash account is debited by the amount of the cash received. The corresponding account credited depends upon the source from which the cash was received. For example, the sales account is credited to record sales or in the case of a government organization, if cash is received for user fees, the corresponding amount credited could be "non-tax revenue".

Posting from the Cash Receipts Journal

Posting the entries from the cash receipts journal, sometimes called a cash blotter in public sector organizations, to the ledger varies slightly from the procedure used for posting from the general journal.

Posting Credit Entries

In the posting reference column of each ledger account, the letters "CR" are written to show when an amount has been posted from the cash receipts journal or cash blotter to a particular ledger account.

Totaling the Cash Receipts Journal

To determine the amount that must be posted from the cash receipts journal or cash blotter to the cash ledger account at the end of the month or accounting period, the cash journal or cash blotter must be totaled and ruled as follows: (1) Rule a single line under the last figure in the amount column. (2) Write the last date of the month or accounting period in the date column. (3) Write "cash debit" in the amount credited column. (4) Write "total receipts" in the explanation column. (5) Add the amounts in the amount credited column and prove the addition. (6) Rule a double line under the date, posting reference and amounts credited columns to show the blotter or journal is completed for the month.

The Reader Should Remember: that a fundamental principle of effective cash management, in both private and public sector firms, should be to *deposit all cash receipts intact as soon as possible,* and most likely at the end of each business day.

17

Processing Cash Payments

OBJECTIVE OF CHAPTER SEVENTEEN

The objective of this chapter is to provide the reader, course or workshop participant with the precise steps to be followed while processing cash payments from a company. This chapter may be considered unique from the government of Canada's point of view, as the majority of the government's cash payments are made via the common service agency, PWGSC.

INTRODUCTION

Any system which exists to control cash must include both cash payments and cash receipts. The owner of a business wants to be certain that payments are made for the correct amount, not paid more than once, to the correct payee and then only for goods and/or services actually authorized, ordered and received in a usually good condition. In addition, each employee wants to avoid the suspicion should there be a cash shortage.

THE CASH PAYMENTS JOURNAL

Accounting and financial systems must provide for adequate controls which ensure the authorized, accurate, efficient, honest and speedy processing of cash payments.

PRINCIPLES FOR THE CONTROL OF CASH PAYMENTS

The following principles should be adhered to as they form an integral part of any system designed for controlling cash payments. (1) *Check and authorize the bill.* No bill or invoice should be paid until it has been duly authorized. In the government of Canada this authorization is done under Sections 33 and 34 of the *Financial Administration Act,* that goods and/or services were duly authorized on the bill after they have been received and that the amount of the invoice is computed correctly. (2) *Pay by cheque, bank draft, credit or debit card.* Since all cash receipts should be deposited intact in the bank, no payments should ever be made directly or indirectly from cash receipts. Sometimes, which may prove later on to be hazardous, employees ask a cashier to cash a personal cheque. This should never be done. *All* payments, with the exception of petty cash and imprest cash, must be made either by cheque, bank draft, credit card or debit card. The petty cash and imprest cash are established and replenished by cheque. (3) *Use pre-numbered* cheques. Pre-numbered cheques should be used to provide an audit trail on all cheques issued. Voucher cheques should be kept on file so that every cheque can be accounted for numerically. (4) *Divide the responsibility.* For proper control, the responsibility for handling cheques and recording disbursements should be divided so that the work of one employee involved in cash handling may be checked *against* that of another. Specifically, for example, in the government of Canada, the same individual may not authorize a single document using both Sections 33 and 34 of the *Financial Administration Act.* (5) *Prepare a randomly operated cash proof.* When all cash receipts have been deposited in the bank and all the bills that should be paid have been by cheque, at least two independent records of cash receipts and payments are made available. The business has a record of receipts in the cash receipts journal and disbursements in the cheque book(s) or petty or imprest cash book(s). The bank has a record of all deposits and withdrawals in the current account. When the business receives a copy of the bank's record in the form of a monthly bank statement, the business should prepare a bank reconciliation statement to verify the accuracy of both accounts, the bank's and the company's.

Posting from the Cash Payments Journal

The accounts detailed in the cash payments journal appear individually in proper ledger accounts. These balances are summarized in the DFS and the detailed in the CFMRS for the government of Canada. The postings usually take place at intervals during the month. To identify those entries already posted, the source codes used for payments made by the government of Canada can vary between a number of three digit numeric fields such as 133, 134 and 144. In the posting reference column of the cash payments journal these source numbers sometimes appear next to each item as they are posted. In the ledger accounts, the letters "CP" and the number of the payment are sometimes also written in the posting reference column to indicate the entries which have been posted from the cash payments journal to the ledger.

THE CASH PROOF

Introduction

Any method used to verify that the amount of cash recorded equals the amount of cash handled is known as a **cash proof.** One example of a cash proof is the total shown on the cash register tape, or the amount recorded, as compared to the amount in the cash drawer, or the amount of cash handled. Still another example occurs when the balance in one's chequing account or savings account is confirmed with the balance on the corresponding bank statement(s).

Cash Over and Short

When cash is handled in over the counter transactions, differences sometimes occur between the amount of cash that is recorded or the cash register tape. The amount of the cash in the drawer might be more than the amount shown on the tape or less. When the reason for a discrepancy cannot be traced to an error, it may be found that the difference was caused by a mistake in making change.

Verifying the Cheque Book Balance

Under an effective system of cash control, all cash receipts are deposited in a chequing account and all payments are made by cheques drawn against that account. The cheque books still, which carry a summary record of all the deposits to and withdrawals from the account, serve as source documents for the journal entries. Postings are made to the cash accounts from the cash receipts journal or cash blotter only at the end of each month. At that time, a figure representing the debits is posted to the cash receipts journal and the figure representing the credits to the cash payments journal.

COMMON HUMAN ERRORS MADE WHILE RECORDING AMOUNTS

Some of the common human errors which occur when recording amounts are: (1) The accountant or bookkeeper or enters more than once the original amount. This type of error occurs when one makes errors while entering or miscopies a number. (2) The accountant or bookkeeper changes the magnitude of the figure(s) entered. This type of error occurs when the initial digit is written in every column.

The Reader Should Remember: the cash payment maxim of making payments on their due date, and not too early or too late, is important. Random instead of regular proof of cash balances such as petty cash is also paramount.

Payroll Accounting

OBJECTIVE OF CHAPTER EIGHTEEN

The objective of this chapter is to present to the reader and the course or workshop participant the complex yet inter-related steps that result in gross pay, deductions and finally the net pay made to the employee. In the government of Canada, pay is handled by a Central Pay System, with DND having a pay system for its military employees and DFAIT dealing uniquely with its rotational staff.

INTRODUCTION

In a very small business the owner him or herself might do all the work required to operate her or his business. In most firms, the work is done by employees, who are paid salaries and wages for the services they provide. By federal and provincial Canadian law, employees are required to maintain accurate records for: (1) all salaries and wages paid to their employees; and (2) certain authorized and statutory deductions that are made from the employees' pay. Thus, any firm, regardless of its size, must have a system for maintaining payroll records.

Payroll refers to salaries and wages paid to employees for a certain period of work. The *pay period* usually refers to bi-weekly, semi-monthly or monthly intervals of remuneration. Payroll data remain important because: (1) They must be collected in order to determine the amount of salary or wages due employees on payday. (2) They are needed to record appropriate expenses involved with salaries and wages; and (3) Records determine statutory and other payments to be made to government agencies and other groups.

The firm's accounting system must establish effective controls over the payroll such as: (1) proper safeguards; and (2) necessary funds withheld from earnings. Payroll accounting may also be considered a vital element in the internal control of cash. In the government of Canada, an organization named Central Pay is a subsidiary of the common service agency, PWGSC.

COMPUTATION OF EARNINGS

To calculate an employee's *net pay*—the amount paid to her or him, the payroll clerk needs to determine the employee's net earnings, that is the amount actually earned and the employee's various *payroll deductions,* which in turn are amounts to be subtracted from the gross pay and usually remitted by the employer to a third party such as a government. N. B. With payroll in the government of Canada, most of these calculations are initiated by a Human Resource or Personnel Office, on a Personnel Management Information System (PMIS) and the deductions done by the Central Pay maintained by PWGSC.

Computation of Gross Earnings

Various plans are used in firms to determine gross earnings of the employees. These include the salary plan, hourly rate plan, piece rate plan, commission plan and salary commission plan.

Hours of Work and Wages

Two factors influence an employee's hours of work and her or his wages: (1) legislation; and (2) the contract of employment.

Under the terms of the *British North America (Constitution) Act, 1867,* to enact labour legislation which remains largely the purview of the provinces, provincial law varying from province to province, sets the maximum hours of work and the minimum wage levels. However, an employee may elect to offer a contract of employment to his or her employee with a different salary and wage rate often supported by the local collective bargaining unit.

Deductions from Gross Earnings

After the employee's gross earnings have been computed; various deductions must be made from this amount. These deductions include statutory deductions, such as the Canada Pension Plan; Income Tax (federal and provincial) and unemployment insurance; deductions required by collective bargaining agreements, such as union dues; and voluntary deductions for items, such as life insurance and hospital premiums. For large industrial plants, accountants generally assign an order of priority to each type of authorized deduction that may be made from an employee's pay. Here is one of the priority plans used in the government of Canada.

The order of priority assigned to each type of authorized deduction that may be made from an employee's pay cheque remains as follows: A. Statutory requirements: (1) Canada Pension Plan, or Quebec Pension Plan; (2) federal, provincial and territorial income taxes; (3) employment insurance; (4) garnishments, assignments, and government demands; B. Collective bargaining agreements: (1) union unilateral fees; (2) union dues; and C. Voluntary deductions: (1) miscellaneous deductions; (2) group insurance; (3) medical services plan; (4) hospitalization plan; (5) company pension plan; (6) Canada Savings Bonds; (7) community services, such as the United Way; and (8) credit union.

Contribution Tables

In an accounting system, the amount of contribution to be withheld from the earnings of an employee is usually determined by contribution tables. The tables are issued by Canada Revenue Agency, Taxation Division, and are reviewed each calendar year.

Federal, Provincial and Territorial Income Tax Deductions

The federal government and each of the provincial and territorial governments all levy taxes on wage earners within various jurisdictions. By law, employers are required to withhold a percentage of their employees' earnings for income taxes and periodically to make payments to the proper collecting governments.

The amount of income tax withheld depends on the amount of an employee's earnings, upon the number of exemptions he or she claims, and upon the province or territory in which he or she resides. Generally, an employee may be allowed the following exemptions: (1) one basic exemption; (2) one married or equivalent exemption; and (3) one exemption for each dependent.

PAYROLL RECORDS AND PROCEDURES

When the payroll has been computed, the data must be recorded by the firm so that it has the payroll option to report to the various federal, provincial and territorial tax authorities, and to other agencies involved in payroll deductions.

The employer is required to keep certain payroll data at least for the number of years stated in the legislation of his or her province or territory. In addition the employer must conform to the requirements laid down in the *Income Tax Act*. They include that an employer must receive permission from the government before he or she may destroy her or his receipts of employees' earnings.

Payroll Records

Two payroll records that are commonly kept to satisfy these requirements are the payroll register and the employee earnings record.

Paying the Payroll and Preparing the Payroll Return

Most firms establish regular paydays. The payday by necessity follows a few days after the end of the pay period so that the payroll department can complete the payroll and prepare it. In the government of Canada, the payroll of the military personnel of the Department of National Defence is held secretly and separately from that of the department's civilian employees.

The Reader Should Remember: most collective agreements determine the size of gross salaries and wages while statutes often determine deductions. The Department of National Defence and the Department of Foreign Affairs and International Trade both have unique methods of handling payroll.

Processing Purchases of Merchandise

OBJECTIVE OF CHAPTER NINETEEN

The objective of this chapter is to demonstrate to the reader and course or workshop participant the steps to be followed when processing purchases of merchandise in a firm, with a parallel focus being made on the authorities needed in public sector firms in the government before purchases of merchandise or services are processed.

INTRODUCTION

Firms that obtain revenue through the purchase and sale of goods and services are known as merchandising businesses. These firms may be retailers, who sell directly to consumers, or wholesalers who sell to retailers and sometimes large consumers. The goods purchased for resale are known as merchandise. The merchandise that a business holds is known as merchandise inventory. In any merchandising business, regardless of its size or the nature of its operations, some system may be established to control the way in which the merchandise is purchased and handled.

There has been a radical assessment of the appropriate methods of inventory management in recent years, with a greater emphasis on 'requirement' rather than 'replenishment' of inventory. The emergence of 'just-in-time' (JIT) systems, has led to a number of advantages. These advantages include reductions in inventory levels, and hence lower inventory carrying costs, better control over inventory lines and fewer production line stoppages.

Inventory policy should be analyzed in terms of the balance between the benefits and costs associated with greater efficiency and lower inventory levels. The costs encountered include holding costs, stock-out costs, re-order costs---as well as the costs of any computer system and the personnel required to operate it. In the government of Canada, "materiel management" to which this process is referred, has taken on a whole new operational and bureaucratic life of its own.

A SYSTEM FOR THE CONTROL OF PURCHASES

In any accounting or financial system designed to control the purchase of merchandise, forms and procedures must be established for these seven operations: approval and authority to purchase merchandise; ordering the merchandise; receiving the merchandise; paying for the merchandise; accounting for the merchandise; storing the merchandise; and using the merchandise.

Approval of and Authority for Purchasing Merchandise

In most organizations, the approval of and the authority for purchasing is usually vested in particular functions, or provided in the company's executive committee minutes. In the government of Canada, authority to purchase merchandise may be delegated by the minister to individual positions in the organization.

Ordering the Merchandise

In small businesses, all the activities involved in ordering the merchandise may be handled by the owner. In a large organization, however, the ordering operation is usually handled by a special purchasing department, headed by a purchasing agent. In the government of Canada, this is the step while exercising spending authority that may fall under "Initiation" of spending authority. Regardless of the size and nature of the firm, the ordering operation usually involves: determining what good or service needs to be bought; selecting the supplier; and placing the order.

Receiving the Merchandise

When the merchandise is received from the supplier, it must be unpacked, inspected and counted; recorded as being received; and moved to the storage or sales area of the department or responsibility centre which submitted the purchase requisition.

In the government of Canada, when the merchandise which has been received has been proven to be what was ordered and has passed the necessary inspection(s), it then may be authorized by the individual in the position exercising the commensurate spending authority under Section 34 of the *Financial Administration Act.* All of these activities comprise the third major operation of the purchasing procedure—receiving the main merchandise.

This process remains unique to the government of Canada, as items must be received on or before March 31 of each fiscal year. Then and only then will the item(s) bought and received may be charged to the current fiscal year, not to any past or future fiscal years. It must be remembered that Parliament, through the *Annual Appropriation Act*, only approves spending for twelve months at a time.

Storing the Merchandise

The merchandise which a firm holds on hand for sale or for use is known as *inventory*. Since goods are continually being purchased, sold, stored or used, the inventory level changes frequently. An effective system of controlling purchases also provides for controlling the amount of items held in storage; keeping an accurate, up to date record of inventory; and storing goods as to avoid reduction, complete or partial loss in value.

Using the Merchandise

Whenever merchandise is used, inventory is sometimes reduced. In the government of Canada, usage of stores should not occur until an individual in the appropriate temporary or permanent position exercises her or his delegated authority as per Section 34 of the *Financial Administration Act.*

Keeping Up-To-Date Inventory Records

Some firms maintain a continuous day-to-day record of each item stored in their merchandise inventory. This type of system is also known as a *perpetual* inventory. Firms also use a *periodic* type of inventory. With the latter method, the merchandise is counted regularly, usually at the end of a particular accounting period.

THE PURCHASES JOURNAL

Introduction

Before a firm can sell merchandise, it must spend money buying goods to be resold. The amounts paid for the purchases are known as *costs*. The amounts received for the sale of the merchandise are considered to be *revenues*. That relationship between costs and revenues determines whether a business will turn a *profit* or *loss* from which it has to pay operating expenses. Should there be no gross profit, the company will either *break even* or suffer a loss.

Accounting for Purchases of Merchandise

To generate a gross profit, a merchandising firm must sell its goods at a price higher than it pays for them. Purchasing goods for sale is much like incurring another type of expense while operating a business. However, until these goods are sold or used, they still remain a type of current asset which the firm owns. Also, until this asset is sold or used, its cost decreases the owners' equity.

PWGSC, the government of Canada's principal purchasing agency, uses a step by step process to buy goods and services. These steps include setting checkpoints for clearance at varying levels of authority, depending on the value of the contract. Canada is also subject to various trade agreements, the more recent being the Agreement on Internal Trade (AIT), the World Trade Organization Agreement on Government Procurement (WTO-AGP), and the North American Free Trade Agreement (NAFTA). These agreements have implications for suppliers to the Canadian government.

An example of this type of accounting entry covering purchasing goods or services may show thus:

WHAT HAPPENS

Cost of merchandise increases. The asset cash decreases. The liability accounts payable sometimes increases.

ACCOUNTING PRINCIPLE

To decrease the owners' equity, debit the account. To decrease an asset or increase a liability, credit the account.

ACCOUNTING ENTRY

Debit: Purchases

Credit: Cash or Accounts Payable

Trade Discounts

Many wholesalers and manufacturers publish catalogues of their products and retail prices. They offer deductions from this *list price* to dealers or individual customers who purchase large quantities. These deductions are called *trade discounts*.

By offering trade discounts, a business can adjust the prices at which it is willing to bill its merchandise without changing the list price as quoted in the catalogue. The trade discount can also be increased so as to offer merchandise to the dealer at a lower cost. Trade discounts *ARE NOT RECORDED* in the accounting records because they are used only to determine the *net* purchase price.

THE ACCOUNTS PAYABLE

The general ledger of a large firm such as the Royal Bank of Canada, Nova Corporation or the government of Canada would become very crowded if it contained separate accounts for all its assets, liabilities, contra accounts, control accounts, owners' equity, expenses and revenues for these reasons: (1) only one individual could post at any one time; (2) the trial balance would be extremely long and cumbersome; and (3) if the trial balance were out of balance, finding the error which caused the imbalance situation could prove to be extremely difficult.

Therefore, to avoid such difficulties, one may use control accounts and divide the general ledger into separate subsidiary ledgers such as accounts payable, accounts receivable, fixed assets and inventory.

TRANSPORTATION IN AND PURCHASES, RETURNS AND ALLOWANCES

Most accountants generally agree that the cost of merchandise acquired for resale must logically include any cost of transporting goods from the seller's place of business to the buyer's.

It is a *generally accepted accounting principle* that the full cost of merchandise includes the amount paid to the seller plus any transportation charges for the delivery of the goods. The costs include FOB destination, FOB supply point and any other costs for transporting the goods.

MAKING PAYMENTS TO CREDITORS

The inclusions on a purchase order or purchase invoice which may vary from customer to customer to determine the agreement between the buyer and the seller as to when the invoice is going to be settled.

Credit Periods

For most firms, the credit period begins with the date of the invoice. N/30 means the payment is due 30 days from the invoice date. N/EOM means the payment is required at the end of the month in which the purchase was made.

Cash Discounts

As a means of encouraging customers to pay their invoices during the first part of the credit period, many firms offer a cash discount, which entitles the purchaser to deduct a certain amount from the face of the invoice if he or she pays the bill within a specific period. When applied to a purchase invoice is called a *purchase discount*. The latter is not recorded at the time of an invoice is journalized, as the buyer gets the discount *only* if he pays the invoice within the discount period.

Making Payments

A transaction such as this may be analyzed as follows: (1) If the creditor's account shows a credit balance, that amount must be debited to show the same has been satisfied in full. (2) The cash must be credited for the exact amount paid. (3) Any difference between the credit balance and creditor's account and the amount of the account goes to the debit of the purchases discount account temporarily.

Thus a combination of the transportation in and purchases discount accounts is eventually removed from the purchases account.

Recording Purchase Discounts in the Cash Payments Journal

Cash payments are recorded in the cash payments journal. As we may have seen from the previous analysis, the entry payment of cash with a purchase discount involves the accounts payable control account and the individual creditor's account, a credit to the purchases discount account and a credit to the cash account.

Posting from the Cash Payments Journal During the Month

Each amount in the general ledger debit column of the cash payments journal is posted individually to the appropriate account in the general ledger. The account numbers are recorded in the posting reference column to indicate that the amounts have been posted to the general ledger.

Postings at the End of the Month

At the end of the month, all the money columns are footed, a check made of the equality of debit and credit totals while being checked with an adding machine with a tape. The total of the general ledger is **not** posted because the amounts individually to accounts in the ledger. On the contrary, the totals found in the payable debit column and the purchases discount credit column are posted to the debit side of the controlling account and the purchases account respectively in the general ledger. The total of the net credit column is posted to the credit side of the cash account and the cash account the number beneath the double line.

Summary of Transactions Involving Purchases

A number of operations are involved in the function of purchasing: An approved and authorized purchase invoice was submitted to the accounting department for journalizing. Sometimes the full amount of the invoice was paid when it fell due. At other time, a deduction for purchase returns or allowances was made for the total amount of the invoice. Alternatively, a deduction for purchase discounts was also made.

The Reader Should Remember: the basic steps when purchasing goods and services and more specifically relate their interrelationships to materiel management in the government of Canada.

$$20$$

Processing Sales on Credit

OBJECTIVE OF CHAPTER TWENTY

The objective of this chapter is to present and describe to the reader and the course or workshop participant the practical steps which may be used in processing sales on credit. In addition, it must be noted that two types of revenue or sales are usually processed by government of Canada departments and agencies.

INTRODUCTION

The revenue of a merchandising business is generated mainly by the sale(s) of merchandise. Some firms generate cash sales only; others both credit sales and cash sales. This chapter focuses on credit sales. Previously the focus was on cash sales.

A SYSTEM FOR CONTROLLING CREDIT SALES

Accounting systems used by merchandising firms vary according to the nature and size of each business. However, every business must have a system that provides for processing timely, efficiently, effectively, economically and accurately both the merchandise for delivery to the customer(s) and the data for recording the sales transaction. Every system must ensure that: (1) The customer's order is properly received and properly approved or disapproved. (2) The goods ordered are taken from stock, packaged and shipped. (3) The customer is accurately and timely billed for the merchandise.

Receiving and Approving the Order

Orders for merchandise reach a firm in a number of ways: They may come on *sales order forms* that are filled out by salesmen who call on customers and solicit orders. They may come in as *purchase order forms*, or by *letter*.

When an order is received by the order department, the salesman verifies all the information submitted to the customer and provides any additional information, such as a catalogue number or unit price, and will expedite the filling of the order. The sales clerk enters all the necessary data on a pre-numbered, multiple copy form known as a *shipping order*, prepared on the basis of a purchase order submitted to the person or firm delivering the merchandise to the participant, usually a firm. The credit department determines whether or not the customer is a good credit risk, that is, whether he or she is likely to pay the bill when it falls due.

Packing and Shipping the Merchandise

When the shipping order arrives in the stockroom, a shipping clerk assembles the items and forwards them to the customer. In the United Kingdom this assembly process is known as "picking". When he or she does so, he or she indicates on the packing slip and all remaining copies whether or not he or she is sending the full quantity of the item (s) ordered. This event is particularly vital to a public sector firm, whose receipt date of an actual item received, usually triggers the authorization of a purchase of a good or service under Section 34 of the *Financial Administration Act*.

The sales invoice may sometimes look a lot like a completed copy of the shipping order, except it lists only those items actually received, and shows how much the customer really owes. Even though a firm sends an invoice at the time that the merchandise is shipped, most businesses find it useful to send the customer a statement of her or his account periodically. The statement that the teller sends the customer looks something like the customer's ledger account. For example, if the statement is issued at the end of the month, the statement may show: the balance due at the beginning of the month; all charges for sales during the month; all deductions for payments received for goods returned during the month; and the current unpaid balance.

Receipts or a packing slip, other than an invoice, are generally useful for triggering the year end practice in some government departments and agencies entitled: "Payables at Year End" or PAYE. According to the Treasury Board of Canada's PAYE policy, when goods or services are received by the firm on or before March 31 and the related invoice is not yet presented for payment, the invoice may be presented in the near or distant future for payment. At March 31, the relevant appropriation is reduced and debited; the PAYE account is increased and credited. Whenever the invoice is presented for payment, the PAYE account is decreased and debited and the cash or bank account is decreased and credited. Any difference one way or another between the actual amount presented for payment and the original PAYE set up earlier on at March 31 should not be debited or credited against the current year's appropriation by the organization's financial officer, but all differences should be netted for all departments and agencies and the final combined amount entered against a single government of Canada account: "Adjustment(s) to previous years" by the Minister of Finance. This is because monies voted by Parliament and later on allotted by the Treasury Board of Canada are only authorized and approved for a single fiscal year. Parliament alone has the ultimate authority to move monies between votes or appropriations or from one fiscal year to another.

The Reader Should Remember: the procedures for dealing with sales for cash and credit may exclude the use of "Suspense" accounts; and the straightforward, simple and correct method of accounting for PAYE transactions.

21

End of Period Adjustments

OBJECTIVE OF CHAPTER TWENTY-ONE

The objective of this chapter is to lead the reader, course or workshop participant through the complex steps which comprise the closing of a particular accounting period. This process can be somewhat trying in public sector firms. At Citizenship and Immigration Canada (CIC), its administrative and financial branches maintain a calendar year (at December 31) closing date for the Unemployment Insurance sector and a fiscal year (at March 31) closing date for its remaining sectors. In essence, CIC then may carry out two separate closings of its combined books in any one fiscal year (April 01 to March 31).

INTRODUCTION

A transaction is simply a financial event resulting from the financial impact of an economic event or operation which has an effect on one or more asset, liability, contra, control or owners' equity accounts. The data generated by all of these transactions during an accounting cycle is processed by the accounting system; and the results then reported on financial statements. Although the procedures which are followed vary according a firm's size, complexity and nature, every accounting system begins by collecting data from the transaction(s) to be processed.

Beginning the Accounting Cycle

With all forms of accounting systems, such as PWGSC's CFMRS or a departmental or agency DFS, four steps always comprise the start of an accounting cycle: Step 1: Find the origin of the data. Step 2: Journalize. Step 3: Post. Step 4: Prove the ledger. The general theory followed in each accounting cycle is that one must be able to follow the trail of each transaction through these four steps.

Find the Origin of the Data

The original record of each business transaction is the *source document.* Some examples of source documents are cash register tapes, cheque stubs, credit memoranda, journal vouchers, purchase invoices, purchase orders, remittance slips, sales invoices and sales slips. The data is "captured" from these source documents at the time the transaction occurs. Authorization of these documents, whether under Section 32, 33 or 34 of the *Financial Administration Act* in the government of Canada, does NOT constitute the creation of source documents. These kinds of necessary authorizations provide the *authority* for *future* economic actions that may result in future events such as the receipt or disbursement of cash, or a promise pay or receive cash later, from which in turn an accountant or bookkeeper may use the created source documents to generate transactions.

Journalize

Though not always done, as in a lot of instances with such financial systems as Free Balance, CDFS, CFMRS, Oracle and SAP, when most of the source documents are posted directly to the general ledger, once the accountant or bookkeeper has entered the data from the source documents, this information becomes ready for entry into the accounting records. The accountant or bookkeeper may also journalize transactions in the general journal or subsidiary journals such as the cash receipts journal or cash blotter.

Post

In addition the accountant or bookkeeper may then transfer these entries to a ledger or book of final entry. Some small businesses only need a general ledger. Larger businesses need subsidiary ledgers as well. These organizations may also use a general ledger for asset, contra, control, liability, expense, revenue, and owners' equity accounts; an accounts payable sub-ledger or accounts with creditors, and an accounts receivable sub-ledger for accounts with debtors.

Prove the Ledger

When all the entries have been posted in the subsidiary ledger(s) and the general ledger, a proof must be made of the accuracy of these postings. First, a schedule of accounts receivable, listing the name of each customer and the amount he or she owes the firm, is made from the accounts receivable ledger. The total on this schedule is then compared with the balance of the accounts receivable control account in the general ledger to prove the accuracy of the postings to the accounts receivable sub-ledger. A similar schedule is prepared for accounts payable, and the total also having been compared with the balance in the accounts payable control account. Similar processes are undertaken in the government of Canada for each of the PWGSC control or bank accounts held in each DFS and PWGSC's CFMRS. A trial balance is then struck for all of the general ledger accounts to show that the total of all the debit balances equal the total of all credit balances.

Merchandise Inventory Account

One of the largest and most valuable assets of a retail store or Canadian government departments such as Fisheries and Oceans (DFO) and National Defence (DND) or a wholesale firm such as Provigo is the inventory of merchandise held for use or for resale. An inventory of merchandise comprises goods on hand and available for sale to customers or for use by the company itself. Methods of inventory control and measurement include the *periodic* or the *perpetual* inventory. The main operational points which obtain concerning inventories remain as follows: (1) There exists no day to day record of either the cost of the amount of goods unsold or not used and still on hand or of the cost to the merchant of goods sold to customers or used by the business. (2) A physical count of merchandise on hand is usually made at the end of the accounting period under consideration. (3) If possible, an actual count of merchandise on hand generally occurs after the close of business on the last day of the accounting period under consideration. (4) To arrive at the *cost value* of the current inventory, two calculations are usually required: (a) The quantity of each item is multiplied by an appropriate unit cost, using *one* consistent method such as Average, FIFO or LIFO. (b) Once the total value of each type of item is obtained, a total figure for the entire inventory may be determined by adding the multiple values of all the various types of merchandise. (5) The cost of goods available for sale or use during the accounting period under consideration is determined by adding the amount of inventory at the beginning of the period to the amount of purchases, represented by the net purchase cost, during the period. (6) The cost of goods used results from subtracting the inventory at the end of the period under consideration from the cost of goods available for sale or use. (7) The figure of cost of goods sold or used then helps to determine the gross profit or loss for the accounting period under consideration, and the value of merchandise on hand at the end of the period which in turn appears as a current asset in the balance sheet.

Inventory analysis remains unique in a large government department such as National Defence which holds some of its inventory in a warehouse in Montreal, Quebec, operated jointly with a private sector firm. DND's and DFO's inventory analysis remains a challenge for the personnel in materiel management and finance.

END OF PERIOD ADJUSTMENTS

Introduction

Accountants and financial analysts alike use financial statements to judge the financial position of a firm and the results of its operations. It is paramount, therefore, that these statements accurately report the amount of items owned, all debts, all expenses, costs and revenues. To accomplish this there must be a precise cut off of transactions at the end of the accounting period. PWGSC interacts fiscally with all other government departments and agencies. The timing of cut-offs, whether late or early, remains significant.

Supplies on Hand Account

This type of business transaction usually affects more than one accounting period. In this instance, *prepaid expenses* are the cost of those goods and/or services which are bought to be used in operating the business but remain unused at the end of the accounting period under consideration. Conversely, the cost of these items is sometimes called a *deferred charge* because the expense is deferred or put off until a later period. To record prepaid expenses: (1) Debit an asset account when items are purchased. (2) Determine the unused portion at the end of the accounting period under consideration. (3) Debit an expense account for the portion of supplies used. In addition, credit the same asset account as in Step 1 for the portion of supplies used.

WORKING EXAMPLE 21-A:

Samuel L. Bell, Chartered Accountant, draws a cheque at the beginning of an accounting period, on June 1, 2XX7 for $ 500, representing several months of office supplies.

WHAT HAPPENS	ACCOUNTING PRINCIPLE	ACCOUNTING ENTRY
The asset office supplies on on hand increases by $ 500	To increase an asset: debit the account	Debit: Office supplies on hand: $ 500
The asset cash decreases by the same $ 500	To decrease an asset: credit the account	Credit: Cash: $ 500

WORKING EXAMPLE 21-B:

At the end of the accounting period on June 30, 2XX7, Samuel L. Bell counted the office supplies on hand. The physical count showed there were $ 300 of supplies still on hand, meaning that $ 200 ($ 500 - $ 300) worth were either used, lost or broken during June, 2XX7. Therefore an adjusting entry was made to transfer the amount of used supplies ($ 200) from the asset account, office supplies on hand to the expense account, supplies used.

WHAT HAPPENS	ACCOUNTING PRINCIPLE	ACCOUNTING ENTRY
Expense decreased owners' equity by $ 200	To decrease owners' equity, debit the account	Debit: Supplies used: $200
The asset account, Supplies on hand, decreases by $ 200	To decrease an asset, credit the account	Credit: Supplies on hand: $ 200

The Prepaid Insurance Account

Many of the firm's assets, such as equipment and buildings, are usually insured against loss through fire, flood, storm or theft. The premium of an insurance policy is paid out at the beginning of the insurance period; therefore it is paid in advance. Should the policy be in force for more than one accounting period, the insurance premium remains a prepaid item. When the premium is paid, the amount debited to the asset account: prepaid insurance. When each portion of the insurance premium expires, it becomes an actual expense.

WORKING EXAMPLE 21-C:

Samuel L. Bell, Chartered Accountant, issues a cheque for $ 900 to pay premium of his firm's liability insurance, and to carry him and his staff against losses due to human error.

WHAT HAPPENS	ACCOUNTING PRINCIPLE	ACCOUNTING ENTRY
The asset prepaid insurance increased by $ 900	To increase an asset: Debit the account	Debit: Prepaid insurance:$ 900
The asset account cash decreases by $ 900	To decrease an asset: Credit the account	Credit: Cash: $900

As the year progresses at Samuel L. Bell, Chartered Accountant, the liability insurance premium provides a year's coverage of liability insurance. Since the premium has been paid in advance, the premium becomes a prepaid item. Thus each accounting period throughout the year must be charged for the portion of the premium that expires during the period elapsed. Therefore, if the accounting firm, Samuel L. Bell, Chartered Accountant has an accounting period of one month, the cost of the insurance expired for the month of June would be 1/12 of the annual premium of $ 900 or $ 75. At the end of June, an entry would be made to transfer one month's insurance ($ 75) from the prepaid insurance account to the insurance expense account.

WORKING EXAMPLE 21-D:

Record the amount insurance expired during the month of June.

WHAT HAPPENS	ACCOUNTING PRINCIPLE	ACCOUNTING ENTRY
Expense decrease owners' equity by $ 75	To decrease owners' equity Debit the account	Debit: Insurance expense:$ 75
The asset account insurance decreases by $ 75	To decrease an asset: Credit the account	Credit: Prepaid insurance: $ 75

The balance of the prepaid insurance account at July 1 will be $ 825. This represents eleven months' insurance that has not been expensed ($ 75 x 11 = $ 825). Through this adjusting entry at the end of each monthly period, the asset account prepaid insurance will contain the amount of the remaining prepaid insurance and the insurance expense account that will expended by the end of the annual or fiscal period.

In addition to the supplies on hand, prepaid insurance, and also prepaid rent, a firm may have other expenses that require adjusting at the end of the accounting period. The basic principle for all adjustments for prepaid items is the same: (1) Record the prepaid amount to the appropriate account. (2) At the end of the accounting period, determine the amount of the asset that been used during that accounting period. (3) Transfer the amount of the expense from the asset account to the appropriate expense account.

These kinds of expenses include bad debs and depreciation. Bad debts expense maintains a contra account named allowance for doubtful accounts and depreciation one called accumulated depreciation.

Bad Debts

This sub-topic discusses adjustments to record a decrease in the current asset account, accounts receivable, due to some accounts becoming not collectible. Such an adjustment is necessary to report accurately the assets on the balance sheet and the expenses on the income statement. A seller, of course, only wants to extend credit only to those customers who will be able to repay their debt. Therefore, the firm's credit department investigates the credit rating and credit record of the customer. However, in spite of careful investigation, a firm can still expect accounts receivable known as *bad debts* to remain not collectible. Western Diversification Canada, because of large amounts due the department from repayable contributions, may have significant bad debts. In addition, Citizenship and Immigration may have amassed large amounts of bad debt from Canadians in some provinces having been overpaid contributions of social benefits. These delinquent debit accounts are known as *bad debts*, balanced with the credit side contra, asset reduction, negative asset, or valuation, or valuation accounts of *allowance for doubtful accounts.*

A *bad debt* arises when it is decided that there is usually no chance of recovering the debt. It might that the debtor has gone into liquidation himself, or has left the country without paying the debt and is not planning to return! A bad debt write off is always against a specific debtor.

Accounts which a firm may be unable to collect usually cannot be easily identified in the accounting period when the commensurate sale(s) is (are) made. In fact, these sometimes are not determined until several months or even a year more, after the actual sale. Therefore, two methods are used to acknowledge losses due to bad debts. (1) The direct write off; and (2) the estimated.

The *direct write off method* records bad debt loss *when* it occurs. Some people frequently criticized this method because they believe it contravenes the matching principle: the revenue from the sale recorded in one accounting period, but the expense is recorded in another.

Furthermore, (1) the net income shown on the income statement is incorrect for the period of the sale and is also incorrect for the period of the write off. (2) The amount of the accounts receivable shown in balance sheet will be overstated until the account is written off.

Finally, it is a *generally accepted accounting principle* that revenues and expenses must match each other whenever the revenue is realized (matching principle).

With the *estimated method*, the actual loss due to the bad debt(s) can be determined only *after* all attempts to collect the debt(s) have failed. Bad debt losses are recorded *before* they occur. The resulting adjusting entry could be as follows:

Debit: Bad debts expense	Credit: Allowance for Doubtful accounts

The allowance for doubtful accounts account may be, as mentioned earlier, classified under a number of different names: an asset reduction account, a contra account, a negative asset account and a valuation account. Another contra account that may be considered is the accumulated depreciation with its opposite expense account: depreciation expense.

Depreciation

Most assets of a business, be it a sole trader, partnership or limited company, should be depreciated. The usual exception is freehold land, as this will usually appreciate or increase in value over time. *Depreciation* writes off an asset during the period that is expected to benefit from its use. Three main methods depreciation are in use: *straight line, reducing balance* and *capital cost allowance* methods. The true meaning of the word depreciation is best expressed in this principle:

It is generally acceptable accounting principle that depreciation is a process allocating the cost of a fixed asset over its estimated life.

Emphatically, depreciation is **not** a process of evaluation. Under the *straight line method*, annual depreciation is calculated as follows: (1) Subtract the estimated disposal value from the original cost of the fixed asset to determine the total depreciation. (2) Divide the total depreciation by the total number of years of the estimated life of the fixed to thus obtain the annual depreciation. The amount of depreciation charged is the same for each year of use. The disposal of the fixed asset occurs when the asset is sold, traded or scrapped. This method is calculated thus:

$$\frac{\text{Cost minus estimated value}}{\text{Numbers of years expected use}} = \frac{\$\,10{,}000 - \$\,256}{4} = \$\,2{,}436 \text{ per annum}$$

The *reducing balance method* would give a larger charge for depreciation in earlier years, and a smaller charge in later years. This method is favoured a lot with automobile dealers, who just love depreciating their inventory by a significant percentage the second the machine is sold and rolls off the lot. With the *capital cost allowance method*, under Canadian income tax legislation, a business is permitted to include in the expense section of its statement of income an allowance for depreciating most of its fixed assets. Finally, the Taxation Division of Canada Revenue Agency divides fixed assets into various classes, with each class being assigned a maximum percentage of depreciation. In some respects, however, these two seemingly similar contra accounts perform different functions.

The *allowance for doubtful accounts* reduces the current asset to a realizable value. *Accumulated depreciation*, on the other hand, shows that a portion of the original cost has expired and has been recorded as an expense.

Amortization should be recognized in a rational and systematic manner appropriate to the nature of a capital asset with a limited life and its use by the enterprise. As a result of this vagueness, a variety of amortization methods are acceptable for use in practice, such as straight line [this method recommendation by the Treasury Board in its Accounting Standard No. 3.1], declining balance, etc...

The Reader Should Remember: there are different main methods used to amortize or depreciate capital assets and write off uncollectable debts.

22

Completing the Accounting Cycle

OBJECTIVE OF CHAPTER TWENTY-TWO

The objective of this chapter is to present the reader and the course or workshop participant with a short review of the six (6) steps of the accounting cycle as it is used in a firm towards the end of the close of every accounting period. These steps not only appear in but also are reflected as a mirror image by each federal government department or agency and PWGSC in their respective financial systems. The names of general ledger accounts are similar, specifically the control or bank accounts. The early or late closing ties and/or dates effected by each department or agency as each interfaces with PWGSC need to be also monitored carefully.

INTRODUCTION

As previously mentioned in this text the beginning phases of the accounting cycle are: Starting Point: Find the origin of the data. Step 1: Journalize. Step 2: Post. Step 3: Prove the ledger. It is also important to note that *revenues must be always matched against expenses in the same accounting period.* In this chapter, the author also examines and provides some working examples of how those end of period adjustments are placed in the permanent accounting records in order to complete the accounting cycle. These adjustments are within the time period of any one month.

COMPLETING A WORKSHEET

When the trial balance shows the correct balance of all accounts, the financial statements can be prepared directly from the trial balance. However, the balances must be adjusted before any statements are prepared. Most accountants prefer to prepare the trial balance on a worksheet to also compute adjustments. The use of spreadsheets such as those generated by Lotus 3.1 and Microsoft Excel can prove invaluable in such an exercise.

The Worksheet

The worksheet is a columnar form, excellent for being prepared on a computerized spreadsheet, and resembles the trial balance introduced earlier on in this text. Additional columns have been, however, introduced to assist the accountant or bookkeeper in computing the amounts of the adjustments; and in sorting and classifying the accounts used in preparing either the profit and loss statement or the balance sheet periodically. Therefore the worksheet should have these columns: (1) the trial balance section; (2) the adjustments section; (3) the adjusted trial balance section; (4) the income statement section; and (5) the balance sheet section.

The following procedures should be used: Step 3a: Complete the trial balance section; Step 3b: Complete the adjustment section; Step 3c: Complete the adjusted trial balance section; Step 3d: Complete the income section; Step 3e: Complete the balance sheet; Step 3f: Complete the other financial statements section.

PREPARING THE FINANCIAL STATEMENTS

Introduction

Previously on the worksheet, the data has been sorted according to the statements on which they appear and the revenue or net loss that has been computed. Therefore it is relatively easy to prepare financial statements.

Step 4A: Prepare the Income Statement

The income statement reports the results of operations conducted by a firm during the accounting period under consideration. In a large merchandising firm one could see sections such as the revenue; the cost of goods sold; the total expenses; the gross profit or loss; the operating expenses; and the net income or net loss.

Step 4B: Prepare Balance Sheet, Statement of Owners' Equity

The balance sheet shows the financial position of the business as at the end of the accounting period under consideration. The statement of owners' equity reports the changes in the owners' equity of the firm during the accounting period under consideration.

Step 4C: Prepare Other Statements

Prepare other statements at the time. The *Handbook of the Canadian Institute of Chartered Accountants*, *the Handbook of Public Sector Accounting Auditing Board, the Treasury Board Standards 3.1*, and *the Financial Information Strategy Manual* all provide a comprehensive list and working examples of the statements required to be prepared by private and public sector firms.

COMPLETING THE ACCOUNTING CYCLE

After the financial statements have been prepared, it is important that the permanent records of the firm in their ledger accounts contain the same information as calculated on the worksheet. The procedure for bringing general ledger accounts up to date is known as adjusting and closing the books. The following are the final steps: Step 5a: Making the adjusting entries; and Step 6a: Prepare a post closing trial balance.

The Reader Should Remember: the details of these six steps which comprise the accounting cycle remain important. This could reduce the likelihood of incidences of human error.

23

Accrual versus Appropriation Accounting

OBJECTIVE OF CHAPTER TWENTY-THREE

The objective of this chapter is to guide the reader and workshop or course participant through the policies and examples of practices that show the similarities and differences of accrual accounting, in essence, implementing GAAP, GAPSAP, and appropriation accounting; and exercising delegated authority, during the day to day operations of government departments and agencies in the federal government of Canada.

INTRODUCTION

This text began by describing the unique theory of how exercising delegated authority, implementing generally accepted accounting principles and financial management function as a combined, integrated process in Canadian government organizations. Finally, the related policies, practices and examples are presented in this third to last chapter. *The Financial Information Strategy Manual,* developed and designed by the Treasury Board Secretarial provides the guidelines for the day to day principles to be applied during the function of this integrated process.

This chapter: defines the differences between accrual accounting, accounting for authorities, and reporting by objects; describes a variety of accounting transactions; and indicates how to classify and code them with rationale supported in certain scenarios. [The practical example used throughout this chapter is an imaginary service line in the Canadian government named the Royal National Police within an imaginary government department called the Ministry of Solicitors and Barristers. In addition, the example also outlines the reporting and presentation requirements for departmental financial statements. Note that the coding used in these scenarios which comprise the working example has been adapted from the one used by the Treasury Board of Canada in the 2007 issue of its *Financial Information Strategy Manual.*] The remaining sub-sections which comprise this chapter include: accounting principles, assets, contra accounts, control accounts, expenses, liabilities, net assets, net liabilities, and revenue.

ACCOUNTING PRINCIPLES

To finally arrive at peparing a feasible set of financial statements, certain basic accounting principles need to be generally recognized and understood before individual accounting transactions can be analyzed, prepared, approved, authorized and entered.

Going Concern

Applying the *going concern* principle expects a department or agency to continue to operate in the foreseeable future with no intentions to cease operations. The implications of this going concern principle remain critical. The historical cost principle would be of limited use if it were not for the going concern principle. For example, amortization, bad debts, depreciation, capital cost allowance and allowance for doubtful accounts policies only work in a going concern situation.

General Definition of Accrual Accounting, Accounting for Appropriations and Other Authorities and Reporting by Object

With the full implementation of *The Financial Information Strategy (FIS)* as at April 01, 2001, departments and agencies were required to account for economic events specific to their organizations on: an accrual accounting basis, an authority basis to identify the appropriations or other authorities, and an object of expenditure basis. These three requirements are not only similar but paradoxically dissimilar. Therefore they need to be considered separately.

Accrual Accounting

Accrual accounting recognizes transactions when the underlying economic event occurs, regardless of whether cash is received or paid. With accrual accounting, transactions are classified as assets, liabilities, owners' equity, revenues or expenses---in essence, following the changes that may be made to the *accounting equation.* It should be noted that within the classification coding of accounts, *Financial Reporting Accounts* **(FRAs)** have been developed as separate accounts in the department's Chart of Accounts in order to code transactions for accrual accounting purposes. It should be remembered that a direct linkage exists between the accounting equation and FRAs.

Accounting for Appropriations and Authorities

As stated earlier in this text, an appropriation or a vote is an authority to pay money out of the CRF. It is clear then that the authority provided by an appropriation or vote is required *before* monies can be spent by government organizations. Some authorities are given in the form of annually approved limits through appropriation acts. Other authorities come from other legislation in the form of statutory spending authority for specific purposes: for example, employee benefits, the minister's salary and motor allowances, revolving funds, etc. *Appropriation authority* is the means by which Parliament controls the outflows of money from the CRF. However, a number of transactions are charged to a current year appropriation but do *not* affect the CRF until a later date or not at all, such as: charges made by one government department on another; and write-offs, forgiveness, etc. of loans, investments or advances. N. B. It should be remembered that some government organizations which are still not compliant to FIS requirements follow neither these principles nor recommended policies and associated practices.

Reporting by Object

To measure the impact of government transactions on the economy, expenditures are classified according to the type of resources or goods and services acquired, revenue earned or transfer payments or grants and contributions made. Identifying detailed economic objects, combined with information from other sectors of the economy, makes possible economic analysis on a national basis, of the effects of government spending. The economic objects are the **basis** of codes for the object classification and are required for government wide statistical purposes. They may also be used at the lowest working level by departments as departmental *line objects*, but departments and agencies often need more detail for their own purposes. As introduced earlier in this text, these object classifications may include categories, sub-categories, reporting, economic, source, class and department line objects. *Standard* objects are the highest level used for Parliamentary reporting by all departments and agencies.

Historical Cost

Under GAAP transactions and events are recognized in financial statements as the amount of cash or cash equivalent paid or received or the fair value ascribed to them when they occurred. Historical cost provides financial statement users with a stable and consistent benchmark on which they can rely on to establish historical trends.

Matching Principle

The matching principle requires that revenues and expenses be accrued. In other words, they are recognized as they are earned or incurred, not just when they are received or paid or when they affect an appropriation.

Materiality

Materiality is a term used to describe the significance of financial statement information to users. To determine whether an item or aggregation of items is material, the following factors should be considered: the size, nature and cumulative effects of the item.

Substance over Form

Financial statements should present the economic substance of transactions and events even though their legal form may suggest a different treatment. Thus, transactions and events are accounted for and presented in a manner that conveys their substance rather than necessarily their legal or other forms.

ASSETS

Assets, what a department **owns**, are economic resources controlled by a government as a result of past transactions or events and from which economic benefits may be obtained. Assets have three essential characteristics. They embody a future benefit that involves a capacity, singly, or in combination with other assets to provide and services. The government can control access to the benefit. The transaction or event giving rise to the government's right to, or control of, the benefit has already occurred.

Cash

From a departmental perspective, cash includes cash on hand, cash in transit and cash on deposit.

SCENARIO 23-A SERVICE LINE RECEIVES MONEY FOR SERVICES RENDERED

The Royal National Police receives a cheque for $ 30,000 in the mail from the Provincial Government of Alberta for policing services rendered.

JOURNAL ENTRIES

	FRA	AUTH	OBJ	Amount $
Dr. Cash In Hand Awaiting Deposit Record By RG	11125	R300	5299	$ 30,000
Cr: Accounts Receivable – Non Tax Revenue	11125	R300	5399	$ 30,000

SCENARIO 23-B ORGANIZATION RECEIVES AN OVERPAYMENT

The Ministry of Solicitors and Barristers receives $ 1,000 from Grand and Toy. It is discovered that this is an overpayment.

JOURNAL ENTRIES

	FRA	AUTH	OBJ	Amount $
Dr. Cash In Hand Awaiting Record Deposit by RG	11125	R300	5299	$ 1,000
Cr. GST Refundable Advance Account	13392	G111	8171	$ 48
Cr. Operating Expenses	513XX	n/a	n/a	$ 952

Receivables

Receivables are financial assets in the form of claims held against customers and others for money, goods or services.

Accounts Receivable

Accounts receivable may be classified as short-term receivables that are normally, but not necessarily, expected to be collected within a year. An allowance for doubtful accounts, because of a bad debt, can be established as a percentage of accounts receivable or by setting up an aging schedule.

SCENARIO 23-C --- SALE OF GOODS

The Ministry sells information products to an outside party or $ 500. This sale represents non-respendable revenue, as it is outside the department's vote netting or net voting authority.

JOURNAL ENTRIES

	FRA	AUTH	OBJECT	AMOUNT$
Dr. Accounts Receivable	11221	R300	399	$ 565
Cr. PST Payable	21151	R300	6299	40
Cr. GST Payable	21134	R300	6299	25
Cr. Non Tax Revenue	41150	R300	4299	500

SCENARIO 23-D THE INVOICE IS PAID IN FULL

	FRA	AUTH	OBJECT	AMOUNT$
Dr. Cash In Hand	11215	R300	5299	565
Cr. Accounts Receivable	11221	R300	5399	565

SCENARIO 23-E ESTABLISH AN ALLOWANCE FOR DOUBTFUL ACCOUNTS

Using its experience with its debtors, and also aging the accounts receivable, Royal National Police decides to set up allowance for doubtful accounts for $ 20,000.

JOURNAL ENTRIES

	FRA	AUTH	OBJECT	AMOUNT$
Dr. Bad Debt Expense	51732	F412	3462	$ 20,000
Cr. Allow for Dbtfl. Accounts	21223	F412	2299	$ 20,000

Loans Receivable

A loan receivable is a financial asset of a government (the lender) represented by a promise by a borrower to repay a specific amount, at a specified amount, at a specified time or times, or on demand, usually with interest but not necessarily.

SCENARIO 23-F LOAN MADE TO AN ABORIGINAL GROUP

The Royal National Police makes a loan of $ 10,000 to a northern aboriginal organization to finance the construction of a modern half way house for runaway teenagers.

JOURNAL ENTRIES

	FRA	AUTH	OBJECT	Amount$
Dr. Loans Receivable – Aboriginal Band	11222	F414	5402	$ 10,000
Cr. RG Payment Control Account	61DDD	R300	6135	$ 10,000

Accountable Advances

Accountable advances are issued as per Section 38 of the *Financial Administration Act* and the Accountable Advance Regulations. Excluded are payments made in advance in accordance with Section 34 (b) of the *Financial Administration Act.* There are two categories of accountable advances: standing advances and temporary advances other than standing advances.

SCENARIO 23-G ISSUANCE AND SETTLEMENT OF A STANDING ADVANCE

A police inspector, an employee of the Royal National Police, who travels regularly, is issued a standing advance of $ 3,000. On his return from a trip, his manager, the Police Commissioner, authorizes his travel report using Section 34 FAA authority. The Chief Financial Officer authorizes his actual travel expenses of $3,718 for payment under Section 33 of the FAA.

JOURNAL ENTRIES

	FRA	AUTH	OBJECT	Amount$
Dr. Standing Advance	13315	H181	5030	$ 3,000
Cr. RG Payment Control Account	61DDD	R300	6135	$ 3,000
Dr. Operating Expense	51321	B11A/B12A	XXXX	$ 3,540
Dr. GST Refundable Advance	13392	G111	8171	$ 178
Cr. Standing Advance	13315	H181	5030	$ 3,000
Cr. RG Payment Control Account	61DDD	R300	6135	$ 718

Inventories

Departments use two different types of inventories: consumable and those held for resale. *Consumable inventories* are items of tangible property that are to be consumed in a future year directly or indirectly in the delivery of program outputs. *Inventories held for resale* are physical items that will be sold, or used to produce a product which will be sold, for example, raw materials, in the future in the ordinary course of business to parties outside of the government's reporting entity. The physical quantities of inventory at period ending may be done either by the *periodic system* where an actual physical count of goods is taken at the end of each period for which financial statements are prepared; or the *perpetual* system where purchases are debited directly to the inventory control account and concurrently entered into the detailed inventory records. As items of inventory are issued, the transaction is recorded in the accounts so that it carries a perpetual or continuing balance of the goods that should be on hand at each date.

SCENARIO 23-G PURCHASING AND ISSUING MATERIEL UNDER A PERPETUAL INVENTORY SYSTEM

The Ministry of Solicitors and Barristers purchases spare parts for its automobiles in the amount of $ 40,000. That invoice price includes freight charges of $ 400. Assuming that the firm, Solicitors and Barristers uses a perpetual system, its accountants record purchases and issues directly in the inventory as they occur. The stores section issues $ 15,000 of inventories.

JOURNAL ENTRIES

	FRA	AUTH	OBJECT	Amount $
Dr. Operating Expense	51321	F112	3452	$ 15,000
Cr. Inventory Held	15110	F312	3452	$ 15,000

JOURNAL ENTRIES USING A PERIODIC SYSTEM OF INVENTORY

Dr. Operating Expense	51321	B11A/B12A	1267	$40,000
Dr. Operating Expense	51321	B11A/B12A	210	400
Dr. GST Refundable Advance	13392	G111	8171	2,020
Cr. RG Payment Control Account	61DDD	R300	6299	$42,420

SCENARIO 23-I INVENTORY COUNT IS LOWER THAN RECORDS INDICATING POSSIBLE OBSOLENCE: WRITE-OFF REQUIRE

The Minister of Solicitors and Barristers performs a physical count of its inventory under a perpetual inventory system and determines that there are fewer inventory items present than there should be according to their records. In this instance the Ministry must write off that portion of its inventory that is no longer available to it. Note that shortages would scarcely be detected under a periodic inventory system as the business does not maintain a current record of the inventory balance. The physical count determined that the count was lower than the perpetual inventory records balance by $ 800 and $ 700 worth of inventory items were obsolete.

JOURNAL ENTRIES

	FRA	AUTH	OBJECT	Amount$
Dr. Losses	51733	F112	3452	$ 1,500
Cr. Inventories	15110	F312	3452	$ 1,500

SCENARIO 23-J INVENTORY COUNT IS HIGHER THAN RECORDS INDICATE – OVERAGE

When the Ministry of Barristers and Solicitors performs a physical count of its inventory, occasionally there is more inventory present than there should have been according to the perpetual inventory account balance. Such overages are usually the result of a record keeping error. Note that overages would scarcely be detected under a periodic inventory system as a current record of the inventory balance is not maintained. Any excess inventory would result in a reduction to the cost of goods sold, for inventories for resale, or operating expense, for consumable inventories, as part of the year-end adjustment to record the ending inventory balance. A physical count determined that the count was higher than the perpetual inventory account balance by $ 600.

JOURNAL ENTRIES

	FRA	AUTH	OBJECT	Amount$
Dr. Inventories	51733	F112	3452	$ 600
Cr. Operating Expense	51324	F315	346/3452	$ 600

PAYMENTS INCLUDING PREPAID AND DEFERRED CHARGES

Prepayments comprise contract payments before the receipt of the goods and/or services, advance payments under the terms of contribution agreements, prepaid expenses and deferred charges. Contract advances made prior to the receipt of goods and services shall be charged to expense in the period in which all the eligibility criteria have been met or the goods and service received as applicable. Advance payments under contribution agreements, in accordance with the Policy Transfer Payments may be made where it is essential to achieve program objectives and is specifically provided for in the agreement. As the disbursement is for expenses to be incurred in the future, the payment is recorded as a prepayment and is recognized as an expense once the eligible costs have been incurred. A prepaid expense or a deferred charge is an allocation to current and/or future periods of past costs where benefits are to be realized, and prepaid expenses provide future benefit(s) over a shorter period of time than do deferred charges. Where appropriate, amortization of any deferred charge or prepaid expense will be charged as an expense on a systematic and rational basis related to use. The balance of any prepaid expense or deferred charge shall be written off to expense in the period with no future benefits.

SCHEDULE 23-K PREPAID EXPENSES

Solicitors and Barristers Canada rents space in an office building in Kingston, Ontario for $ 15,000 per month. However, the owner of the building, Queen's University, demands that all of the tenants of the building prepay at least one year's rent. At the time Solicitors and Barristers pay the Queen's the desired amount of prepaid rent, there are four months left in the fiscal year. The rent consumed by Solicitors and Barristers in Kingston by fiscal year end is also recorded.

JOURNAL ENTRIES

	FRA	AUTH	OBJECT	Amount$
Dr. Prepaid Expense Rent	14110	B11A/B12A	511	$ 180,000
Cr. GST Refundable Advance	13392	G111	8171	$ 8,571
Cr. RG Payment Control Account	61DDD	R300	6299	$ 171,429
Dr. Rent Expense	51321	F119	3459/0511	$ 60,000
Cr. Prepaid Expense	14110	F313	3459/0511	$ 60,000

SCENARIO 23-L ADVANCE PAYMENT UNDER A CONTRIBUTION AGREEMENT

On April 15, 2XX1, Solicitors and Barristers Canada makes an advance payment to a group of Queen's University law students conducting research and development at Kingston Penitentiary in the amount of $ 30,000. This contribution is to cover eligible expenses for the next 6 months.

JOURNAL ENTRIES

	FRA	AUTH	OBJECT	Amount$
Dr. Prepaid R & D Expenses	14120	B15A/B11A	2041	$ 30,000
Cr. RG Payment Control Account	61DDD	R300	6299	$ 30,000
Dr. R & D Expenses	51119	F119	3459/2041	$ 30,000
Cr. Prepaid R & D Expenses	14120	B15A/B11A	2049	$ 30,000

SCENARIO 23-M PAYMENTS IN ADVANCE OF RECEIVING GOODS

Barristers and Solicitors enters into a contract with Grand and Toy for goods where the customer requires the Ministry to make a payment in advance of receiving these office supplies in accordance with Section 34 (b) of the Financial Administration Act. The amount of the payment is $ 10,500 (including GST). The goods are received at the Millhaven Institution.

JOURNAL ENTRIES

	FRA	AUTH	OBJECT	Amount$
Dr. Prepaid Expenses	14110	B11A/B12A	1XXX	$ 10,000
Dr. GST Refundable Advance	13392	G111	8171	$ 500
Cr. RG Payment Control	61DDD	R300	6299	$ 10,500
Dr. Operating Expense	51119	F119	3459	$ 10,000
Cr. Prepaid Expense	14110	F313	3459	$ 10,000

CAPITAL ASSETS

Capital assets are tangible assets that are purchased, constructed, developed or otherwise acquired and are held for use in the production or supply of goods, delivery of services or to produce program outputs; have a useful life beyond one fiscal year and are intended for use on a continuing; and are not intended for resale in the ordinary course of business. For the government of Canada, capital assets have the following characteristics: beneficial ownership and control clearly rest with the government; and the asset is used to achieve government objectives.

For government of Canada accounting purposes capital assets generally include all assets treated as capital assets under the Public Sector Accounting and Auditing Board (PSAAB) recommendations and GAAP in Canada. The Treasury Board Standard 3.1 on capital assets recommends that these assets have an initial historical cost of $ 10,000. Departments and agencies may choose a lower or higher threshold value.

SCENARIO 23-N PURCHASE OF A TANGIBLE CAPITAL ASSET

Solicitors and Barristers Canada purchased from Jim Key Motors and received a GM truck for $ 25,000 on January 31, 2XX6. Delivery costs are an additional $ 600 and the GST is $ 1,280. Payment does not take place until the following fiscal year, on April15, 2XX7. The truck has a useful life of 10 years with no estimated residual value.

JOURNAL ENTRIES

	FRA	AUTH	OBJECT	Amount$
Dr. Vehicle	16133	B14A	1261	$ 25,000
Dr. Vehicle	16133	B14A	210	$ 600
Dr. GST Refundable Advance	13392	G111	8171	$ 1,250
Cr. Accounts Payable	21111	R300	6299	$ 26,850
Dr. Amortization Expense	51433	F111	3451	$ 2,500
Cr. Accumulated Amortization	16233	F311	7061/7099	$ 2,500

SCENARIO 23-0 DISPOSAL VIA SALE OF TANGIBLE ASSETS

On May 1, 2000, Solicitors and Barristers purchased computer hardware for $ 32,000 with an estimated service life of five years an estimated residual value after five years of $ 2,000. The Ministry uses straight-line amortization and decides to sell the asset on November 1, 2XX7 for $ 8,000. Under a different scenario the computer hardware is sold for $ 3,000.

JOURNAL ENTRIES

	FRA	AUTH	OBJECT	Amount$
Dr. RG Deposit Control Account	61DDD	R300	5299	$ 8,000
Dr. Accumulated Amortization	16222	D321	4843	$ 27,000
Cr. Computer Hardware	16122	D321	4843	$ 32,000
Cr. Gain On Disposal Of Assets	42411	D321	4843	$ 3,000
Dr. RG Deposit Control Account	61DDD	R300	5299	$ 3,000
Dr. Accumulated Amortization	16222	D321	4843	$ 27,000
Dr. Loss On Disposal Of Assets	51511	D321	4843	$ 2,000
Cr. Computer Hardware	16122	D321	4843	$ 32,000

SCENARIO 23-P WRITES OFF A TANGIBLE CAPITAL ASSET

A Toyota Camry valued at $ 30,000 owned by Ministry is involved in a pile up on the highway. The automobile is a complete write off. The useful life of the automobile was estimated at 10 years and the accumulated amortization balance at the time of the accident was $ 25,000. The Director General of Finance decided that the vehicle had no future benefits to offer the Ministry and should be written off immediately. Melodge Monnedge, the insurance company in Toronto with which the Camry was insured, decided that based on the red book, they would pay the Ministry $ 8,000 for the automobile.

JOURNAL ENTRIES

	FRA	AUTH	OBJECT	Amount$
Dr. Accumulated Amortization	16233	F351	7099/3425	$ 25,000
Dr. Loss On Disposal Of Assets	51512	F351	7099/3425	$ 5,000
Cr. Automobiles	16123	F351	7099/3425	$ 30,000
Dr. RG Deposit Control Account	61DDD	R300	5299	$ 8,000
Cr. Gain On Disposal of Assets	42411	D321	4843	$ 8,000

LIABILITIES

Liabilities are what a business *owes*. They are financial obligations to out-side organizations and individuals as a result of transactions and events on or before the accounting date. They are the result of contracts, agreements or legislation in force at the accounting date that require the government to repay borrowings or to pay for goods and services acquired prior to the accounting date. *PSAAB Handbook* 1500.39

SCENARIO 23-Q   PURCHASE, RECEIPT, AND SETTLEMENT OF INVOICE RE: SUP-PLIES

Solicitors and Barristers' office in Alexandria, Ontario purchases and receives $ 1,000 in supplies from IKRA. The Ministry later on settles its invoice with the supplier.

JOURNAL ENTRIES

	FRA	AUTH	OBJECT	Amount$
Dr. Operating Expense	52513	B11A/B12A	11XX	$ 1,000
Dr. GST Refundable Advance	13392	G111	8171	$ 50
Cr. Accounts Payable	21111	R300	8299	$ 1,050
Dr. Accounts Payable	21111	R300	8299	$ 1,050
Cr. RG Payment Control Account	62DDD	R300	6299	$ 1,050

DEFERRED REVENUES

Deferred revenues or unearned revenues are monies received in advance from parties external to government for whom a government entity will pro-vide specified goods or services in the near future. Deferred revenues related to specified goods and services are usually recorded in specified purpose accounts. These unearned revenues may arise from the sale of goods and services from the following types of goods and services outside parties: rights and privileges; lease and use of public property; services of a non-regulatory nature; services of a regulatory nature; and sales of goods and services of both a regualtory and non regulatory nature; sales of goods and information products; and other fees and charges, etc...

INTERNAL TRANSACTION – NON TAX REVENUES

There is no conceptual difference between transaction with external parties and government departments but there are procedural differences. The major difference is that for sales of goods and services, the billing department, or creditor, does not have to wait for payment by the invoiced department, or debtor. Instead, the creditor is deemed to have been paid when a transaction is processed by the Interdepartmental Settlement functionality of the Standard Payment System (SPS/IS). Simply put, the Seller collects.

OPERATING EXPENSES

The majority of transactions that a department will record relate to operating expenses, and most of those for salaries and wages. In addition to the proper accrual accounting treatment, it is important to ensure that these operating expenses are charged to the correct appropriation or authority whether it is a program vote, statutory authority, or a specified purpose account, etc... It should be also noted that some expenses, for example, amortization, bad debts and provision for accumulated vacation pay are not charged to an appropriation. As well, it is important to ensure that the appropriate economic object is selected to reflect the nature of each transaction.

The Reader Should Remember: That the unique but important nature of policies, practices and procedures are outlined in official documents such as the CICA Handbook and FIS Manual. These publications should be followed wherever accounting is practiced in a Canadian government organization.

24

Financial Analysis

OBJECTIVE OF CHAPTER TWENTY-FOUR

The objective of this chapter is to demonstrate to the reader, course or workshop participant that financial analysis can be done to financial statements after they have been produced, showing how financial planning may be put into practice; and how working capital could be managed.

INTRODUCTION

Financial planning is the process of estimating the amount of financing required to continue a firm's operations and for deciding when and how the funds should be financed.

Without a reliable procedure of estimating financing needs, a government department or private company may run out of sufficient funds to pay for its obligations. In addition, it is completely intolerable for a responsibility centre manager to overspend the amount allotted for a government of Canada organization. Individual responsibility centre managers may negotiate the amount of spending done by a subordinate, peer and superior fellow managers, and often transferring the necessary funds, as long as two things do not occur: neither individual allotments nor the total of all allotments approved for spending in each department exceeds the amount allotted by the Treasury Board of Canada under Section 31 of the *Financial Administration Act,* or voted by Parliament in the *Appropriation Act.*

By definition, net working capital is the amount of money left after current liabilities have been subtracted from current assets:

Net working capital: Current assets – current liabilities

In other words, net working capital can also be thought as the portion of current assets that could be financed through long-term borrowing or owners' equity. Responsible management of a firm requires constant monitoring of its operations. One way to measure the liquidity, debt situation, and profitability of a firm is to engage in financial ratio analysis. This analysis can serve as a basis for financial planning and also provide a tool for monitoring performance. Ratio analysis helps to reveal the overall condition of a firm.

FINANCIAL PLANNING

The success and solvency of a firm cannot be guaranteed merely by successful individual projects or by increasing revenues. A liquidity crisis, that is, a shortage of cash to pay financial obligations, always threatens a firm. Since access to ready cash may often be controlled by a higher and outside power, small and medium sized firms are in a greater danger of possible cash shortages than larger companies, which usually have a wider range of financing alternatives. In the government of Canada, where the majority of the financing in most instances stems from Parliamentary votes via Treasury Board approval, funding is restricted to votes and allotments, with legal authority to switch from one vote or allotment to another vote or allotment needed ultimately by Parliament voting the change, this restricts the availability of cash even further. This does not mean that large organizations do not have as many problems. Three examples that may be cited are the Rolls Royce Company in the United Kingdom, the government of New Zealand and the Chrysler Corporation. Comparing future cash receipts with future cash payments on a monthly basis determines the financing surplus or deficit each month. The result is a cash flow budget through which future financing of the firm may be predicted. Table 24-1 shows a format that may be used to estimate required cash.

Table 24-1 A Format To Estimate Required Cash

Month	Payments	Monthly Cash Flow	Opening Cash	Ending Cash	Cash Reserve	Surplus or Deficit	NOTES
Bal. fwd.							
April							
May							
June							
July							
August							
September							
October							
November							
December							
January							
February							
March							

In the *cash turnover* method, there are no significant changes in operating expenditures from one period to another. Annual operating expenditures are defined here as total cash expenditures, or expenditures such as purchases of goods and raw materials and payment of salaries, interest, etc. *Cash turnover* is the number of times that firm's cash is collected, or turned over, in a year. Cash turnover is calculated as follows:

$$\text{Cash turnover} = \frac{360 \text{ days}}{\text{Days between purchasing raw materials, collecting sales or funding}}$$

Or simply:

$$\text{Cash turnover} = \frac{360 \text{ days}}{\text{Cash cycle}}$$

Note that the *cash cycle* refers to the number of days that pass between the purchase of raw materials, etc. and the collection of sales and funding proceeds.

SCENARIO 24-A USING THE CASH TURNOVER METHOD

PROBLEM: Suppose the cash cycle of a firm is 72 days. Assuming that the firm has annual expenditures of $ 600,000, determine required cash of the firm for the year.

SOLUTION: Using the equation presented above, calculate the cash turnover:

$$\text{Cash turnover} = \frac{360 \text{ days}}{72} = 5$$

To determine the minimum cash required, you divide the annual expenditures of $ 600,000 by the firm's cash turnover:

$$\text{Minimum cash required} = \frac{\$ 600,000}{5} = \$ 120,000$$

Therefore, the firm must keep minimum cash balance of $ 120,000 throughout the year to maintain its liquidity. Keeping a balance below $ 120,000 will create a shortage of cash and possibly lead a bankruptcy, in a private sector organization and an overspending of a department's allotment in the case of a public sector firm.

ANALYSIS OF SOURCES AND USES OF FUNDS

In financial *planning* and control, it is essential to understand how funds have been generated and where they have been used. The study is called the *analysis of sources and uses of funds*. Without a good understanding of the sources and uses of funds, and the changes that occur in these sources and uses, management cannot evaluate what the firm has done or in what direction it is going.

Sources of Funds

- A decrease in assets, an increase in liabilities or an increase in capital.

Uses of Funds

- An increase in assets, a decrease in liabilities or a decrease in capital.

Table 24-2 shows a change in a balance sheet account may be a source or use.

Table 24-2 Sources And Uses Of Funds

Transaction	Source	Use
If assets (increase)		X
If assets (decrease)	X	
If liabilities (increase)	X	
If liabilities (decrease)		X
If capital (increase)	X	
If capital (decrease)		X

SCENARIO 24-B ANALYZING SOURCES AND USES OF FUNDS

ANALYSIS: Table 24-3 indicates that the sources of funds for the government of Canada as at March 31, 2XX3 were cash, loans receivable, accounts receivable, depreciation, long term debt and investment in Canada. The generated funds were spent to acquire more inventories and fixed assets and to repay accounts payable, pensions payable and accruals of salaries and wages. Note that the depreciation account has a negative sign, which means that the value of assets owned by the racetrack has decreased. Since depreciation is a decrease in asset value and non-cash (non-appropriation) expenditure offset in investment in Canada, it is viewed as a source of funds.

Table 24-5 is very informative, as it clearly reveals the main sources and uses of funds. For instance, in the case of the government of Canada, reduction of its accumulated deficit generates 64.04% of the total resources. Second to the main source of funds is foreign exchange, which contributes 28.45% of all generated funds. Note that the reduction of its accumulated deficit, foreign exchange, pensions and other liabilities together accounted for 96.09% of the total funds and therefore, are the major sources of funds on which the financing of the government of Canada relies. If any of the government's top level decision-makers think that any of those major sources are not very reliable for future operations, the government may take corrective action and seek new sources of financing in advance.

Table 24-3 Balance Sheet Of The Government Of Canada (Values In Millions of Dollars)*

	2XX1/2XX2	2XX2/2XX3	Sources	Uses
Assets:				
Cash & Acc. Rec.	59,833	62,626	Nil	2,793
Foreign Exchange	52,046	48,950	3,096	Nil
Loans, Inv. & Advncs	21,556	23,748	Nil	2,192
Inventories	6,438	6,113	325	Nil
Tangible Cap. Assets	45,724	47,034	Nil	1,310
Prepaid Expenses	1,200	1,093	107	Nil
Total Assets	186,797	189,564		
Liab & Inv in Canada				
Acc Pay & Acc Liab	81,453	79,384	Nil	2,069
Pensn & Other Liab	180,618	181,004	386	Nil
Unmatured Debt	442,271	439,752	Nil	2,519
Accumulated Deficit	-517,545	-510,576	6,969	Nil
Tot Liab & Inv in Can	186,797	189,564		

Table 24-4 Percentages Of Sources And Uses Of Funds

	Millions Of Dollars	**Percentage**
Sources:		
Foreign Exchange	3,096	28.45%
Inventories	325	2.98%
Prepaid Expenses	107	0.98%
Pension And Other Liab.	386	3.55%
Accumulated Deficit	6,969	64.04%
Total Sources	**10,883**	**100.00%**
Uses:	-	-
Cash And Acc. Rec.	2,793	25.66%
Loans, Inv. & Advances	2,192	20.14%
Total Capital Assets	1,310	12.04%
Acc. Pay. & Acc. Liab.	2,069	19.01%
Unmatured Debt	2,519	23.15%
Total Uses	**10,883**	**100.00%**

Table 24-5 Ranking Of Sources And Uses Of Funds For The Government Of Canada

Rank	Sources	Percentage	Rank	Uses	Percentage
1	Reduced Deficit	64.04	1	Cash & Acc. Rec.	25.66
2	Foreign Exchange	28.45	2	Unmatured Debt	23.15
3	Pens. & Other Liab.	3.60	3	Loans, Inv. & Adv.	20.14
4	Reduced Inventory	2.98	4	Acc. Pay. Accrd. Liab	19.01
5	Prepaid Expenses	0.97	5	Tangble. Cap. Assets	12.04

Table 24.5 also indicates that the generated funds are spent mainly on cash and accounts receivable (25.66%), unmatured debt (23.15%), loans, investments and advances (20.14%) and accounts payable and accrued liabilities (19.01%). If this pattern of spending is not a desired one, upper level decision-makers in the government of Canada may correct the situation before the shortage of funds for other purposes becomes an issue. Because it can reveal such vital information, the analysis of the sources and uses of funds is an integral part of any sound financial planning and control system.

USES AND TYPES OF RATIOS

Although there are a substantial number of individual ratios, they usually fall into five major categories: liquidity, activity, debt, profitability and market.

An asset's degree of *liquidity* depends on how quickly that asset can be converted into cash without incurring a substantial loss. The *current* or *liquidity* ratio is the relationship between current assets and current liabilities:

$$\text{Current ratio:} \quad \frac{\text{Current assets}}{\text{Current liabilities}}$$

In eliminating the less liquid inventory category and concentrating on assets more easily converted into cash, the *acid-test* [or *quick*] *ratio* determines whether a firm could meet its creditor obligations sales were to drop catastrophically:

$$\text{Acid-test ratio:} \quad \frac{\text{Current assets} - \text{inventories}}{\text{Current liabilities}}$$

Activity ratios determine the speed with which a firm can generate cash if the need arises. The *average collection period* of time a firm must wait before receivables can be translated to cash. Note that cash sales are excluded from total sales:

$$\text{Average collection period:} \quad \frac{\text{Accounts receivable}}{[\text{Annual credit sales}/360 \text{ days}]}$$

The counterpart to accounts receivable is accounts payable. To find out the *average payment period* for accounts payable, you simply do the same thing you did for accounts receivable --- that is, divide annual purchase, without cash purchases into accounts payable:

$$\text{Average payment period:} \quad \frac{\text{Accounts payable}}{[\text{Annual credit purchases}/360 \text{ days}]}$$

Inventory turnover is important to a firm because inventories are the most liquid form of current assets besides cash. The *inventory turnover ratio* is calculated as follows:

$$\text{Inventory turnover:} \quad \frac{\text{Cost of goods sold}}{\text{Average inventory}}$$

Another way of analyzing the ability of a firm to convert inventories into cash employs the *inventory conversion ratio,* which tells us how many days it takes to convert inventories into cash:

$$\text{Inventory conversion to cash period [days]:} \quad \frac{360 \text{ days}}{\text{Cost of goods sold}/360}$$

A firm may borrow money for short-term purposes, mainly to finance working capital, or for long-term reasons, mainly to buy plant and equipment. The debt **ratio** indicates the percentage of total assets that is financed by debt:

$$\text{Debt ratio:} \quad \frac{\text{Total liabilities}}{\text{Total assets}}$$

A more familiar debt ratio involves the relationship between long-term debt and owners' equity. This is called the *debt-equity ratio*:

$$\text{Debt-equity [D/E] ratio:} \quad \frac{\text{Long-term debt + value of leases}}{\text{Owners' equity}}$$

The **long-term debt/total asset ratio [LD/TA]** relates debt to the total assets of a firm, and can provide useful information regarding the degree to which the firm finances its assets with long-term debt:

$$\text{LD/TA ratio:} \quad \frac{\text{Long-term debt}}{\text{Total assets}}$$

It is also important to find out how well a firm can pay its interest. For this purpose, you can use the **times interest-earned ratio:**

$$\text{Times interest-earned ratio:} \quad \frac{\text{EBIT}}{\text{Annual interest expense}}$$

The *gross profit margin* shows how efficiently a firm's management uses material and labour in the production process:

$$\text{Gross profit margin:} \quad \frac{\text{Sales} - \text{Cost of goods sold}}{\text{Sales}}$$

The *operating profit margin* shows how successful a firm's management has been in generating income from the operation of the business:

$$\text{Operating profit margin:} \quad \frac{\text{EBIT}}{\text{Sales}}$$

The *net profit margin* is generated from all phases of a business. In other words, the ratio compares net income with sales:

$$\text{Net profit margin:} \quad \frac{\text{Net profit after taxes}}{\text{Sales}}$$

The *return on investment ratio* [ROI] was invented by Pierre Dupont of the Dupont Corporation for the firm's own use. However, this ratio is used by major companies as a convenient way to measure the combined effects of profit margins and total asset turnover:

$$\text{ROI:} \quad \frac{\text{Net income}}{\text{Sales}} \quad \text{X} \quad \frac{\text{Sales}}{\text{Total assets}} \quad : \quad \frac{\text{Net income}}{\text{Total assets}}$$

FINANCING WORKING CAPITAL

By definition, *net working capital* is the amount of money left after current liabilities have been subtracted from current assets:

Net working capital: Current assets – current liabilities

Therefore, net working capital can also be thought of as the portion of current assets that should be financed through long term borrowing or owners' equity. Current assets usually fluctuate from month to month. During months when sales are relatively high, firms usually carry a lot of inventory, accounts receivable and cash. The level of inventory declines when there is less selling activity. The timing of high and low inventory basically depends on the nature of the product. The decision whether to finance assets with short term or long term loans is a choice between monitoring risk and maximizing profits. The volume of accounts receivable is usually determined by the credit standards of the company. The main purpose of inventory management is to determine and maintain the level of inventory which will ensure that the customer orders are satisfied in sufficient amounts and on time. Accounts payable can be viewed as free loans from suppliers. In the absence of accounts payable, the firm has to borrow money or to use its own equity to pay suppliers' bills.

The Reader Should Remember: financial planning is referred to as the process of estimating future financial needs and identifying how previous funds were financed and for what purpose they were spent. The three basis methods to estimate future needs are the percentage of sales method, the cash budget method, and the cash turnover method. The analysis of sources and uses of funds reveals how a firm has been financed and how its resources have been spent. In a very conservative approach to financing working capital, fixed assets, the minimum level of current assets, and a portion of seasonal requirements are all financed by long term debt and equity. The benefits of lowering credit standards are the profit from additional sales; the costs are additional bad debts and greater financing costs for additional accounts receivable. The benefits of raising credit standards are reduction of bad debts, lower financial costs for accounts receivable; the cost is reduction of profits from sales. The purpose of inventory management is to determine and maintain the level of inventory that will ensure satisfaction of customer orders in sufficient quantity and on time. A cash discount is an acceptable offer of how its benefit [or the cost of not using the cash discount] exceeds the cost of borrowing. You can analyze a firm's financial statements by engaging in ratio analysis and/or by standardizing the financial statements. The intelligent use of ratios requires that we apply them in association with other information. Financial statements can be interpreted by calculating financial ratios, which are divided into four major categories: liquidity, debt, activity and profitability.

25

Selected Unusual Topics In Accounting, Delegation of Authority and Financial Management In The Government of Canada and Profit-Making Organizations

OBJECTIVE OF CHAPTER TWENTY-FIVE

The objective of this chapter is to introduce the reader, the course and workshop participant to a selected group of unusual topics which have a direct and indirect impact on accounting, delegation of authority and financial management in profit and non-profit making Canadian businesses.

INTRODUCTION

This chapter comprises some selected unusual topics in the government of Canada and public sector accounting and finance. These topics include: Activity-Based Costing; Human Resource Accounting; Materiel Management; Major Financial Systems such as SAP, Oracle-Based Systems; Provincial Sales Tax

(PST); Goods and Services Tax (GST); Harmonized Sales Tax (HST); Corporate Governance; and other unusual requirements such as deadlines set by the Auditor General of Canada and the Treasury Board of Canada for compliance to GAAP.

UNUSUAL BUT DIRECTLY RELATED ISSUES

Activity-Based Costing (ABC)

Activity-based costing (ABC) is a method of allocating costs to products and services. It is generally used as a tool for planning and control. This is also a necessary tool for value chain analysis.

Traditionally, cost accountants had arbitrarily added a broad percentage on to direct costs to allow for indirect costs. However, as the percentages of overhead costs had risen, this technique became increasingly inaccurate because the indirect costs were not caused equally by all the products.

Consequently, when multiple products share common costs, there is a danger of one product subsidizing another. This kind of cross subsidization is not allowed between products and services produced in any one government department or agency.

The concepts of ABC were developed in the manufacturing sector in the United States during the 1970s and the 1980s. During the time the Consortium for Advanced Manufacturing, now known simply as CAM-1, provided a formative role for studying and formalizing the principles that have become more formally known as Activity Based Costing. Robin Cooper and Robert Kaplan, proponent of the Balanced Score Card, brought notice to these concepts in a number of articles published in the *Harvard Business Review* beginning in 1988. Cooper and Kaplan described ABC as an approach to solve the problems of traditional cost management systems. These traditional costing systems are often unable to determine accurately the costs of production and of the costs of related services.

The ABC method of costing views a business as a series of activities, each of which absorbs resources. Extremely useful in a public environment, where resources are voted basically for absorption by program activities, business or service lines, the method suggests that the products in the business that cause these activities, and these activities in turn consume costs. The use of ABC should help to define the level of activity, by trying to identify the forces behind the costs that is, 'cost drivers'.

With ABC, in stark contrast to absorption costing where the product is costed by the addition of fixed overheads, a term coined by Alfred P. Sloan of General Motors and Pierre Dupont of Dupont Chemicals, to the direct or variable costs of the product or service, for example, materials and labour, to give full cost of the product or service. The main problem with absorption costing surfaces when overheads are often apportioned on some arbitrary or inappropriate basis. An example of this would be using labour hours as the basis of overhead apportionment when the business is highly capital intensive. Then the use of machine hours as the basis might be more appropriate.

ABC seeks to categorize costs as either short term or long term variable costs. Short term costs are essentially those that traditional costing systems would call variable costs---they are volume related and change directly with the volume of production. Long-term costs also vary with measures of activity, but not immediately.

It should be remembered when attempting to categorize costs as variable, semi-variable or semi-fixed, and fixed, that all fixed costs become variable in the long run. Proponents of ABC argue that this system reflects more accurately the true cost of a particular product, enabling management to make better decisions relating to pricing and product profitability. The critics argue that ABC can be extremely time consuming and sometimes difficult to identify the cost drivers.

Activity based management (ABM) is an approach to management in which process managers are given the responsibility and authority to continuously improve the planning and control of operations by focusing on key operational activities. ABM strategically incorporates activity analysis, ABC, activity-based budgeting, life cycle and target costing, process value analysis and value chain analysis.

In the government of Canada, the Treasury Board has issued a policy document called *"Guide to the Costing of Outputs"*. The process described in the document outlines a 'road map' for the costing outputs with the following steps: 1. Define the purpose of the cost accounting exercise. 2. Define the outputs to be costed. 3. Determine the cost base. 4. Determine the required cost allocation process. 5. Select allocation bases. 6. Perform calculations.

Human Resource Accounting

Rensis Likert and the R. G. Barry Corporation in the United States are known in human resource circles for the theory introduced on accounting for human resources. Likert presented the concept of the cost of human assets such as soccer, hockey, football and cricket players. He referred to them as they might be shown on the firm's balance sheet, especially if the contracting or employing organization depended more on human beings than on capital assets to generate its revenues. Likert's idea was extended from the fact that the large amounts of money paid out in remuneration could be somehow capitalized, in the same manner as how the historical cost of fixed assets such as land, buildings, other equipment, furniture and fixtures was entered as tangible assets at the time of their purchase and later on depreciated or amortized.

Materiel Management

In the majority of public sector organizations, or especially where large dollar amounts of materiel are used to generate revenues for the firm, a distinctive link usually exists between accounting, finance and the substantive organization within the company that controls the amounts of materiel purchased, used and maintained at optimum levels. Materiel or supplies, like fixed assets and human resources are accrued assets which have been converted from cash. These items are just in another state of liquidity. Thus the amounts invested should be monitored, controlled and husbanded with an almost equal amount of prudence and probity as cash.

Sometimes, more often than not, in large government organizations such as Fisheries and Oceans and National Defence, a significant amount of cash invested in fixed assets, the latter of which, unlike inventories, may have been capitalized.

Major Financial Systems Used in Government Departments and Agencies

Canadian government departments and agencies have always maintained, purchased and/or developed accounting and financial systems for organizational use. One senior financial systems analyst at National Defense in the United States government is reputed to have said:

> "...There is no private sector developed system which may easily be converted for use by public sector organizations. Conversely, no public

sector organization has yet developed a piece of software of the calibre of say, Microsoft Power Point...."

Public sector developed systems include software packages such as CDFS, CFMRS, FINCON and PC & MAINFRAME FOCUS. Private sector developed systems used by or now currently in use by Canadian government organizations include AMS, MSA, Oracle and SAP.

Whatever the financial system used by an individual department or agency, there should always exist an economic, effective, speedy interface between such a system and PWGSC's CFMRS. Diagrammatically, this interface should appear as follows:

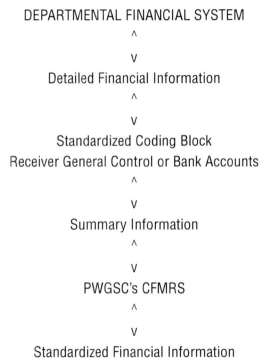

DEPARTMENTAL FINANCIAL SYSTEM

^

v

Detailed Financial Information

^

v

Standardized Coding Block
Receiver General Control or Bank Accounts

^

v

Summary Information

^

v

PWGSC's CFMRS

^

v

Standardized Financial Information

Sales Taxes

Sales taxes, the incidence of which may be legally thrust upon individual non-government organizations (NGOs) and/or governmental organizations alike, may be highlighted under Provincial and Territorial Sales Tax; Goods and Services Tax; and The Harmonized Sales Tax.

Provincial and Territorial Sales Tax (PST)

In most Canadian provinces and territories, a provincial or territorial sales tax at a rate determined by each province or territory, is levied on the Canadian consumer. The province of Alberta is a notable exception. The rate of the PST is controlled by a continuum of the annual settlement of sales generated long ago by the fur and other consumable items which are usually divided by type.

Goods and Services Tax (GST)

This tax was first introduced in Europe as a *Value Added Tax*. It was later on levied by an earlier Canadian federal government. The tax follows the concept of Value Added Tax imposed on residents of some EEC countries such as the United Kingdom and Italy.

The government of Canada uses the taxed consumer as a tax collector. In the general ledger of relevant organizations these types of accounts are maintained: GST In, GST Out and Bank or Control accounts. A practical example of how this taxation function obtains is as follows:

SCENARIO 25-A GST OR HST FUNCTION

An imaginary government Department XYZ sells taxable items to the tune of $ 100,000. On these items, at the GST rate of 5%, the organization collects on behalf of the Canada Revenue Agency, GST totaling $5,000. During the same fiscal period under consideration, Department XYZ purchases taxable items that total $ 40,000 on which the 5% GST or $ 2,000 has been paid out. The resulting general ledger accounts in the books of Department show the following:

RELEVANT T-ACCOUNTS

RG Deposit Control Account	Sales	GST In
105,000　　｜	｜ 100,000	5,000　｜ 5,000
RG Payment Control Account	Purchases	GST Out
｜　42,000	40,000 ｜	2,000　｜ 2,000
｜　5,000		

At the end of the fiscal period, on settlement date, the amount of GST to Canada Revenue Agency by Department XYZ is $5,000 - $2,000 = $3,000.

Harmonized Sales Tax (HST)

In certain Canadian provinces, such as New Brunswick, the PST and GST are together to form the Harmonized Sales Tax (HST). The accounting practices for the HST are similar to those used in the recording and reporting of the GST. In addition, certain laws, policies, practices, and regulations determine on which items HST will be levied.

Corporate Governance

Some years ago, on both sides of the Atlantic, a number of companies pulled some rather unsavoury accounting and financial stunts involving collusion and fraud at the highest levels of the firms' administration. These miscreants included organizations such as Enron, Northern Telecom and World Com. These chunks of financial flummery and skullduggery occurred in Canada, the United States and the United Kingdom. One disastrous situation resulted in the demise of the United States branch of the international Big Five accounting firm, Arthur Anderson. It would seem now that the majority of the firm's clients have been farmed out other big five firms. Senior executives at Enron were indicted.

In a bold attempt to discourage such a recurrence in the United States, Congress passed the Sorbannes-Oxley Act. This biting bit of legislation has had a definite impact on a firm's accounting systems with a more direct result being felt and seen on its internal control policies, practices, and systems. The Canadian Parliament recently passed *The Federal Accountability Act.*

OTHER UNUSUAL FINANCIAL SYSTEMS AND TOPICS

Other unusual systems and topics have surfaced on the accountancy, financial management and systems landscape. These include the ABC spin offs---Activity Based Management, Activity Based Budgeting, Target Costing and the Balanced Score Card. In 1992, Robert S. Kaplan and David Norton introduced the latter, a concept used to measure a company's activities in terms of its vision and strategies, meanwhile giving the firm's managers a comprehensive view of the business' performance. The Treasury Board of Canada continues to significantly influence financial management in the government of Canada while introducing policies such as the *Financial Management Accountability Framework*. This framework is intended to translate the vision of modern public service management, as established in the document *Results for Canadians* into support of management expectations; and the new controls on managing transfer payments, specifically grants and contributions. In addition, from the earliest days of computerization, the writing of programs for accounting activities has been given a high priority, with almost every aspect of accounting now being covered by software programs and packages of varying sorts. It is impractical to describe them all. However, those programs include those appearing in the following groups: small business packages, for example, MYOB; the larger business software and packages, for example, AMS, Oracle and SAP; upgraded business software; and software packages developed by government organizations, for example, CFMRS and CDFS.

Compliance to the Objectives of the Financial Information Strategy (FIS) Handbook, CICA Handbook, PSAAB Handbook and the Treasury Board Accounting Standards

In the late 80s, with the challenges brought about by an old detailed maintenance and reporting system used by departments and agencies and simultaneously owned by PWGSC called the Central Accounting System (CAS) and its sub-ledgers named the Department Reporting System (DRS) and the Central Agency Information System (CAIS), a then Deputy Auditor General for Canada was concerned that the proposed replacement of the approaches used by this system could not be dealt with feasibly by most departments and agencies. Specifically, the CAS, CAIS and DRS were either two old, did not reconcile easily with each other individual systems operated by departments and agencies or were producing untimely, duplicated detailed information which was also being maintained and reported on by individual department and agency systems. In addition, departments and agencies embarked on the goal of increasing the level of user fees and cost recovery collected.

This goal was intended to augment the dwindling appropriations being voted them each fiscal year by Parliament. Unfortunately, because of the strict legalities and regulations which needed to be adhered to as laid down by the *British North America Acts* as early as 1867, and supported and augmented annually by the *Annual Appropriation Act* and controlled and monitored day to day by the *Financial Administration Act*, these laws and regulations restricted the re-spending of user fees and cost recovery collected by decision makers. In addition, government departments and agencies not only used an ancient and outmoded method of accounting referred to as "modified accrual accounting"; but the classification and coding system in use was functionally inadequate; and the accounting and financial system had not been designed to account for the GAAP processes such as the capitalization of assets.

During this period of accounting, financial management and systems hiatus, some key decisions were made and acted upon which included: the Auditor General for Canada recommending in his 1984 Report to Parliament that departments and agencies implement full accrual accounting, including the capitalization of assets; the formation of the Public Sector Accounting and Auditing Board; the publication of the Report on the Modernization of Comptrollership; and a senior financial manager at PWGSC, Dr. Phil Charko, devising and creating the fledging ideas of tenets of the Financial Information Strategy (FIS). FIS's objectives were set out in the main to: implement full accrual accounting; adapt a classification and coding structure which would accommodate the first objective; and change drastically government accounting and financial systems which would also accommodate the first objective.

Further, the Canadian Institute of Chartered Accountants, in connection with the Public Sector Accounting and Auditing Board, created, designed and published the *Public Sector Accounting and Auditing Committee's Handbook (PSAAC) Handbook.* To crown it all, the Treasury Board of Canada not only revamped its old and outdated *Guide to Financial Management,* but replaced it with the *Comptrollership Manual*, and finally with the *Financial Information Strategy Manual*, the latter two documents including sections on government Accounting Standards. Eventually, the Board directed that all departments and agencies be set an official deadline by which they should be compliant to FIS objectives, policies and practices, including those appearing in the *CICA Handbook*, the *PSAAC Handbook* and the Treasury Board's Accounting Standards.

Accounting, Auditing and Financial Management Stardard Setting in Canada

The *CICA Handbook* contains and maintains standards for financial accounting and auditing, as laid down by the Accounting Standards Board and the Auditing Standards Board (AusB) of the Canadian Institute of Chartered Accountants. The *CICA Handbook* is the major source of accounting and auditing standards in Canada. Its authority is enhanced because it enjoys a special legal status. For example, Regulation 44 of the *Business Corporations Act* states:

"...The financial statements referred to in paragraph 155(1)(a) of the Act shall, except from time to time, of the Canadian Institute of Chartered Accountants set out in the CICA Handbook..."

The Accounting Standards Board is authorized by the Board of Governors of the Canadian Institute of Chartered Accountants to publish reports on its own responsibility. The CICA'S Board of Governors has also authorized the AusB to publish reports on its own responsibility. There is also a third CICA standard setting body, the *Public Sector Accounting and Auditing Committee (PSAAC)*.

The following points should also be noted about the process of setting standards for the *CICA Handbook*: The Accounting Standards Board publishes accounting standards "...on its own authority..." New standards require the approval of at least two-thirds of the members of the Board. Two-thirds or more of the Board's members must be members of the CICA. While not mentioned explicitly in the terms of reference, it should be noted that exposure drafts enable interested parties to react to a proposed standard before it is finalized. Membership on the Accounting Standards Board is voluntary, that is, these are not full time, salaried positions. The *CICA Handbook* says little about how a particular topic is placed on the agenda of the Accounting Standards Board. It should be apparent that the issuance of a new standard will require considerable time. Also, the *Emerging Issues Committee (EIC)* was established in 1988 by the Accounting Standards Board to provide a forum for the timely review of emerging accounting issues that are likely to receive divergent factory treatment in practice in the absence of some guidance. In the main, one could say that, similar to the exercise of delegated authority, the various steps taken to create a new standard seem to suggest that the process is quite "political".

According to the *Securities Act* of Ontario, the role of the *Ontario Securities Commission* may be summarized as regulating all securities trading in Ontario, including both the securities themselves and the exchanges on which they are traded. Prior to 1978 the *Securities Act* provided a detailed description for the contents of the financial statements of companies whose securities were publicly traded. However, in 1978, the Act recognized the *CICA Handbook's* Accounting and Auditing Recommendations as the appropriate authority for standards of financial reporting. Currently, an OSC National Policy Statement No. 27 (1992) states that GAAP

"...has the meaning ascribed to this term by the CICA Handbook..."

The Reader Should Remember: the significance of standard setting resulted in adherence to generally accepted accounting principles (GAAP).

Quizzes, Problems, Case Studies & Projects

QUIZZES

[All allocation time for quizzes: introduction: 10%; group work: 50%; presentations and review: 40%]

Quiz number one – True and false

Approximate total time required: 35 minutes

Are these statements true or false?

* During a hearing a before the Public Accounts Committee of the government of Canada, the Chairman, a member of Her Majesty's Loyal Opposition, asked a senior official at to the Department of Public Works and Government Services Canada the following question: "...*Did you have the authority to do what you did...?*"

* In public sector organizations, anything may be decided, approved or authorized by a majority of executive committee members.

* The *BNA Acts 1867* to *1995* are a series of Acts of Parliament of the Dominion of Canada portraying a political relationship between Canada and the United Kingdom.

* In 1982, Canada repatriated its constitution and entrenched it within the Charter of Rights and Freedoms.

* The names of the *British North America Acts 1867* changed from time to time as each provided larger amounts of users equal legal counsel from the government of the United Kingdom.

* British North America was another name for the Dominion of Canada.

Quiz number two – True and false

Approximate total time required: 20 minutes

Are these statements true or false?

* The Treasury Board of Canada comprises six civil servants.

* The Treasury Board Secretariat is the administrative arm of the Treasury Board and comprises civil servants with varying aspects of expertise.

* The Office of the Comptroller General is part of the Treasury Board while the latter is in session.

* Supply periods coincide exactly with the times when Parliamentarians take their holidays.

* The Receiver General for Canada is also the Minister of Public Works and Government Services Canada.

Quiz number three – Treasury Board and the Expenditure Management System

Approximate total time required: 60 minutes

* Name the six politicians comprising the Treasury Board.

* Which members of the Treasury Board are appointed by virtue of their politically appointed office?

* Which two agencies in the government of Canada share the ultimate power to delegate authority?

* What functions related to the Consolidated Revenue Fund do the Minister of Finance and the Receiver General for Canada perform respectively?

* Name the key functions of the Expenditure Management System.

* Define the following terms: ARLU, EID, EMS, EMIS, and MRRS.

Quiz number four – Financial systems in the government of Canada

Approximate total time required: 25 minutes

* Name the systems in the government of Canada's official compendium of systems approved for department or agency used by the Treasury Board of Canada.

* Is it true or false that in the days prior to the development of CDFS by PWGSC, the FINCON system, which PWGSC had also created, was not used by its creating organization?

* Discuss, citing practical examples, how authority is delegated from the Minister to her or his Deputy Head and then to positions in a particular department or agency.

Quiz number five – Cash journal

Approximate total time required: 20 minutes

Combine the two sentences which would most likely go together.

* The bookkeeper posts "cash in hand" as a debit on the first page of the journal.

* With debits on the left side and credits on the right side.

* As a credit on the other side of the page.

* As ledger postings are made, the diagonal lines are not always drawn.

Quiz number six – Concept of debit and credit

Approximate total time required: 25 minutes

* How important is Father Luca Pacioli to the development of the concept of double entries?

* Discuss the importance of cash being always entered inwards on the left and outwards on the right.

Quiz number seven – Delegation of authority, capital, etc...

Approximate total time required: 30 minutes

* Is this statement true or false? "...Authority is delegated from the Minister to the deputy minister and then to persons employed by a particular department or agency..."
* What is a balance sheet?
* What is capital?
* What is working capital and what does it do?
* What is the difference between: a. working capital; b. capital owned; and c. capital employed?
* Distinguish between current assets and fixed assets.
* What are liquid assets?
* What is profit?
* What effect will profit have on: a. the assets of a business; and b. the capital of a business?
* What effect do drawings have on the balance sheet?
* What is a liability?

Quiz number eight – Bookkeeping, trial balance, types of accounts

Approximate total time required: 50 minutes

* Explain the seven stages of double entry bookkeeping.
* What are the characteristics of a ledger account?
* Name the two sides of an account.
* What do you understand by a real account, a personal account and a nominal account?
* What are the rules for making entries in real accounts when we buy an asset or sell a worn out asset?
* What are the rules for making entries in personal accounts?
* What are the rules for entering losses and profits in nominal accounts?

*   What is meant by 'closing an account'?

*   What is a trial balance?

*   Describe five types of errors, which do not show up in a trial balance.

Quiz number nine – Inventories

Approximate total time required: 20 minutes

*   Given that opening inventory is $ 500; purchases $ 6,000; sales $ 9,350 and closing inventory is $ 480, set out a cost of goods sold account to find the gross profit. Express the gross profit as a percentage of: (a) selling price; and (b) cost price.

*   If the beginning inventory is $ 250; sales $ 8,000; ending inventory $ 300 and gross profit 25% of the selling price, find the value of the purchases.

*   When the beginning inventory is $ 500; purchases $ 9,200; ending inventory $ 780 and gross profit is 100% of the cost price, find the value of the sales.

Quiz number ten – Cost of goods, freight, purchases, etc.

Approximate total time required: 20 minutes

*   What items usually appear in a cost of goods account?

*   How does one deal with freight in on a cost of goods account?

*   How does one deal with purchases and returns allowances?

*   How are sales discounts treated?

*   How do overhead expenses appear in the final accounts?

*   How does one treat salaries and wages expense?

Quiz number eleven – Types of inventory

Approximate total time required: 60 minutes

* What do you understand by the terms FIFO and LIFO?

* What do you understand by the term WIP?

* Give reasons why it may be impractical to count inventory [take stock] on the last business day of the financial year.

* Outline the principles for arriving at the inventory valuation: (a) When the inventory is counted *before* the end of the year; and (b) When the inventory is counted *after* the end of the year.

* Outline the importance of the purchases figure in arriving at the valuation of the inventory on hand.

* Why is it most important to record carefully details of inventory movements towards the end of the financial year? What impact could it probably have on PAYE in the government of Canada's books?

* How does one find the cost price of the cost of goods sold?

* What do you understand by the rate of inventory turnover?

Quiz number twelve – Using journal and ledger folios

Approximate total time required: 60 minutes. [N. B. Participants attempting this quiz may find it difficult to complete without the appropriately ruled paper].

* Alistair Cooke is in business as a grocer. Some of his transactions are listed below. Please tabulate a statement showing the subsidiary ledger into which they would be entered and name the accounts which receive either immediately or ultimately, the relevant debit and credit entries.

Paid rent by cheque.

Sold good to Francois Gibbons on credit.

Bought goods from Club Trix Wholesale on credit.

Sold goods to Albert Renfrew who paid in cash.

Ronald Mirabel's cheque which Cooke had deposited into the business' current account at the Caisse Populaire was returned, marked: "Not Sufficient Funds" with an accompanying bank charge.

Purchased from Gatineau Motors a supply of gasoline and motor oil, for cash.

Cashed a cheque drawn on the Caisse Populaire to replenish the funds in the petty cash drawer.

*   You need to have your reply follow as far as possible this format:

Transaction	Subsidiary Ledger	Account Debited	Account Credited
Paid rent	Cash journal	Rent expense	Bank

*   Write up the purchases journal, sales journal and goods returned journal from the following transactions of Mendel & Co. Furniture Manufacturers. GST is to be taken at 5% on all items, after purchases discount, if any, has been deducted.

2XX1

April 04 Sold on credit to Pierre Dunscombe: 8 fireside chairs at $ 85 each; 6 bedroom chairs at $ 45 each; 2 wardrobes at $ 55 each. [All items are subject to 40% sales discount.]

April 06 Purchased on credit from Canadian Lumber some planks of timber valued at $ 340.

April 08 Purchased on credit from Friendly Furniture Ltd. 5 gyp rock sheets for $ 215.

April 09 Sold on credit to Walter Taitt: 2 bedroom suites style B at $ 199 each; 2 bedroom suites Type Q at $ 311 each. [All items subject to 40% sales discount.]

April 12 Sent a credit note to Pierre Dunscombe for an overcharge of $ 3 each on the wardrobes sold to him on April 4th.

April 14 Purchased on credit from Drew Specialty Supplies: 40 yards Rexene at $ 4 per yard; plastic bindings for $ 31. [All items on the invoice were subject to 45% purchase discount.]

Sold on credit to Better Furnishings Ltd: 5 occasional tables at $ 45 each; 12 television chairs at $ 22 each; 6 television tables at $ 30 each; 4 tea trolleys at $ 36 each; and 4 telephone tables at $ 31 each. [Sales discount of 40% on all items.]

Quiz number thirteen – Cash discount, cash journal, etc.

Approximate total time required: 45 minutes

* How is cash discount recorded in the ledger?

* How does the cash journal perform the function of a subsidiary journal?

* What are contra entries in the cash journal?

* How do we deal with discounts allowed?

* Distinguish between sales or purchases and cash discounts.

* What is the function of the petty cash, or imprest cash or Departmental Bank Account?

* A typewriter bought for $ 90 has been entered in the cash account. What is the corresponding debit or entry for this?

* What effects do cash discounts have on the profit of a business?

* Name the necessary accounts for cash discount in a general ledger.

* Would you consider a fixed asset ledger a subsidiary ledger and why?

Quiz number fourteen – Preparing a bank reconciliation

Approximate total time required: 20 minutes

* The following information was available when Jimmy Hendricks began to reconcile his bank balance on May 31, 2XX8: balance per depositor's books: $ 1,638; balance per bank statement: $ 2,420; deposit in transit: $ 150; cheques outstanding: Number 650, $ 300 and Number 654, $ 240; collection of a $ 400 note plus interest of $ 8; collection fee for note: $ 10; bank service charge: $ 6.

* Prepare the bank reconciliation statement

Quiz number fifteen – Bank reconciliation

Approximate total time required: 30 minutes

* What is a bank reconciliation statement?

* Why is a bank reconciliation statement necessary?

* What are the main points of difference that could arise between a bank statement and a firm's account with a bank?

* How can we have cheques that have not been credited by the bank?

* Explain why cheques may not be presented for payment.

* What items sometimes omitted from the cash journal does one usually enter in the cash journal before preparing the bank reconciliation statement?

* Explain how you would deal with a bank overdraft on: (a) the bank company's account; and (b) the bank statement, when preparing a bank reconciliation statement.

Quiz number sixteen – General journal and entries, etc.

Approximate total time required: 20 minutes

* What is a general journal?

* What is a journal entry?

* How does one set about journalizing a transaction?

* Give some examples of transactions that require journalizing.

* What do you understand by a composite journal entry?

* What is a narration and what does it do?

* What is complex, not complicated but unique about journal entries made at DND?

Quiz number seventeen – Accruals and prepaids

Approximate total time required: 20 minutes

* A credit balance brought down on a salaries and wages account represents a liability; explain how this can arise.

* A debit balance brought down in an insurance account represents an asset. How and why? What other accounts may have the possibility of showing a debit balance either as an expense or an asset?
* A credit balance brought down on the rent account may also equal to what?

Quiz number eighteen – Provision

Approximate total time required: 30 minutes

* What do you understand by the accounting term "provision"?
* Give two reasons why the proprietor of a business should create a provision for doubtful accounts?
* What are the entries in the general ledger on creating a provision for doubtful accounts?
* Explain the entries necessary to increase a provision for doubtful accounts.
* Explain the entries necessary to decrease a provision for doubtful accounts.
* How does a provision for doubtful accounts appear in a balance sheet?
* What do you understand by the term 'net accounts receivable'?
* What is the difference between a bad debt and a provision for doubtful accounts?

Quiz number nineteen – Amortization, capital cost allowance and depreciation

Approximate total time required: 30 minutes

* Describe the main entries generally used for depreciation or amortization accounts.
* Explain the terms depreciation and amortization.
* Explain the method(s) used to calculate amortization and depreciation.
* What do you understand by a "sale of asset" account? Where is this

account usually employed?

* When does a gain or loss on disposal of an asset arise?

* What is the difference between an amortization and a depreciation account?

Quiz number twenty – Suspense accounts, trial balance

Approximate total time required: 30 minutes

* Does a balanced trial balance prove that the books are absolutely correct?

* What types of errors will a trial balance not disclose?

* How does one go about normally correcting errors not disclosed by a balanced trial balance?

* What is a suspense account? When is it sometimes used? In your opinion, should it ever be used?

* When would a suspense account, if used, be opened with: (a) a debit balance; and (a) credit balance?

* What is the effect on the trial balance of posting the total of the "discounts allowed" account to the credit of the discounts received account?

* What is the effect on the trial balance of posting the total of the "discounts allowed" account to the debit of the discounts received account?

Quiz number twenty-one – Departmental accounts, overhead

Approximate total time required: 20 minutes

* What do you understand by departmental accounts? How do they function in the government in Canada?

* Name two common methods of apportioning overhead expenses.

* What are the important points to remember when overhead expenses are paid in advance?

* Why are departmental accounts essential when responsibility centre managers are sometimes assessed at each financial period ending during the individual department's performance evaluation?

Quiz number twenty-two – General ledger, sub-ledgers
Approximate total time required: 45 minutes

* Name the main subdivisions of the general ledger.

* Give another name for the sales sub ledger.

* Give another name for the accounts payable sub ledger.

* What accounts would you expect to find in the purchases sub ledger?

* What accounts would you expect to find in the sales sub ledger?

* Outline the main advantages to be derived from the use of computerized accounts receivable and accounts payable sub ledgers.

* Explain how it is possible to have *two* valid accounts for the same individual.

* What is a "running balance" account?

* Explain what you understand by the term "set off".

* What accounts would you expect to find in the general ledger?

* What action is usually taken on the sales and purchases sub ledgers at the end of each month?

* What can be the effect on the sales sub ledger control of a personal account for an account receivable which has a credit balance at month-end?

* Name the debit control accounts which the Receiver General for Canada maintains.

* Name the credit control accounts which the Receiver General for Canada maintains.

* In what main types of financial systems are those RG control accounts kept?

Quiz number twenty-three – Capital, net profit, net worth, etc.
Approximate total time required: 30 minutes

* What is the relationship between net profit and capital?

* How would you treat drawings when determining net profit?

* What effect does new capital introduced into a firm have on profits?

* How are accounts such as 'Invalid Vote Suspense' or 'Accounts Receivable OGD Suspense' or 'Accounts Payable OGD Suspense' dealt within the government of Canada's accounts?

Quiz number twenty-four – Cash flow

Approximate total time required: 30 minutes

* What is the main purpose of a cash flow statement?

* Why is net profit sometimes treated as an inflow of cash?

* What is the effect on cash flow of an increase in accounts payable and in inventory?

* How is the annual charge for depreciation dealt with in a cash flow statement?

* How dangerous is it in the government of Canada for a responsibility manager's career should him or her to overspend the 'cash' made available for spending by Parliament or the Treasury Board?

Quiz number twenty-five – Cash budget

Approximate total time required: 20 minutes

* What is the main purpose of a cash budget?

* On what basis are the figures for a cash budget usually computed?

* What is meant by the 'usual cycle of receipts and payments'?

* How are the following dealt with in a cash budget: depreciation and acquisition of assets?

* In what ways do accounting ratios help to understand business results?

Quiz number twenty-six – Fundamental accounting theory

Approximate total time required: 20 minutes

* What are the three fundamental elements of accounting theory?

* What do you understand by: measurement, classification and coding?

* Distinguish between recording and reporting.

* Explain the meanings of: accruals, prepayments, prudence and probity.
* What does PSAAB mean?

Quiz number twenty-seven – Inventory

Approximate total time required: 15 minutes

* The lower the value of ending inventory, the ____ the gross profit.
* Determining ending inventory by lower of cost or market is done at the _____ at the end of the period.
* When it appears that inventory is obsolete or broken, it should be reported at its_____.

Quiz number twenty-eight – Income Statement

Approximate total time required: 20 minutes

* Prepare an income statement based on the following information: Fees income, $ 38,000; Supplies expense: $ 16,000; Salaries expense: $ 12,000; and Miscellaneous expense: $ 7,000.

Quiz number twenty-nine – Balance Sheet

Approximate total time required: 20 minutes

* From the following information, prepare a balance sheet as at December 31, 2XX7: Cash: $ 6,000; Accounts receivable: $ 3,000; Supplies: $ 1,000; Equipment: $ 14,000; Accounts payable: $ 2,500; Notes payable: $ 1,500; Mortgage payable: $ 12,000; and Capital as at December 31, 2XX7: $ 8,000.

Quiz number thirty – Closing Entries

Approximate total time required: 20 minutes

After the adjusting entries have been posted, some of the accounts which appear in the general ledger of Samuel L. Bell, Chartered Accountant have the following balances as at December 31, 2XX8. Prepare the required closing entries:

Cash $ 4,000

Accounts Receivable   9,000

Computer 5,400

Accumulated Depreciation: Computer   3,900

Accounts Payable   900

Samuel L. Bell, Capital   20,000

Samuel L. Bell, Drawings   15,000

Revenue And Expense Summary   Nil

Fees Earned   43,000

Other Income 20,000

Salary Expense   21,000

Rent Expense 1,500

Supplies Expense 2,500

Depreciation Expense—Computer   1,300

Office Expense   700

PROBLEMS

[Allocating time to solve problems: Introduction: 5%; Group work: 45%;
Presentation & wrap up: 50%; Case study and project time is allocated
to each case and each project separately]

Problem number A – Set up ledger accounts

Approximate total time required: 30 minutes

Set up the necessary ledger accounts and record the following information
into these accounts. Allow two or three lines for the expense accounts and four
lines or more for all other accounts. When the ledger accounts have been established, journalize the closing entries and post them in the general ledger.

Account Title	Account Number	Debit Entries	Credit Entries
B. Kinsey, Capital	301	Apr 12 J3 $700	
Revenue and Expense	399	Nil	Nil
Sales	401	Nil	Apr 01 J1 $3,100
			Apr 25 J4 $1,900
Rent Expense	501	Apr 01 J1 $ 4,000	
Advertising Expense	502	Apr 15 J3 $2,225	
Utilities Expense	503	Apr 20 J4 $150	
Miscellaneous Exp	504	Apr29 J5 $80	

Problem number B – Owners' equity

Approximate total time required: 30 minutes

* Explain why the owners' equity on a balance sheet is not the same for the
  owners' equity in the capital account after closing entries have been made.

* What are the two major kinds of owners' equity accounts used during
  an accounting period? When are they used? Why do they not have the
  same nomenclature or quite the same meaning in public sector financial
  statements?

* Why is it necessary to transfer the balances from the temporary accounts to the capital account at the end of an accounting period?

* What does a debit balance to the revenue and expense summary represent? What entry is required to transfer this debit balance to the capital
  account?

* What is the purpose of striking a post closing trial balance? How is it prepared?

* Briefly explain each of the six steps in the accounting cycle.

Problem number C – Fundamental elements of accounting
Approximate total time required: 40 minutes

* What are the fundamental elements of accounting?

* Why does a business need complete accounting records?

* What are a chartered accountant, a certified management accountant and a certified general accountant? What are some of their professional duties?

* What is an asset? Give five examples from the organization which employs you.

* What is an expense? Give five examples from the organization which employs you.

* What is a liability? Give five examples each from a private sector and a public sector firm.

* What is revenue? Give five examples from a private sector and from a public sector firm.

* What is owners' equity? What other accounting items describe it? What is it called in a government of Canada firm?

* Francois Filbert, an electrician from North Battleford, Saskatchewan owns a company which has assets totaling $ 70,000 and no liabilities. What is the company's owners' equity? Explain how you arrived at your answer, relative to the accounting equation.

* Why do we need a balance sheet? What are its main components?

* What accounting item is common to both a balance sheet and an income statement?

Problem number L-B 1 – Language of business, part 1

Approximate total time required: 30 minutes

Accounting has been defined as the "language of business." Below are some of the basic terms which comprise that language. Do you understand the meaning of each? Can you define each term and use it in an original sentence, where possible involving the firm, responsibility, profit or cost centre in which they are employed?

Source document	Liability	Accounting equation	CA
CGA	Creditor	Limited liability	CMA
Accounts payable	Dividend	Value	Proxy
Data processing	Asset	Auditor	Bank loan
Cash	Liquidity	Accounts receivable	CPA

Problem number L-B 2 – Language of business, part 2

Approximate time required: 30 minutes

The following items are important. Do you know the meaning of each? Can you define each item and use it in a sentence, preferably referring to your responsibility, cost or profit centre?

Transaction	Net income	Accounting period
Revenue	Net loss	Fiscal period
Expense	Financial statement	Fiscal year

Problem number D – McGrunder's Trucking

Approximate total time required: 55 minutes

On December 31, 2XX1, Sean McGrunder owned a small trucking business, McGrunder's Trucking with the following assets and liabilities:

Cash in the company's petty cash, $ 230; a positive balance in a current account at the Caisse Populaire, Gatineau, Quebec, $ 6,770; a second-hand Toyota truck with a red book value of $ 10,850; office furniture with a possible net book value of $ 6,585; accounts receivable from the government of Canada of $ 2,900 which Sean knows is 100% collectible; accounts payable to Rhona Hardware Supply on Merivale Road, Nepean of $ 3,560; and Grand and Toy Office Supply at the Bayshore

Shopping Centre, Nepean, Ontario of $ 260. A bank loan is payable to a local branch of the TD Canada Trust in Nepean, Ontario of $ 30,000. Office buildings and a garage with an historical value of $ 150,000 are partly financed with a mortgage on the same buildings with a mortgage at a local branch of the Bank of Nova Scotia on Richmond Road, Ottawa in the amount of $100,000. Any imbalance in the firm's accounting equation [*assets = liabilities + owners' equity*] has been entered on its books either as a debit to a Goodwill account or as a credit to Sean McGrunder, Capital account.

* Prepare a balance sheet as at December 31, 2XX1 for McGrunder's Trucking in such a way as to show within the balance sheet: total fixed assets; total current assets; total current liabilities; Sean McGrunder, Capital; and total liabilities and owners' equity.

Problem number E – Francine Jardine, Certified General Accountant

Approximate total time required: 40 minutes

Mademoiselle Francine Jardine, Certified General Accountant, started a tax preparation and financial consulting firm on January 1, 2XX2 in the town of Anjou, Quebec. With a large volume of business expected from the government of Quebec's Regie Automobile, Mlle. Jardine is confident her firm will remain a going concern. The single proprietorship owns premises valued at $ 55,000; a new Toyota Camry automobile was purchased one year ago for $ 32,750; office and tax preparation inventory has a market value of $ 8,500; office furniture fixtures bought on credit at the Brick Warehouse at $ 2,850; petty cash currency and chits totaling $ 100; and a positive current account balance of $ 5,000 at the local Banque Nationale du Canada on Maisonneuve Est in downtown Montreal. Mlle. Jardine keeps but does not audit her own firm's books. She has entered in the firm's general ledger any imbalance in its accounting equation [*assets = liabilities + owners' equity*] either as a debit to a goodwill account or a credit to Francine Jardine, Capital account. During the first two weeks of the month of January, Mlle. Jardine undertook the following transactions on behalf of her firm:

January 05 Purchased inventory supplies from Grand and Toy for $ 500 on credit.

January 08 Sold services of $ 2,300 to the Government of Quebec for cash.

January 09 Paid utilities of hydro, gas, water and telephone for $ 450 by cheque.

January 12 Hired her niece Natasha Gibbon for two weeks and owes the latter $ 1,050.

January 13 Bought and paid for by cheque a new piece of computer software for $ 3,500.

January 14 Sold services of $ 2,500 to the government of Quebec on credit.

*   Make the relevant changes to the accounting equation and prepare a balance sheet as at January 15, 2XX2.

Problem number F – The Passport Office

Approximate total time required: 30 minutes

Below is an imaginary balance sheet as at January 31, 2XX1 for The Passport Office.

The Passport Office

Balance Sheet as at January 31, 2XX1

Assets			Liabilities and Owners' Equity	
Cash	3,500		Accounts Pay:	Nil
Accounts Rec:	Nil		Queen's Printer	1,200
Govt. of Canada	25		Grand And Toy	40
Supplies invntry.	150		Total Liabilities	1,240
Printing eqpt.	6,100		Owners' Equity:	Nil
Phtcpyng eqpt.	1,200		Retained Erngs.	9,735
Total Assets	**10,975**		Total Liab & O E	**10,975**

*   Who is the owner of this business?

*   How much cash does the business have?

*   Who owes money to the business? How much is owed?

* What computer equipment does the business own?

* What is the total value of all the assets owed by the business?

* To whom does the business owe money?

* How much money is owed to each creditor?

* What equity in the assets does the business own?

* When was the balance sheet prepared?

* Solve the accounting equation for the Passport Office.

Problem number G – Queen's Printer

Approximate total time required: 55 minutes

* The following data reflects the financial position of the Queen's Printer on June 30, 2XX1. Set up an accounting equation to classify this financial data. Once you have determined the kind and amount of each type of asset and liability, use the equation to find out the owners' equity.

* When the accounting equation is complete and it is in balance, prepare the balance sheet as at June 30, 2XX1. The Queen's Printer has $ 2,800 in cash; the Passport Office owes it $ 275; it owns printing supplies recorded at $ 250; owns a computer costing $ 1,950; owes Grand and Toy $ 345; owns printing equipment costing $ 600; owes Toshiba $ 470 and the School of Public Service owes it $ 110.

Problem number H – Role of an accountant

Approximate total time required: 45 minutes

In a format similar to the following, list five businesses in your community for each type of business indicated by the columnar headings:

Profit-making organizations		Non-profit making organizations	
Produces goods	Sells goods	Sells services	Provides services e. g.
ALCAN	Grand & Toy	Bell Telephone	The Ottawa Hospital

* What is the role of an accountant in a business?

* Each source document can be the basis of many different reports in a

business. Suggest one report that could be obtained from the information below.

Example: Cheque stubs --- total amount of money paid out.

Source documents to be analyzed from which reports may be produced: sales slips; purchase invoices; payroll clock cards; cheques; deposit slips.

Problem number I -- Newspaper ads

Approximate total time required: 30 minutes

*   For a current newspaper, such as the *Vancouver Sun*, *Edmonton Journal*, *Winnipeg Free Press*, *Toronto Star*, *Globe and Mail*, *Ottawa Citizen*, *La Presse* cut out and bring to class some classified advertisements with jobs for accountants, accounting clerks, bookkeeper, and/or finance officers. From those advertisements, obtain and list the following information: title of position; salary range; education required; knowledge required; experience asked for (if any); and type of work to be done.

Problem number J – Community Garage, Part I

Approximate total time required: 25 minutes

On April 1, 2XX1 Rosalind Moreau signed a contract to purchase the Community Garage from Michel Jacques. For the purchase price of $ 600,000, Rosalind acquired the following assets: Building $ 350,000; Goodwill $ 50,000; Equipment $ 50,000; and Land $ 150,000. The firm owes Robert Jackson $10,000; Moreau took $250,000 from her personal bank account at the TD Canada Trust, to make a down payment of $ 160,000 and deposited the balance of $ 90,000 in the account of the Community Garage at the local branch of the Bank of Nova Scotia to operate the business.

*   Set up an accounting equation [*assets* = *liabilities* + *owners' equity*] to classify this data, just as you did in previous problems. Then prepare a balance sheet for the business as at April 30, 2XX1.

Problem number K – Community Garage, part 2

Approximate total time required: 40 minutes

During May, 2XX7, the following changes occurred in the assets, liabilities and owners' equity of the Community Garage owned by Rosalind Moreau [See previous problem number J]:

Moreau invested an additional $ 20,000 in the firm.

A payment of $ 10,000 was made to Robert Jackson.

Moreau borrowed $ 1,000 from her personal bank and added it the equity in the company.

An addition of $ 20,000 was made to the firm's building. The Community Garage paid $ 10,000 to Rhona Construction, but still owes the builder $ 10,000.

* Compute the company's bank balance at the local branch of the Bank of Nova Scotia on May 31, 2XX1. Using the information provided in this problem and that provided in earlier relevant problems in this text, prepare a balance sheet as at May 31, 2XX1 to reflect the changes which took place during May, 2XX1.

Problem number L – Sean Higgins' Civic Garage

Approximate total time required: 30 minutes

The April 30, 2XX1 balance sheet for the Civic Garage, owned and operated by Sean Higgins, revealed the following information: Cash $ 900; Equipment: $ 5,000; Accounts Payable: $ 3,000; and Sean Higgins, Capital: $ 2,900. During May, 2XX1 the garage was involved in the following transactions:

Sean Higgins bought equipment on credit for $ 200; Sean Higgins invested an additional $ 1,000 in the business; Sean Higgins paid $ 300 to a creditor on account; Sean Higgins withdrew $ 60 from the bank for his personal use; Sean Higgins bought equipment for $ 100; and Sean Higgins returned equipment purchased for $ 50 and was paid in cash.

* On a form like that below, show what happens to the accounting equation a result of May's transactions, recording each transaction, *mentally checking* the equality of the accounting equation. The first transaction appears as an example:

	Assets		Liabilities And	Owners' Equity
	Cash	Equipment	Acc. Pay.	S. Higgins, Captl.
Opening Balance	900	5,000	3,000	2,900
Transaction	Nil	+ 200	+200	Nil
Closing Balance	900	5200	3,200	2,900
Total Assets		6,100	Total Liab. & O.E.	6,100

Problem number M – Transactions and fundamental elements

Approximate total time required: 45 minutes

* Give five examples of transactions that a business might have.

* What happens to the fundamental elements when an owner invests cash in a business?

* What happens to the fundamental elements when cash is paid on an account receivable?

* What happens to the fundamental elements when an owner withdraws cash from a business?

* Why do expenses decrease the owners' equity?

* What happens to the fundamental elements when cash sales are made?

* Compare the balance sheet and the income statement as to their form and fashion. The income statement covers a period of time, whereas the balance sheet is for a particular date. What is the purpose of having two statements? What item appears on both the income statement and the balance sheet at the end of the accounting period?

Problem number N – Debit and credit entries

Approximate time required: 40 minutes

* Determine the debit and credit for each of the following transactions. On a form similar to the following, show what happens to the fundamental elements in each transaction and which accounts are involved: *Example: Bought tools for $ 50 each.*

Debit entry		Credit entry	
What happened	Account debited	What happened	Account credited
Asset increased	Inventory: Tools	Asset decreased	Cash

Returned tools purchased for $ 10 in cash.

Paid $ 75 to a creditor (an account payable) on account.

Received $ 120 from a customer on an account receivable.

Bought tools for $ 50 on credit.

Paid $ 40 to settle an account payable.

Bought tools for $ 80 in cash.

Bought supplies inventory for $ 20 on credit.

Received $ 60 from a debtor (an account receivable) on account.

Bought supplies inventory for $ 10 in cash.

Paid wages of $ 250 in cash to store clerk, William Gantry.

Problem number L-B 3 – Language of business, part 3

Approximate time required: 40 minutes

* The following terms are important. Do you understand the meaning of each? Can you define each term and use it in an original sentence, preferably with a practical example from your responsibility centre.

Account	Crediting the account	Account balance	Transfer payments
T-account	Credit balance	Investment in Canada	Appropriation
General ledger	Double-entry principle	Business transaction	Allotment
Debiting the account	Capital account	Authority	Vote

Problem number O – Effect on accounting equation: A = L + OE

Approximate total time required: 35 minutes

*   On a form similar to the following show what happens to the fundamental element in each transaction and which accounts are involved.
Use the signs A+, A-, L+, L-, OE+, OE- to indicate increases or decreases in the assets, liabilities, and owners' equity accounts.

Example: Melvin Peters started a financial consulting business in
Cornerbrook, Newfoundland with $ 4,000 in cash. Mr. Peters had with-
drawn the funds from his personal bank account at a local branch of
the Bank of Nova Scotia on Water Street in Cornerbrook in the province
of Newfoundland.

Debit entry		Credit entry	
What happened?	Account debited?	What happened?	Account credited?
A+	Cash	OE+	M. Peters, Capital

Bought equipment for $ 600 on credit from Staples Business Depot on
Duckworth Street in downtown St. John's.

Sold services for $ 2,000 on credit to Timothy Lindsay.

Paid $ 750 in cash for rental of office space on Reed Street South in
Cornerbrook.

Received $ 3,000 in cash from the sale of services to the Canadian
Coast Guard base at Vlesingen.

Received $ 1,000 from Timothy Lindsay on account.

Melvin Peters invested an additional $ 1,000 in the business.

Received $ 1,100 in cash from the sale of services to the Newfoundland
Constabulary.

Paid $ 450 to the Newfoundland Telephone Company for telephone
services.

Sold consulting services on credit to the Faculty of Commerce at Memorial University.

Problem number P – Scratch and Dent Store, St. John

Approximate time required: 30 minutes

* The Scratch and Dent Store in St. John, New Brunswick can sell a Frigidaire freezer for $ 850 on a credit sale of net 30 days. The manufacturer will pay the shipping charges to the store. If, however, the store purchases a carload of 500 freezers, the cost is reduced by $ 200 each. The lower price results from the quantity price offered by the manufacturer and the reduced transportation costs of a carload shipment. Sales have increased gradually, and the store is expecting a 20% increase in sales in the coming year. Would you recommend that the store purchase a carload of freezers? Explain the reason(s) for your answer.

Problem number Q – Poonabit Shoe Store

Approximate total time required: 30 minutes

The accountant set up one revenue account for the Poobabit Shoe Store in Prince Albert, Saskatchewan. The account is credited for all the sales and debited for all the sales returns, discounts and allowances. In this way, only the balance of the Sales Account is shown on the income statement. This becomes a problem at Xmas, 2XX2 when a particular bad batch of shoes was almost nearly all returned, severely depleting the amount reported in the Sales account for December, 2XX2. The manager of the store wants to know the actual dollar amount of sales and sales returns for the month of December.

* Why would the store manager want to know the total of sales returns?

* How could the accountant rearrange the records to provide this information?

* In your judgment were the sales returns too high? How could the store manager determine if they were excessive? What steps could he take to reduce the amount of returned goods?

Problem number R – Sources and uses of funds: ABC Co.

Approximate total time required: 40 minutes

* Using the following data, compute the sources and uses of funds and interpret your results:

Balance Sheet of the ABC Co. (in 000's of dollars)

Assets:	Year 1	Year 2
Cash	100	200
Loans Receivable	50	110
Accounts Receivable	40	42
Inventories	80	110
Fixed Assets	90	95
Depreciation	(30)	(34)
Total Assets	**330**	**523**
Liabilities & Ownrs' Equty:		
Accounts Payable	45	46
Notes Payable	45	45
Long Term Debt	20	210
Owners' Equity	220	222
Total Liab. & Ownrs. Eqty.	**330**	**523**

Problem number S – Cash required

Approximate time required: 30 minutes

* Determine the minimum cash required if a firm's total annual expenditures are $ 2,000,000 and the cash cycle is 60 days.

Problem number T – Surplus cash or deficit: Almonte Engineering Works

Approximate time required: 30 minutes

* Determine the cash surplus or deficit for a particular month for the Almonte Engineering Works, given the following information: receipts, $ 100,000; payments, $ 60,000; beginning cash, $ 10,000; and cash reserve, $ 5,000.

Problem number AA – Halifax Distributing

Approximate total time required: 40 minutes

The Halifax Distributing Company acquired a new truck on April 1, 2XX6 for $ 65,000. The accountant estimated that the truck has a useful life of 5 years. The trade-in value at the end of this period is approximated to be $ 5,000. The straight line method of calculating depreciation is being used in the firm's accounting records.

* What is the depreciation expense for 2XX6?

* What is the monthly depreciation expense?

* What will be the balance in the account Accumulated Depreciation --- Delivery Truck at the end of 2XX7?

* At the end of 2XX6?

* What will be the unexpired cost, at net book value of the delivery truck in balance sheet as at December 31, 2XX6? At the end of 2XX7?

Problem number LB-4 – Language of business, part 4

Appropriate total time required: 40 minutes

* The terms below are important. Do you understand the meaning of each? Please define each term and use it in original sentence with reference to the operations of your employing responsibility centre.

Drawing account	Prepaid expense	Obsolescence
Taxpayer investment	Bad debts	Allocation
Cost of goods sold	Contra asset account	Plant and equipment
Perpetual inventory	Grants & contribution allotment	Operating budget allotment
Periodic inventory	Material management	Minor capital allotment
Controlled capital allotment	Operating expenditure vote	Program vote
Statutory vote	Special allotment	Disposal value
Frozen allotment	COGS available for sale	Aging accounts receivable
Responsibility centre	Profit centre	Cost centre

Problem number LB-5 – Language of business, part 5

Approximate total time required: 60 minutes

* The terms below are important. Do you understand the meaning of each? Please define each term and use it in an original sentence with reference to the operations of your employing responsibility centre.

Drawing account	Prepaid expense	Obsolescence
Investment in Canada	Bad debts	Allocation
Cost of goods sold	Contra asset account	Plant and equipment
Perpetual inventory	Materiel management	Accumulated depreciation
Periodic inventory	Replacement cost	Fixed asset ledger
Allowance for doubtful accounts	Book value	Historical cost
Statutory vote	Special allotment	Frozen allotment
Amortization	Capital cost allowance	Physical deterioration
Early cut off period	Late cut off period	Depreciation

Problem number BB – Rustic Furniture Store

Approximate total time required: 25 minutes

Christina Peczecktrosky owns the Rustic Furniture Store in Saskatoon, Saskatchewan. Christina estimates that if she follows an extremely liberal policy of granting credit to just about everyone who asks for it her total sales will be $ 5,000,000 for the year and she may lose about 8% of her credit sales as noncollectible. She expects that the store's annual dollar gross profit at about 25% of sales will be these dollar amounts before and after the deduction for bad debts:

Credit sales	$ 5,000,000
Estimated gross profit (approximately 25% of credit sales)	1,250,000
Less: approximate bad debt losses (8% of credit sales)	(400,000)
Estimated gross profit after bad debt losses	850,000

She estimates that she would have the following credit sales resulting bad debt losses if she followed credit which were less liberal:

Very strict	Sales: $ 2,000,000	Losses: ¼%
Moderately strict	Sales: $ 3,000,000	Losses: 1%
Strict	Sales: $ 4,000,000	Losses: ½%
Lenient	Sales: $ 4,500,000	Losses: 5%

*   At an expected gross profit of 25% on sales, which credit policy will yield the most profit after losses?

Problem number CC – Crown Assets Disposal

Approximate total time required: 35 minutes

Crown Assets Disposal, located in Sault Ste Marie, Ontario, owns one delivery truck. Last fiscal year, 2XX5/2XX6, the vehicle was driven 400,000 kilometres, making 250,000 stops. Operating costs were as follows:

Depreciation	40,000
Fuel and other expenses	20,000
Insurance	4,400
Licenses	900
Storage	4,800
Drivers' Salaries and Wages	115,000
Drivers' Contribution to Employee Benefit Plan	18,000

The responsibility centre manager, having delegated most of the spending authority for the annual budget under Section 34 of the *Financial Administration Act*, is considering selling the truck and using two alternate providers: renting an alternative from the National (Tilden) Car Rental Company, Rent-A-Truck branch in town or using Acme Delivery Services. National's annual charge is $12,000 plus $1.60 per kilometre for the first 50,000 kilometres, $1.40 per kilometre for the next 50,000 kilometres, and $1.20 per kilometre after that. All the truck's expenses are also paid. None are listed as outstanding. The accounts payable has a zero balance at the end of the last accounting period. Acme Delivery Services will pick up and deliver in any area, however, at $3.00 per stop.

* What action would you recommend that the responsibility centre manager take regarding the truck?

Problem number DD – FIS accounting standards: Weckworth's Clothiers

Approximate total time required: 120 minutes

The *Financial Information Strategy* Manual issued by the Treasury Board Secretariat states that "...consistency does not mean that different organizations must apply the same accounting standard methods. This may be thought to improve comparability between departments. However, requiring such uniformity may result in dissimilar circumstances between departments being reported as being similar. For example, amortization policies should be developed on the basis of what best reflects consumption of the asset in its particular operating environment. There maybe different operating environments in each department..."

The manual also states that "...to measure the impact of government transactions on the economy, expenditures are classified according to the type of resources (goods and services) acquired, revenue carried of the transfer payments made. Identification of detailed economic objects, combined with information from other sectors of the economy, makes possible economic analysis, on a national basis, of the effects of government spending. The economic objects are the basis for the object classification and are required for government-wide statistical purposes. They may be used by departments as department line objects but departments may need more detail for their own purpose..." Clearly then, regardless of the variety of program activities combined to form a department, at the economic object level, government expenditures become comparable by type.

In the private sector, surveys are frequently made to compile averages for the expenditures made by various types of businesses. These surveys are made by the Microsoft Corporation, the National Cash Register Company, and others. One such survey, made of a large number of men's clothing stores, showed the average expenditures for stores with a comparative sales volume as follows: (Percentage is based on total sales):

Cost of goods sold	64.0%
Expenses:	Nil
Advertising	3.0%
Bad debts	0.2%
Depreciation and insurance	1.5%
Miscellaneous	1.8%
Rent and occupancy	3.5%
Supplies used	1.0%
Taxes and fees	1.0%
Wages, salaries, etc.	19.5%
Net Income	4.5%

Anne Weckworth operates a clothing store in Timmins, Ontario similar in size and sales volume to that which was reported earlier in this problem. Her income statement for 2XX6 is shown below. [Note that certain expense items have been grouped so that a comparison can be made with those appearing in the survey mentioned above]. The percentages shown are based on the revenues resulting from sales. At the end of each quarter, Ms. Weckworth prepares an income statement and compares her business's actual expenditures with those in the budget. On September 30, 2XX7, Weckworth's Clothier's expenses for the first nine months of the year for the following selected items are listed as follows:

Advertising	22,080
Wages and salaries	261,370
Supplies used	13,160

* If Ms. Weckworth is to keep within her planned budget for the year, what is the most she can spend on these items during the remaining three months of the year?

Weckworth's Clothiers

Income Statement

For The Year Ended December 31, 2XX6

Revenue From Sales	1,256,000	100.0%
Cost Of Goods Sold	818,910	65.2%
Gross Profitability	437,090	34.8%
Expenses:	-	-
Advertising	52,750	4.2%
Bad Debt Loss	16,330	1.3%
Depreciation & Insurance	32,660	2.6%
Miscellaneous Expense	17,850	1.4%
Rent and Occupancy	77,890	6.2%
Supplies Used	8,500	0.7%
Taxes And Fees	10,050	0.8%
Wages And Salaries	194,680	15.5%
Total Expenses	410,710	32.7%
Net Income	26,380	2.1%

Problem number L-B 6 – Language of business, part 6

Approximate total time required: 30 minutes

* The following items are important. Do you understand the meaning of each? Can you define each item and use it an original sentence regarding the financial operations of your employer?

Cash	Deposit in transit	Cheque
Dishonoured cheque	Certified cheque	Debit memorandum
Negotiable instrument	Service charge	Blank endorsement
Bank reconciliation statement	Restrictive endorsement	Disbursement
Encoding	Petty cash voucher	Crossing
Imprest cash journal	Coding	Departmental bank account
Classification	Inter-departmental voucher	Bank statement
Section 32 *FAA* Authority	Section 33 *FAA* Authority	Section 34 *FAA* Authority

Problem number EE – Regal Parking Lot

Approximate total time required: 35 minutes

The manager of the Regal Parking Lot located at the corner of Reed and Abercombie Streets in Lacombe, Alberta charges $ 1.50 for the first hour of parking and 75 cents for each additional half hour, but to a maximum of $ 5.00. The lot is in the limit of the shopping district. Two large department stores in the area have arranged for their customers to get special rates which are highly competitive with those levied by the Regal Parking Lot. Up to six o'clock, most customers park for almost an hour; after six, each averages three (3) hours.

There is an attendant on duty from 8am to 12pm, seven days a week. When a customer drives into the lot, he or she pays and locks her or his own car. The attendant then gives her or him a ticket on which the arrival time at the lot is written. When the customer returns to retrieve her or his automobile, he or she surrenders the ticket, on which the attendant writes the time of departure and the commensurate parking fee. The attendant subsequently turns in the tickets with the copies of the cash receipts tendered earlier to the paying customers.

*   The owner has been suspicious that his attendants have not been turning in all the cash they may have collected. Can you or your syndicate group suggest a system to prevent this eventuality?

*   A number of customers who park daily from 9am to 5pm have asked for a special weekly rate. What factors should be considered in acceding or not to their request?

Problem number FF – Northern Supermarket

Approximate total time required: 20 minutes

The Northern Supermarket in Yellowknife, Northwest Territories opens daily from 9am to 9pm, except on Sundays, when its opening hours are only from 1pm to 2pm. The supermarket's daily cash receipts amount to several thousands of dollars during weekdays but only several hundreds on Sundays. These takings are placed in an office safe at the end of each business day. These receipts are then deposited in the bank the following morning. However, the receipts for Friday and Saturday are banked on Monday morning. On the weekend there is usually from $ 20,000 to $ 25,000 in the safe. The manager of the store recognizes the danger of a hold up during the day or a robbery of the safe during the night.

* What safeguards might the store manager take to protect these cash receipts?

Problem number GG -- Safeguarding public monies
Approximate total time required: 20 minutes

It is sometimes necessary in the remote north western city of Whitehorse, Yukon Territories, because of the law, the collective agreement, etc., to pay salaries and wages in cash. The comptroller of the north-western branch of the Canada School of Public Services has to assure herself that the risks associated with the handling of cash are always minimized.

* If you were that FI-03, list the protective steps you would take to ensure the safety of these situations: (1) delivery of funds to the department's head administration office; (2) stuffing pay envelopes; (3) adequate safekeeping of funds prior to payment; (4) issuing pay envelopes; and (5) handling pay envelopes.

Problem number HH -- Shipment of water coolers
Approximate total time required: 20 minutes

The Warren Brothers, who own and operate the Northwestern Edmonton Mall in Alberta, purchased a shipment of water coolers to be used in the mall's Honeysuckle Rose Hotel from the Camrose Manufacturing Company. The invoice for the orders totaling $ 360,000 is dated May 1, 2XX1, and has term of net 30 days. On May 11, 2XX1, the company does not have sufficient cash to pay this latest invoice; but it will certainly have the money by June 1, 2XX1. In order to take advantage of the preferred 2% discount, Mr. Alexander Warren is considering borrowing from the Principal Banking Group in Edmonton the money to pay the invoice. The company has a good credit rating and can borrow the necessary amount of 6% interest. Mr. Warren wants to know the answer to pay the invoice by May 31. The following facts must be considered: the amount Mr. Warren needs to borrow is the amount that he would need to pay the invoice on May

11; and the interest on the bank loan will be calculated for only 20 days because there ARE 20 days...The invoice is therefore being prepaid by 20 days.

* What is your recommendation to Mr. Warren?

Problem number II – Tugs and Lighters Canada

Approximate total time required: 20 minutes

An imaginary federal government department named Tugs and Lighters Canada located in Sioux Ste Marie, Ontario, Canada carries out the following functions during the month of April, 2XX1:

* The department purchases and receives $ 2,500 in supplies from Marine Merchants Limited on April 15, 2XX1. The department settles its invoices with Marine Merchants Limited for the supplies it bought earlier on April 25, 2XX1.

* You are an FI-03, a finance officer employed in the accounting department of Tugs and Lighters Ltd. Kindly prepare the required journal entries following the principles laid down in Section 1500.39 of the *PSAAB Handbook.*

Problem number JJ – Greenhouses Canada

Approximate total time required: 60 minutes

A manager at an imaginary federal government department, Greenhouses Canada, located above Quidi Vidi Lake in St. John's, Newfoundland, has been delegated the authority to approve the purchase of a building for $ 500,000 in cash. The estimated life of the building is 10 years. Amortization is calculated as per the *Treasury Board Accounting Standard 3.1,* on a straight line basis and recorded in the books of the department every six months. The building is purchased on April 01, 2XX1. The manager, on September 30, 2XX6, is also delegated the authority from the Treasury Board via its Circular Number 90XX87 to sell the building for $ 300,000. The building is sold on March 31, 2XX7 for the amount approved by the Treasury Board. $ 150,000 is received in cash the same day and the remainder is promised by the purchaser Private Parks Cornerbrook Limited to be paid when the company's becomes more liquid. The rate of HST levied in the Province of Newfoundland is 13%.

You are the department's finance manager, a FI-03. You purchase a computer from Regional Computers Limited on credit on April 15, 2XX6. Authority for the purchase of this item has been delegated under Section 34 of the *Financial Administration Act.* The computer costs $ 15,000 plus 13% HST. On June 5, 2XX7 Greenhouses Canada accrued salaries and employee benefits to be paid at the end of the ensuing pay period on June 15, 2XX7. Salaries: $ 35,000; employer of federal and provincial taxes of $ 6,000; employer portion of the Canada Pension Plan: $ 5,000; and the employer portion of Unemployment Insurance: $ 4,000.

* Required: Kindly make the necessary journal entries for the above mentioned transactions.

CASE STUDIES

Case Study Number One

Morris Fenty's Bowling Alley

Approximate total time required: 45 minutes

Introduction: 10 minutes

Syndicate work: 15 minutes

Presentation and Wrap up: 20 minutes

Morris Fenty owns a successful bowling alley. Because many customers have to wait a long time for a free alley, Morris decided to add four more lines, at a cost of $ 100,000. Morris wants to borrow the money from a local branch of the Bank of Montreal and makes an application for a loan. He includes a statement quoting one line from the past year's financial statements with the application, showing that the bowling alley's owners' equity is estimated at $ 200,000. The bank replies that it cannot make a decision until it receives additional information showing audited details such as the assets and liabilities of the business.

* Why would the bank request a list of assets and liabilities of the business before it makes a decision?

* What set of financial statements should Morris have submitted with his loan application?

* What factors other than a list of the assets and liabilities do you think the bank will consider while deciding whether or not to float Morris Fenty the approved loan?

Case Study Number Two

Gaspe Gift and Floral Shop

Approximate total time required: 25 minutes

Introduction: 5 minutes

Syndicate work: 10 minutes

Presentations and wrap up: 10 minutes

David Cousineau, the owner of the Gaspe Gift and Floral Shop, examines the balance sheet at the close of the last accounting period and notices that the business has $ 2,500 in cash to invest in another business. The balance sheet for the gift shop as at December 31, 2XX1 follows:

Gaspe Gift And Floral Shop

Balance Sheet

As At December 31, 2XX1

Assets		*Liabilities and Owners' Equity*	
		Bank of Montreal, Gaspe	
Cash	$2,500	Loan Payable	$ 1,000
Accounts Receivable	800	Accounts	Payable:
Inventory For Sale	15,000	J. P. Leger	4,000
Inventory Supplies	500	Guy et Cie	1,500
Display Cases & Eqpt.	6,500	Total Liabilities	6,500
		Owners' Equity:	
		David Cousineau, Capital	18,800
Total Assets:	**$ 25,300**	**Total Liabilities & O. E.**	**$ 25,300**

* Analyzing the situation, do you feel that he can make such a cash withdrawal without placing the flower shop in a difficult financial situation?

Case Study Number Three

Oak Bay Cleaners

Approximate total time required: 35 minutes
Introduction: 5 minutes
Syndicate work: 15 minutes
Presentations and wrap up: 15 minutes

The Oak Bay Cleaners offers a window washing and repair service. The company has regular monthly contracts to wash windows and replace broken windows in several large office buildings in downtown Victoria and the Saanich Peninsula on Vancouver Island in British Columbia. The company also provides window cleaning and window repair services to houses and apartments. The fledging business uses one expense account to record all expenses and one revenue account to record revenues. The owner-manager, Mr. Donald MacKintyre, upon being questioned as to the efficiency and accuracy of the record-keeping he maintains for the company, remarked that he has made considerable improvement in his method of bookkeeping as before he had only one account in which he just entered expenses opposite to his revenues. However, Mr. MacKintyre is now convinced that the system does not provide him with all expense and revenue details he needs to make informed decisions about the present and future operations of Oak Bay Cleaners.

*   What are the various expenses and revenues that such a business would have?

*   Explain why it would be useful to Mr. MacKintyre to know the amounts received for each type of revenue and the amounts spent for each type of expense.

*   What would you suggest that may make the financial records of Oak Bay Cleaners show the total of each major item of revenue and expense?

Case Study Number Four

Mayfair Dress Shoppe

Approximate total time required: 60 minutes

Introduction: 5 minutes

Syndicate work: 30 minutes

Presentations and wrap-up: 25 minutes

Janine Phillipe has worked for six years as a sales clerk in the Mayfair Dresse Shoppe. She plans to open her own shop when she has raised the necessary money to pay for start up expenses.

* What advantages does Janine now have as an employee that she will not have when she becomes the owner of a new dress shop?

* Why would Janine prefer to own a business rather than be employed?

* What advantages and disadvantages will she face as a new owner?

* What major assets will Janine need when she starts her own shop?

* How much capital would you estimate that Janine will need when she opens her own business?

* Where might the information be found to calculate such an estimate?

* What are the various sources from which Janine might obtain the necessary capital to start her own business?

* If Janine's dress shop fails, who is most likely to lose money?

Case Study Number Five

Juan and Vincente Clodomiro

Introduction: 5 minutes

Syndicate work: 15 minutes

Presentations and wrap-up: 10 minutes

Two brothers, Juan and Vincente Clodomiro, each are starting a separate business. Juan has learned to repair automobiles at Algonquin College and has also worked in an auto repair shop. He plans to open a small business which would provide auto repair and maintenance services. Vincente has taken courses in insurance and has passed his real estate broker's examination. He plans to open a real estate firm on a concession basis and also to write insurance policies.

*   Who will need more capital to open a business, Jean or Vincente? Explain why.

Case Study Number Six

Dana Anderson Bookstore

Approximate total time required: 45 minutes

Introduction: 5 minutes

Syndicate work: 25 minutes

Presentations and wrap up: 15 minutes

Dana Anderson owns and operates a thriving bookstore on the campus of Acadia University in Wolfville, Nova Scotia. Dana has two regular employees: Joseph Hamilton and Denis Fortin. The bookstore is profitable, and Mr. Anderson considers opening two more bookstores: at Memorial University in St. John's, Newfoundland and at the University of Moncton in Moncton, New Brunswick. Mr. Anderson plans to place Hamilton in charge of the Memorial location and Monsieur Fortin at Moncton. Mr. Anderson has also assessed the entire situation and believes that the two new bookstores will be successful if properly managed. He is also considering forming a partnership with Messrs. Fortin and Hamilton. Although each of these two employees has cash to invest but neither of them owns any property, each person's performance at Acadia has been honest and reliable. Mr. Anderson believes that as a partnership the new stores will be successful.

*   Does Mr. Anderson's plan of forming a partnership with Messrs. Fortin and Hamilton sound like a good idea?
*   Who stands to lose the most should the venture prove unsuccessful and the stores lose money?
*   What form of business would limit Mr. Anderson's responsibility to his investment?

Case Study Number Seven

Human Resource Management

Approximate total time required: 45 minutes

Introduction: 5 minutes

Syndicate work: 20 minutes

Presentations and wrap up: 20 minutes

Each day the manager of a responsibility centre in the government must make some important decisions. For example, he or she might have to decide whether the organization or the government can afford to settle a large bill today or wait until a later date, or he or she might have to decide whether to purchase a certain item of equipment, hire additional employees, or do without them. To make decisions intelligently, the manager needs useful information. The information usually comes from records of her or his business. Managers in some type of government businesses, however, must make decisions on the reports that come from the job applicant's records. Records must be found to be of acceptable quality; also the information must be accurate. Inaccurate, untimely information is worse than no information at all. You are a human resource manager making the final decision as to whether you are going to hire a new finance manager in your company or not. How can you ensure the application information and that provided by references are usable and reliable?

Case Study Number Eight

Maria Corleone's Bakery

Approximate total time required: 60 minutes

Introduction: 10 minutes

Syndicate work: 30 minutes

Presentations and wrap-up: 20 minutes

Maria Corleone of Saskatoon, Saskatchewan owns and operates a bakery. She sells her baking products by individual customer sale on walk-in by choice, house to house delivery, or to small grocery stores. Maria buys her bakery supplies from several wholesale farms in the surrounding countryside. She rents a building where her bakery is located but owns the baking and delivery equipment, on which there is a mortgage due each month. She withdraws $ 1,000 each month for her personal use from the bakery revenues. A few new customers have been added but in general the total sales have not been good during the past two years. Refer to the comparative balance sheets below; after discuss and answer the questions which follow in point form on flip chart paper:

Maria Corleone's Bakery

Comparative Balance Sheets

As At June 30, 2XX1 And December 31, 2XX1

	June 30, 2XX1	December 31, 2XX1
Assets:		
Cash	410,000	680,000
Acc. Rec.	700,000	400,000
Equipment	25,000,000	25,000,000
Bakery Supp	120,000	150,000
Total Assets	*26,230,000*	*26,230,000*
Liab. & O. E.:		
Acc. Pay.	730,000	400,000
Mort. Pay	9,000,000	11,000,000
M. Corl., Cap.	16,500,000	14,830,000
Tot. Liab & O E	*26,230,000*	*26,230,000*

   *   Identify significant changes that have taken place and have not taken place in the financial position in the bakery in the last six months.

   *   What trend, if any, do these things indicate?

   *   How could the bakery's financial position situation be improved in the future?

Case Study Number Nine

Auditor's Report

Approximate total time required: 45 minutes

Introduction: 5 minutes

Syndicate work: 30 minutes

Presentations and wrap up: 10 minutes

A chartered accountancy firm, with a medium-sized practice in Brandon, Manitoba, was hired to audit the books of a Brandon department store. The firm mailed its auditor's letter after conducting the annual audit of the store. In addition, a copy of this accompanying questionnaire was sent to one of the store's regular customers, a Mrs. Lucille Stewart of 185 Huron Street, North Brandon, Manitoba.

THIS IS NOT A STATEMENT

We are conducting an audit of the books of the North Brandon department store. We are meanwhile making a number of checks to help us determine the accuracy of the store's accounting records. The books show that you have an outstanding balance of the $ 350 in the company's favour. Does this amount agree with yours? Yes_____No_____ If the answer is no, what amount does your records show? $_____ Then return, if possible, this card in the enclosed self-addressed and stamped (franked) envelope.

Messrs. Higginbottham, Hollingsworth and Hinkson

Chartered Accountants, January 15, 2XX3

Please sign here, thank you

_____

Mrs. Stewart replied that the unpaid balance showing in her records was $ 250.

The department store's trial balance was in balance at the time of the audit. Why then, was it necessary for the CA firm to double check with the store's customers?

* If the store had several customers, would it have to contact each one?

* How could such an error to Mrs. Stewart's account have occurred without it showing up in the balanced trial balance?

Case Study Number Ten

Situations

Approximate total time required: 60 minutes

Introduction: 10 minutes

Syndicate work: 30 minutes

Presentations and wrap up: 20 minutes

Here is a list of accounting and financial situations in which a decision-maker may find him or herself while in the government of Canada. Complete the cause and effect actions that may result.

Situation	GAAP Principle	Statutory Authority	Accounting
A mistake of an 0.05 cent error repeats itself 50 times regularly			
Contract for 25K is struck			
Expense budget exceeds revenue budget significantly			

Case Study Number Eleven

Consolidated Revenue Fund

Appropriate total time required: 60 minutes

Introduction: 5 minutes

Group work: 30 minutes

Presentation and wrap-up: 25 minutes

At Confederation, the Dominion of Canada came into existence under the aegis of the *British North America Act, 1867.* As the years passed, other *British North America Acts* were passed in the British Parliament, and most likely, ratified in the Canadian Parliament. In 1982, the then Prime Minister of Canada, the Right Honourable Pierre Elliott Trudeau, repatriated the Constitution and the *Constitution Acts, 1867* came into existence. Coming out of these Acts is the manner in which funds are deposited by the Minister of Finance and managed by the Receiver General for Canada or Minister of Public Works and Government Services Canada. Please discuss in your answer these questions in your individual groups, and prepare to discuss them in the plenary session which is to follow:

* How, if at all, was the CRF affected by the repatriation of the Constitution?

* How important is the Governor General to the availability of funds to generate Supply? Can this influence affect the level of the CRF? If so, how? If not, why not?

* Who is ultimately responsible for the current level of the CRF? Why? Discuss.

Case Study Number Twelve

Ice Roads

Approximate total time required: 70 minutes

Introduction: 10 minutes

Group work: 40 minutes

Presentation and wrap up: 20 minutes

The Department of Fisheries and Oceans (DFO), which comprises a number of program/activities or service lines, the largest of which is the Canadian Coast Guard (CCG), owns, leases, maintains and operates ice roads in the far Canadian north.

Ice roads only exist for part of the fiscal year, usually in the colder winter months. During that frigid period, CCG freezes sections of land, tundra and water on which to create roadways on the ice. These ice routes can cross lakes, land, tundra, seas and other bodies of water making a path for transporting equipment, people and supplies between northern Canadian cities, communities and towns such as Yellowknife, Whitehorse, Norman Wells, Inuvik and Aklavik.

During the non-winter months, when a relatively warm thaw sets in, leaving sometimes only the underlying permafrost, the ice roads only exist as concepts in the minds of administrators and financial officers employed by CCG.

* Can these ice roads be recorded as fixed assets in the books of Canada or DFO or CCG?

* If these assets may be capitalized, would they be subject to amortization, appreciation, depreciation, capital cost allowance, depletion or depreciation?

* What financial policy and rule making organization(s) would be most likely to provide the guiding policies and practices: *American Institute of Public Accountants, The Bank of Canada, Canadian Institute of Chartered Accountants, Certified General Accountants of Canada, International Federation of Accountants, Institute of Chartered Accountants of England and Wales, Institute of Chartered Accountants of Scotland, Public Sector Accounting and Auditing Board, Receiver General for Canada, Society of Management Accountants of Canada or The Treasury Board.*

Case Study Number Thirteen

Westminster Model

Introduction: 5 minutes

Group work: 35 minutes

Presentation and wrap up: 20 minutes

In a previous federal election in Canada, the Progressive Conservative Party lost to the Liberal Party. The leader of the ruling party, Monsieur Pierre Elliott Trudeau was invited by the sitting Governor General to be Prime Minister and to from the next official government of Canada. Before the election, employees in an anonymous Directorate of the House of Commons were separated into two groups: those who had been hired by the House's Human Resources Staff; and those who seemed to have been political appointees. After the election, the apparent political appointees did not want to turn up on the following day.

* What very high level organization in a government adapting the Westminster Model such as Canada may seem to have the same dual roles in the appointment and hiring process?

* What would be your reaction, if you happened to a Senior Responsibility Centre manager in the House of Commons when political appointees appeared to be conveniently missing after an election?

Case Study Number Fourteen

Department QRS

Approximate total time required: 60 minutes

Introduction: 10 minutes

Group work: 30 minutes

Presentation and wrap up: 20 minutes

You are the Deputy Minister of the imaginary Department QRS. During the reading of the government's last Annual Budget speech, you discovered some changes which were going to be made to the program/activity structures of the three Assistant Deputy Ministers who report directly to you. In his budget speech, the Minister of Finance announced as part of the government's fiscal plan that $ 2.3 billion was being transferred from Service Line X, 40% from Service Line Y, and 25% from Service line Z to create a new Service Line R.

* During your group discussion, develop a role play with four other members of your group, you in the role of Deputy Minister and the others, each that of an Assistant Deputy Minister. Make sure that during the plenary session which follows later, that the lead individual presenting the findings of your group is the one who has been playing the role of the Assistant Deputy Minister of the new Service Line R. While answering the question below, ensure consideration is given all relevant information provided.

* What processes, at the strategic management, management control and operational control levels in government, not forgetting the direct and indirect control of your department, must take place to affect this program/activity adjustment? Also ensure that the department's Assistant Deputy Minister of Finance and Administration, Department QRS's Senior Full Time Financial Officer is fully aware of these processes.

Case Study Number Fifteen

Sean MacGregor's Service Station

Approximate total time required: 40 minutes

Introduction: 5 minutes

Group work: 25 minutes

Presentation and wrap up: 10 minutes

Sean MacGregor operates an automobile service station. He sells gasoline, oil, tyres, batteries and other automobile supplies. He also fixes flat tyres, lubricates cars, and does a spot or two of mechanical repair work. He has the help of one part time employee. In the past, MacGregor had enough time to in which to repair vehicles and also handle customer services. No separate record for each of the various phases and types of work was kept. Revenue was shown in one account. Recently, business has been booming. MacGregor finds that he cannot attend to customers and do all the repair work also.

> *   How may the records of the business be organized to help MacGregor make this important decision?

Case Study Number Sixteen

Inter-Provincial Trucking

Approximate total time required: 60 minutes

Introduction: 10 minutes

Group work: 30 minutes

Presentation and wrap up: 20 minutes

The Inter Provincial Trucking Company operates highway trucks among several large Canadian cities in three provinces. The company also owns a number of small trucks for local deliveries. In addition, the company owns warehouses in several cities, maintains a garage for overhauling and repairing its trucks, and has a large central office. To assist in vehicle maintenance, the company owns a wide variety of equipment. Special loading and conveyor equipment has been installed in the warehouses; the main garage is well equipped with tools and machines; the central office holds typewriter, adding machines, calculators, facsimiles, Dictaphones, computers and other office machines. Only one equipment account is being prepared, with equipment recorded in one amount. The president of Inter Provincial Trucking, Don Yearwood, believes this plan does not provide the necessary detailed information.

* Why would the president want detailed information about the company's equipment?

* What change in the records would you suggest to provide detailed information the firm needs?

Case Study Number Seventeen

PWGSC Coding Block

Approximate total time required: 60 minutes

Introduction: 10 minutes

Group work: 30 minutes

Presentation and wrap up: 20 minutes

The following is a transparent, 22-digit, up to the required PWGSC limit, coding block for an imaginary government Department MNZ:

Dept. /Agency	FRA Activity	(GWAC)	Authority	Object (Econ)	Transaction Type
000	00000	00000	0000	0000	0

You are the department's senior full time financial officer, in fact, at the ADM level of management. The department's computerized financial system, run on an Oracle-based platform, has been set up after discussions between you, your staff, the department's system development and maintenance branch and PWGSC. The department's system development committee arrives at the following departmental coding block:

Activity	Responsibility	Source Code
0000	0000	00000

* What kind of system and associated coding block has been developed for departmental use?

* Is Oracle anything like CDFS, GMAX or an SAP based platform?

* What methods do you think are being utilized to shrink the number of digits in the coding block from the standard size of 22 to 13?

* Where do you think the apparently missing fields like: GWAC, FRA, Object and Transaction Type have disappeared to and how can one determine the actual coding and the classification results from this truncated coding block?

PROJECTS

Project Number One

Eaton Employment Service

Approximate total time required: 120 minutes

Introduction: 10 minutes

Group or syndicate work: 80 minutes

Presentations & wrap up: 30 minutes

On October 1, 2XX1, Mademoiselle Jean Sauve bought the Eaton Employment Service from Osvaldo MacPherson. For the purchase price of $ 4,480, Mlle. Sauve received the assets and liabilities listed below:

Eaton Employment Service

Balance Sheet

As At September 30, 2XX1

Assets		Liabilities and Owners' Equity	
Cash	$ 2,400	Accounts payable:	
Accounts Receivable:		Armand L. Pariseau	$ 430
Le Roi et Cie Ltee.	525		
Tyres Inc.	380	Owners' Equity:	
Furniture	1,270	O. MacPherson, Equity	4,470
Office Equipment	325		
Total Assets	**$ 4,900**	**Total Liab. &Owners' Equity: $ 4,900**	

The transactions for October, 2XX1 were as follows:

October 01 Paid $ 160 in cash for rent expense.

October 02 Sold services for $ 240 on credit to the Rex Company Ltd.

October 03 Bought a new typewriter for $ 560 in cash.

October 05 Sold services for $ 2,400 in cash.

October 08 Sauve withdrew $ 600 from the business for personal use.

October 09 Paid $ 160 for newspaper advertising.

October 11 Sold services for $ 5,900 in cash.

October 12 Paid $ 130 to A. L. Pariseau on account.

October 15 Sold services for $ 2,005 on credit to Tyres, Inc.

October 16 Bought furniture for $ 750 on credit from A. L. Pariseau.

October 18 Sold services for $ 850 in cash.

October 19 Returned lamp which was bought for $ 200 on credit from A. L. Pariseau.

October 22 Paid $ 150 for the telephone bill.

October 23 Received $ 150 from Le Roi Cie Ltee on account.

October 25 Sauve withdrew $ 100 from the business again.

October 26 Sauve sold services for $ 1,800 cash to the Rhona Company.

October 29 Paid $ 230 for the hydro electricity bill.

October 30 Sold services for $ 600 in cash.

October 30 Paid $ 120 for newspaper advertising.

* In a general journal make the "opening entries" to record the company's assets, liabilities and owners' equity shown on the balance sheet as at September 30, 2XX1. Remember that Jean Sauve is the new owner as of October 1, 2XX1.

* Open the following ledger accounts for and including: cash; accounts receivable, with individual accounts for each debtor; furniture; office equipment; accounts payable; Jean Sauve Capital; advertising expense; rent expense; and utilities expense.

* Journalize the transactions for the month of October, 2XX1.

* Post the journal entries to ledger accounts.

* Prepare a trial balance.

* Prepare an income statement and a formal balance sheet.

Project Number Two

Department PQR

Approximate time required: 180 minutes

Introduction: 15 minutes

Group work: 120 minutes

Presentation and wrap up: 45 minutes

The following partial trial balance as at March 31, 2XX7 comes from Responsibility Centre Number 203578 in an imaginary government department PQR. You are the department's finance officer at an FI-03 group and level.

* Kindly compute and insert the Investment in Canada or Owners' Equity credit balance and the balancing totals of each debit and credit column.

* Prepare a balance sheet as at March 31, 2007 and the income statement for the fiscal year April 1, 2XX6 to March 31,2XX7.

During the fiscal year April 1, 2XX7 to March 31, 2XX8 the following transactions occurred:

Vote 1 Operating Expenditures Vote	13,500,000
Vote 5 Capital Expenditures Vote	6,700,000
Vote 10 Grants & Contributions Vote	20,360,000
Vote L15 Loans To Canada Post	1,600,000
Contribution To Employee Benefit Plans	5,635,000
Ministry's Salary And Car Allowance (S)	45,000
Revenues Credited To The Vote	(3,560,000)

Treasury Board approved the following allotments under Section 31 of the *Financial Administration Act:*

Operating Budget Allotment	12,040,000
Controlled Capital Allotment	6,200,000
Grants And Contributions Allotment	20,360,000
Special Allotment	5,680,000

Completed Trial Balance

As March 31, 2XX7

Accounts Name	Dr.	Cr.
Cash	5,000	
Imprest Cash	20,000	
Departmental Bank Account	150,000	
Receiver General Deposit Control	750,000	
Receiver General Payment Control		310,000
Receiver General Payroll Control		350,000
Receiver General IS Debit Control	800,000	Nil
Receiver General IS Credit Control		300,000
Receiver General Foreign Exchange Control	15,000	
Other Control Accounts	780,000	
Accounts Payable: Rhona Hardware		500,000
Fixed Assets: Land & Buildings	2,600,000	
Fixed Assets: Furniture & Fixtures	500,000	
Fixed Assets: Computers	700,000	
Accrued Salaries		2,300,000
Accumulated Amortization: Land & Buildings		700,000
Accumulated Amortization: Furniture & Fixtures		210,000
Accumulated Amortization: Computers		250,000
Inventory: Office Supplies	210,000	
Inventory: Materiel	850,000	
Inventory: Work In Progress	950,000	
Inventory: Finished Goods	850,000	
Prepaid Rent	895,000	
Prepaid Insurance	485,000	
Accrued Vacation Liability		2,500,000
Investment In Canada (Calculated)		3,140,000
TOTALS	10,560,000	10,560,000

Based on the delegated authorities granted by the Minister to the department's Deputy Head within the delegation document, your senior administration officer, the five program managers and you, the senior full time financial officer have been delegated "full" authority to: hire and fire employees; contract with third parties (the department's limit delegated by PWGSC is $ 580,000 and implement the four steps of expenditure control as per Section 32, 33 and 34 of the *Financial Administration Act.*

R. C. Number 203578 purchases on credit from Dell Computers a computer system for $ 250,000.

Previously $ 300,000 had been set aside to cover the purchase of the same computer system, so it was committed under Section 32 of the *Financial Administration Act.*

The bi-weekly salary bill for the responsibility centre, which has been accrued, totals $ 370,000. The first actual payroll paid as per the paylist sent from PWGSC is $ 368,857, including the bilingual bonus.

The responsibility centre sells $ 2,500,000 in services for cash to an OGD (Dept X) and $ 1,600,000 on credit to a third party---the British Columbia Provincial Government.

37% of the Accounts Receivable balance as at February 29, 2XX8 proves to be not collectible, according to the internal auditors, Messrs. Spicer and Pegler, Chartered Accountants. This amount has been verified by the department's resident external auditors from the Office of the Auditor General for Canada.

According to the Treasury Board Standards, the department's fixed assets are being amortized on a straight line basis: land [original cost $ 1,500,000, is not amortized] and buildings [original cost $ 1,100,000], purchased on May 1, 2XX2, with an estimated life of 25 years; furniture & fixtures, purchased on July 1, 2XX3 with an estimated life of 10 years; and computers purchased on April 1, 2XX4 with an estimated life of 5 years.

The responsibility centre also purchases $ 600,000 in materiel supplies---half for cash and half on credit. The department deals with Rhona Hardware for all its supplies, materiel and office. The responsibility centre settles $ 100,000 of its accounts payable balance during the fiscal year. As at March 31, 2XX8 when the inventory count was taken, these were the following balances: materiel: $ 370,000; work in progress: $ 400,000; and finished goods $ 500,000.

During the fiscal year also, $ 150,000 was transferred from materiel to work in progress.

$ 80,000 of office supplies was purchased for cash; $ 120,000 was used during the fiscal year.

$ 250,000 more rent was prepaid for cash and the department's year's rent usage cost $ 350,000. $ 360,000 more insurance was prepaid for cash. The department's year's coverage was $ 250,000.

Your finance clerk, a CR-05, has estimated that the PAYE transactions for the responsibility centre as at March 31, 2XX8 totals $ 75,000 made up of salaries earned but not yet settled: $ 40,000; furniture bought and received but not yet paid for: $ 20,000; and supplies received, used by March 31, 2XX8 (FOB destination) but not yet paid for.

* Make all the necessary accounting entries for the fiscal year. Please make note of which fiscal and financial activities did not require accounting entries.

* Prepare a trial balance.

* Make the required adjusting entries.

* Prepare an adjusted trial balance.

* Prepare the relevant period ending statements such as an income statement and a balance sheet, all according to PSAAB's GAAP.

Solutions to Quizzes

Solution to quiz number one – True and false

* True
* True
* False
* True
* True
* True

Solution to quiz number two – True and False

* False
* True
* False
* False
* True

Solution to quiz number three – Treasury Board and EMS

* President of the Treasury Board, Comptroller General, Minister of Finance, Receiver General, and two other Board members appointed by the Prime Minister.
* President of the Treasury Board, Comptroller General, Minister of Finance, and the Receiver General
* PWGSC, Treasury Board

* Minister of Finance controls the CRF; the Receiver General manages the CRF.

* The key features of the Expenditure Management System are: integrating the budget planning process; emphasizing the ongoing review of programs and managing within available resources through allocation; eliminating central policy reserves; introducing departmental business plans to focus on strategic changes to programs and businesses; providing more flexibility to ministers and departments to help them manage within approved resources; improving information on program performance to aid decision-making and facilitate accountability; and recognizing the role of the House of Commons standing committees in reviewing the government's spending priorities for future years and introducing department outlooks.

* ARLU means the Annual Reference Level Update.

* EID means the Expenditure Information Division.

* EMS means the Expenditure Management System.

* EMIS means the Expenditure Management Information System

* MRRS means the Management Reporting and Results System

Solution to quiz number four – Financial systems in the Government of Canada

* AMS, CDFS, Free Balance, GMAX, Oracle, SMA, and SAP.

* True

* Authority is delegated outwards from the minister to the deputy head who in turn delegates temporary or permanent authority to positions in the department or agency. The organization's delegation document plus specimen signature cards are the main instruments used. *Delegatus non potest delegare* is the key element in the process. DND's practice of the delegation of authority has some feasible practical examples.

Solution to quiz number five – Cash journal

* Sentence numbers one and two.

Solution to quiz number six – Concept of debit and credit

* In most accounting and bookkeeping circles, Luca Pacioli is considered to be the 'father' of the concept of debit and credit.

* Cash always comes in on the 'left' and leaves on the 'right'. By following this basic and fundamental concept, the other side of the accounting entry usually remains correct.

Solution to quiz number seven – Delegation of authority, capital, etc...

* Authority is delegated outwards to temporarily or permanently filled positions not persons.

* A balance sheet is a statement showing the financial position of a business at any one point in time. Invented in 1536 by Simon Stevin of Bruges, this statement also shows the assets of a business listed on one side, and its liabilities and owners' equity listed on the other.

* Capital is a term specifically used to indicate the investment of an owner in a firm. Therefore, in the owners' equity of a balance sheet, say, a sole proprietorship such as a chartered accounting firm with a single owner, for example, the term "Albert B. Singleton, Chartered Accountant, Capital" is used to indicate the chartered accountant, Mr. Albert B. Singleton's investment.

* Working capital is the amount of capital made available to meet day to day expenses of running a business. It may be expressed mathematically thus: [(cash + inventories + accounts receivable) – accounts payable].

* Capital owned, the amount owned as at balance sheet date by a business' owner, comprises all the cash and other resources employed in the business.

* Capital employed, the total assets of a business, is the effective amount

that is being used in the firm. It usually comprises the owners' equity funds plus long term debt.

* Current assets are any assets other than fixed assets. These are funds which are either in the company's office safe, or in the bank, or easily converted to cash. Fixed assets are those assets intended for use in a business on a continuing basis. These are permanent items such as land, buildings and equipment. The main distinguishing feature between these two types of assets is the easy manner in which one is convertible to cash as opposed to the other.

* Liquid assets comprise cash and those assets, such as accounts receivable and inventories, which are readily converted to cash, in order to meet the day to day outlays of a company.

* Profit results when revenues exceed expenses during a particular accounting period under consideration.

* Profits may increase both the value of assets and the capital.

* Drawings decrease the owners' equity and the assets, usually cash, simultaneously.

* A liability is that item which a firm owes.

Solution to quiz number eight – Bookkeeping, trial balance, type of accounts

* The main stages of double entry bookkeeping are: (1) preparing a source document; (2) journalizing; (3) posting a general ledger; (4) preparing a trial balance; (5) making adjusting and closing entries; (6) preparing an adjusted trial balance; and (7) preparing financial reports: e. g. an income statement and a balance sheet.

* A ledger account generally shows the increases and decreases in asset, contra, control, liability and owners' equity accounts. In the past these types of accounts were kept in a bound hard cover book. Now they may also be maintained manually, mechanically, electrically or electronically. Their key characteristics revolve around certain advantages: (1) Detailed information relating to transactions is already recorded in journals and source documents, and the information for decision-making purposes. (2) All the information relating to particular person or

business activity may now be found in one place. In the same spot, one can have a summary of one's dealings with each particular customer or supplier. At one glance, one can tell how much one has spent on any individual expense in a particular financial period.

* The two sides of an account are debit, found on the left side; and credit, found on the right side.

* A real account is a balance sheet account that is carried into the following year. It is also a proprietary account. It always represents something we can see, move or touch such as buildings, cash, computers and furniture.

* A personal account is a type of account used by an individual or organization for their own needs. It is usually headed with the name of a business, company, firm or person.

* A nominal account is a type of account which is closed out at the end of the year. In this type of account is also kept a record of transactions for which we have nothing tangible to show.

* At the end of an accounting period, after the income statement has been prepared, the balances left in the temporary accounts must be reduced to zero. This action is necessary so that these accounts can be used to accumulate and summarize revenue and expense data for the oncoming accounting period. In order to reduce these temporary account balances to zero, the amounts found there need to be transferred to some other account, called the revenue and expense summary. This transfer process is known as *closing the accounts.*

* One of the better types of mathematical accuracy is achieved by preparing a summary of the balances of the ledger accounts. This summary, known as a *trial balance,* lists the titles of the accounts followed by accompanying debit and credit balances in the numerical order in which each account appears in the ledger.

* Five types of errors which are not revealed by a trial balance: (1) transaction(s) omitted completely from a journal; (2) transactions entered twice or more; (3) transactions entered correctly in one of the journals posted more than once; (4) transactions entered correctly in one of the journals but posted to the wrong account; and (5) the wrong account is debited or credited. PLEASE NOTE THAT THE TRIAL BAL-

ANCE'S MAIN FEATURE IS TO CHECK WHETHER ALL DEBITS = ALL CREDITS REGARDLESS OF THE LEDGER ACCOUNT(S) TO WHICH THEY HAVE BEEN POSTED.

Solution to quiz number nine – Inventories

* Opening inventory ($ 500) + Purchases ($ 6,000) = Cost of goods available for sale ($ 6,500) – Closing inventory ($ 480) = Cost of goods sold ($ 6,020) – Sales ($ 9,350) = Gross profit ($ 3,330): 35% of Sales; 55.3% of Cost.

* Beginning inventory = $ 250; Ending inventory = $ 300; Sales = $ 8,000; Gross profit = 25% of Selling Price = $ 2,000. Therefore, Cost of goods = Sales – Gross profit ($ 8,000 - $ 2,000 = $ 6,000). Therefore, by formula, Purchases = [(Cost of goods + Ending inventory) – Opening Inventory] = [$ 6,000 + $ 300) - $ 250] = $ 6,050.

* Beginning inventory ($ 500) + Purchases ($ 9,200) = Cost of goods available for sale ($ 9,700) – Ending inventory ($ 780) = Cost of goods sold ($ 8,920) + Gross profit (100% of Sales: $ 8,920) = Sales ($ 17,840).

Solution to quiz number ten – Cost of goods, freight, purchases, etc.

* The cost of goods sold account usually includes: [opening inventory + purchases – closing inventory].

* The freight-in could be the cost of transporting equipment and supplies purchased, hence it may be added to the purchases account, and therefore be part of the cost of the goods sold account.

* Purchases returns and allowances are usually deducted from the purchases account and therefore could become part of the cost of goods sold account.

* Sales discounts may also be deducted from the sales account.

* Overhead expenses are an allocated or apportioned total of indirect expenses which may have appeared as individual expense accounts

before summation, allocation or apportionment.

* Salaries and wages are among those expenses which are usually deducted from gross profit before the latter results in a net profit before dividends and taxes.

Solution to quiz number eleven – Types of inventory

* These terms define two of the main methods used to value inventory held and probably used later on by a firm. FIFO means first-in, first out; and LIFO means last-in, first out.

* The term means work in progress or work in process.

* To ensure that any inventory added to be removed from the stockroom on that last business day is included in the inventory count. Also most firms close their books at the end of each calendar year. Exceptions would be those firms that close their books at the end of a fiscal year which may not coincide with the calendar year ending.

* When an inventory is not counted precisely at the end of the year these kinds of transactions could be missed: (1) Inventory items added after the count, resulting in a real understatement of company profits; and (2) Inventory items removed after the count, resulting in an actual overstatement of the actual company profits.

* The amount of the purchase figure determines the actual dollars calculated in the cost of goods sold and eventually the profit or loss levels of the firm.

* Inventory movement towards the end of year can be easily missed. Hence, a careful recording of the details of inventory movements would ensure the accuracy of not only the ending inventory figure but also the opening inventory figure for the next fiscal year and any resulting profit and loss levels. The impact on PAYE could result in the amounts set up at year end.

* Cost of goods sold = [opening inventory + purchases – closing inventory].

* Inventory turnover may be defined as the amount of times the average annual level of inventory that is sold in any one accounting year.

Solution to quiz number twelve – Using journal and ledger folios

Transaction	Subsidiary Ledger	Account Debited	Account Credited
Worked Example	**Cash Journal**	**Rent Expense**	**RG Pymt. Cntrl. Acc.**
Sold goods on credit	Sales journal	Acc. Rec. F. Gibbons	Sales revenue
Bght goods on credit	Purchases Jnl	Supplies inventory	Acc. Pay.: Club Trix
Sold goods for cash	Sales journal	Cash	Sales revenue
Cheque rtnd. NSF	Cash journal	Acc. Rec. Mirabel	Caisse Pop. Bk A/C
		Bank charge	Caisse Pop Bank A/C
Purchased supplies	Prchs. Journal	Supplies expense	Cash
Rplnsd. petty cash	Petty cash jrnl.	Petty cash account	Caisse Pop Bank A/C

Transaction	Purchases Journal	Sales Journal	Goods returned Journal
Sold stuff on crdt.	n/a	$ 676	n/a
Prchsd stuff on crdt.	$ 340	n/a	n/a
Prchsd stuff on crdt.	$ 215	n/a	n/a
Sold stuff on credit	-	$ 612	n/a
Credit note to Pierre	-	-	$ 6
Purchases	$ 105	-	-
Sold stuff on credit		$ 562	

Solution to quiz number thirteen – Cash discount, cash journal, etc.

* Cash discount is never recorded in any of the books of original entry because money is deducted up front from the price charged, making both selling price and cash received, in essence, smaller.

* There are usually a myriad of cash entries, of cash being received and cash being disbursed. As a result, these need to be summarized in a subsidiary journal before a larger and later summarized fewer volume of entries are then placed in the general journal.

* Contra entries are journal entries made in a cash journal such as allowance for doubtful accounts and cash over and short.

* Discounts allowed, if distinguishable by an individual entry, may

sometimes be added as a kind of contra entry.

* Sales discounts and purchases discounts usually generate debits and credits to contra accounts in which these events are entered. Cash discounts are generally deducted from the selling or purchase price, making the amount received or submitted a lower selling price.

* A petty cash journal keeps a detailed account of small amounts spent on items which are not settled by individual cheques but with cash advanced by the holder of the petty cash in return for I. O. U.'s until the actual amount spent is supported by the invoice(s).

Dr: Office Equipment – Typewriter $ 90.00

Dr: GST Refundable Advance   4.50

Cr: Cash $ 94.50

* They essentially reduce profit levels, unless the volume of sales increases because of the resulting reduction in cost. In this situation, it is assumed that the sale takes place in Ontario.

* None, except the net effect on cash and the opposing expense, revenue, asset or liability account for which cash is being disbursed.

* Yes, I would. It is impractical to maintain all the individual entries for every single asset purchased, sold or made obsolete. Hence the need for a fixed asset sub-ledger, usually kept by individual asset.

Solution to quiz number fourteen – Preparing a bank reconciliation statement

Bank Reconciliation

Balance per bank statement	$ 2,420	Balance per firm's cheque book		$ 1,638
Add deposit in transit	150	Add: Notes receivable	$ 400	
Less: Outstanding cheques:		Interest income	8	
Number 650: $ 300		Less: Collection fee	(10)	
Number 654 240	(540)	Service charge	(6)	392
Adjusted bnk. stmnt. Balance	**$ 2,030**	Adjusted firm's cheque bk. Bal.		**$ 2,030**

Solution to quiz number fifteen – Bank reconciliation

* A bank reconciliation is a balanced statement which takes into account the differences between the customer's version of his or her bank balance and the balance generated by the bank itself.

* To not only identify but to correct any errors either made by the bank or the customer which may have been included with the list of differences mentioned in the previous answer. The main points of difference could be cheques not honoured by the bank; deposits in transit; deposits not yet entered by the bank; bank charges not yet entered by the customer; bank interest not yet entered by the customer; other bank credits not entered by the customer; and errors.

* Cheques may have been lost in the mail or cheques have not been submitted as yet by customers for payment.

* The cheques may have been lost or destroyed; or the payee's unfortunate demise may have occurred between the time of issue of the cheques and their time of honouring.

* Bank charges or bank interest appearing on the bank statement and supported by source documents.

* In both cases the amount of the bank overdraft should be entered in reverse. For example, on the bank account it will be shown as a credit on the reconciliation statement, and in the case of the reconciliation, shown as a debit.

Solution to quiz number sixteen – General journal and entries, etc.

* The firm's book of original entry where debits and credits first occur.

* A journal entry is a listing of accounts accompanied by commensurate dollar figures shown on the left and the right which should be equal. These two lines of information, plus the narrative which follows below, are a short and precise financial representation of an economic event which has occurred as a result of a company's operations.

* On the first line enter the calendar or fiscal year of transaction. On the second line, enter the day and the month of the calendar or fiscal year

of the transaction. On the left side of the third line, enter the account and the amount to be debited. On the right side of the fourth line, enter the account and the amount to be credited. On the fifth or more lines, describe the economic event which has just transpired.

* Samuel L. Bell, Chartered Accountant, invested $ 5,000 in his chartered accountancy firm. The Passport Office sold $ 2,500,000 worth of passports for cash, during the month of June, 2XX3. Grand and Toy sold $5,000 in supplies on credit to the Canadian School of Public Services on April 1, 2XX1.

* A journal entry which comprises one or more debit and one or more credit entries.

* A narration, a statement which is entered on the line below the credit line of a journal entry, describes the company's economic event which took place.

* Journal entries made at DND are usually multiple entries made in Canadian currency and the currencies of the countries in which the department is operating at the time. The difference on exchange balances the entry after conversion of the foreign currency (ies) to the Canadian dollar(s).

Solution to quiz number seventeen – Accruals and prepaids

* The individual making the entry (ies) was probably attempting to accrue salaries and wages. These expenses may have been incurred but not paid for. In addition, the entry may be an attempt to correct an incorrect interpretation of an event involving salaries and wages or just a plain and simple error.

* Insurance may have been prepaid. In other words, the firm may have purchased insurance coverage in advance of excess of what has been used or is to be used during the accounting period under consideration.

* Rent may have been accrued. In other words, the firm may have incurred an item of rent expense but the cash for the rent has not yet been disbursed during the accounting period under consideration.

Solution to quiz number eighteen – Provision

* A provision represents the accounting for an expense that may occur based on historical information.

* The proprietor can ascertain the amount of bad debts which have occurred based on the combined ages of a set of accounts receivable. The proprietor has to assess the amount of bad debts that may occur based on the combined ages of a set of accounts receivable.

* The first line: annual or fiscal year; second line; date of entry of provision; third line: debit of the bad debts expense, followed by an amount equal to the dollar figure found on the 4th line; fourth line: credit: allowance for doubtful expense, followed by an amount equal to the dollar figure found on the 3rd line; and the narration.

* There has been an understatement in the amount of bad debts calculated.

* There has been an overestimation in the amount bad debts calculated.

* As a contra entry to the amount which appears on the left side of the balance sheet as an accounts receivable.

* Account receivable which has been reduced by the contra entry of an allowance for doubtful accounts.

* The bad debt is usually a debit to an expense account and the provision for doubtful accounts is a credit to a contra account.

Solution to quiz number nineteen – Amortization, capital cost allowance and depreciation

* First line: calendar or fiscal year under consideration; second line: month and day of transaction; third line: Dr: amortization or depreciation expense, followed by an estimated amount equal to that appearing on the 4th line; fourth line: Cr: accumulated amortization, followed by an estimated amount equal to that appearing on the 3rd line; and fifth line: the narration.

* Amortization is the allocation of the historical cost of a capital asset over its estimated useful life. Amortization may also be described as the gradual planned reduction in the value of a capital expense.

* Depreciation is a measure of the wearing out, consumption or other loss of a value of a fixed asset arising from use, effluxion of time or obsolescence through technological and market changes. Depreciation should also be allocated to accounting periods so as to charge a fair proportion of cost to each accounting period during the period of the expected life of each fixed asset.

* Two very familiar and much used methods of amortization or depreciation in Canadian government firms are: the straight line method (officially recommended by the Treasury Board of Canada Accounting Standard No. 3.1 for use in government organizations); and the capital cost allowance method (recommended by the Canada Revenue Agency in the *Income Tax Act* for use when preparing annual income tax returns). Under the straight line method, annual depreciation is calculated as follows: Subtract the estimated disposal value from the original cost of the fixed asset under consideration to determine the total depreciation. Divide the total depreciation by the total number of years of the estimated life of the fixed asset under consideration to thus obtain the annual depreciation. The amount of depreciation charged is the same for each year of use. The disposal of the fixed asset occurs when the asset is sold, traded or scrapped. With the capital cost allowance, under Canadian income tax law, a business is permitted to include in the expense section of its statement of income an allowance for depreciating most of its fixed assets. Finally, the Taxation Division of the Canada Revenue Agency separates its assets into various classes, with each class being assigned a maximum percentage rate of depreciation.

* Depreciation is shown in the balance sheet as an accumulated deduction from the original cost of the asset(s), the result of being a net book value of the fixed assets, or stated simply as net assets.

* When an asset is sold, either fully or partially depreciated, the original cost of the asset arrives at a gain or loss on the sale of the asset. In the government of Canada, this is what transpires since departments are required to comply with GAAP, affecting the branch of PWGSC named Crown Assets Disposal and each individual department or agency.

Solution to quiz number twenty – Suspense accounts, trial balance

* No, it does not.

* a. A transaction entered twice or more. b. A transaction entered correctly but posted more than once. c. A transaction omitted completely from a journal. d. The wrong account is debited or credited. e. Two compensating errors.

* By checking actual accounts against budgeted amounts and attempting to account for all differences.

* A suspense account is a "hanging" account. The information is suspended and not debited or credited to a genuine ledger account. It is sometimes used by the government of Canada operations. In reality, a suspense account should never be used.

* If an asset or expense, the resulting balance should be shown in the correct account in the trial balance. If a liability, revenue or owners' equity, the resulting balance should be also shown in the correct account in the trial balance.

* The trial balance could be out of balance doubly on its credit side.

* The trial balance could be out of balance doubly on its debit side.

Solution to quiz number twenty-one – Departmental accounts, overhead

* Departmental accounts, in a private sector organization, can be equated to branch accounts. In a public sector organization, such as the Canadian government, organizational sub-divisions at the program level, usually managed by an assistant deputy head, are known as departments. In provincial and territorial governments they may be known as ministries. In all public sector instances, departmental or branch accounts are maintained. In the private and public sector, the key factor which remains is that most of these organizations are managed by a responsibility centre manager who may be assigned responsibility for his or her organizational unit with the commensurate delegated authority.

* Two common methods of apportioning overhead expenses are by direct labour hours and machine hours.

* Two important points to remember when any type of asset is paid in advance is that the prepaid item is not really an expense, but an asset which is essentially owned by the firm. Expenses are determined by use.

* It is essential that responsibility centre managers are assessed at the end of each financial period ending because the manager may have authorized that those actual expenses be incurred in excess of the budgeted amount. One of the most efficient ways of controlling expenses, though somewhat unusual and effective, is to assess the managers' performance by the amount of expenses incurred when compared to the updated budget. In addition, in the government of Canada, only Parliament has the legal right to authorize expenses in excess of the amounts voted previously during the passing of an *Appropriation Act.*

Solution to quiz number twenty-two – General ledger, sub ledgers

* The main sub-divisions of a general ledger are usually the cash journal; the purchases journal; the sales journal; the accounts receivable sub-ledger; fixed assets sub-ledger, etc…

* Another name for the sales sub-ledger is the sales journal.

* Another name for the accounts payable sub-ledger is the accounts payable control account.

* Accounts expected to be found in the purchases sub-ledger are a listing of supplier purchases; and purchases discounts allowed.

* Accounts expected to be found in the sales sub-ledger are items of goods and services sold; sales discounts; and sales returns and allowances.

* One of the main advantages to be derived from using computerized accounts receivable and accounts payable sub-ledgers is the independent checking of these accounts, which may be accomplished electronically first by the internal auditor(s) and afterwards double checked by the external auditor(s).

* It is possible to have *two* valid accounts for the same individual when there may be an account with his or her name in a sub-ledger and a general ledger simultaneously.

* A "running" balance account is a sort of account which is open and carried forward in a balance sheet as long as the firm remains a viable entity or going concern.

* "Set off" is used to clear transactions and/or balances in one account with those in an opposing account. In the government of Canada "set off" may be used to settle an employee's outstanding debt by removing funds at source from the individual's personal account such as her or his pension or salary credit.

* Accounts one would expect to find in a general ledger include: cash journal, purchases journal, sales journal, accounts payable sub-ledger, accounts receivable sub-ledger, fixed assets sub-ledger, other expense, revenue, owners' equity, current liabilities and long-term liabilities.

* Sales and purchases sub-ledgers are usually reconciled against control accounts at the end of each month.

* Should an account receivable show a credit balance at month-end, this could be an error. Though, a sales sub-ledger account which happens to be debited, could represent an adverse entry in a sales ledger, sub-ledger or not.

* The debit control or bank accounts which the Receiver General for Canada maintains are the Receiver General Deposit Control Bank Account; and the Receiver General IS Debit Control Account and sometimes the Receiver General Foreign Exchange Control Account.

* The credit control or bank accounts which the Receiver General for Canada maintains are the Receiver General Payment Control Account, the Receiver General Payroll Account, the Receiver General IS Credit Control Account, and sometimes the Receiver General Foreign Exchange Control Account.

* The main types of financial systems in which the RG control or bank accounts are kept: individual departmental and agency financial systems: CDFS; and the CFMRS, which is operated by the Receiver General.

Solution to quiz number twenty-three – Capital, net profit, net worth, etc.

* Capital may or may not include net profit depending on how long the firm has been operating.

* Drawings should not be deducted from net profits, but from the capital account(s) of the individual(s) who withdrew the cash.

* New capital changes the amount of the total capital held by the firm. Profits however are determined by the difference between income and expenditure.

* Invalid vote suspense, accounts receivable OGD Suspense or accounts payable OGD suspense or accounts payable may be shown ultimately as assets, liabilities, expenses or revenues.

Solution to quiz number twenty-four – Cash flow

* The main purpose of a cash flow statement is to show how much cash the firm had at the beginning of the accounting period under consideration, the exact amount of cash that flowed in, whether from operations or investments, the cash that flowed out, and the balance of cash which existed at the end of the accounting period under consideration.

* Net profit is sometimes treated as an inflow of cash because usually the difference between all income and expense which results in profit, may be directly associated with the net flow cash during the accounting period under consideration.

* The effect on cash flow of a decrease in accounts payable is an increase in cash flow and an increase in inventory is a decrease in cash flow.

* The annual charge for depreciation is usually not included in a cash flow statement because the depreciation of an asset does not necessarily affect the firm's cash flow.

* It is extremely dangerous in the government of Canada for a responsibility manager's career should him or her overspend the 'cash' made available for spending by Parliament or the Treasury Board. "Cash" made available for spending from Parliament or the Treasury Board of Canada is sometimes used synonymously with the amount of authority given.

Solution to quiz number twenty-five – Cash budget

* The main purpose of a cash budget is to monitor continuously the amount of authority or cash inflowing, outflowing and ultimately made available to a decision maker with the delegated authority in the government of Canada or in a private sector organization.

* The figures for a cash budget are usually computed from a combination of the information provided by the budgeted income statement and budgeted balance sheet.

* The phrase 'the usual cycle of receipts and payments' may be defined as the time associated with the usage of cash by operations and/or investments during the accounting period under consideration.

* In a cash budget depreciation is not usually considered; and acquisition of assets is considered as an outflow of or a decrease.

* Accounting ratios help us to understand business results because they are specifically calculated mathematical relationships between relevant elements of assets, liabilities, expenses, revenues and owners' equity. These ratios or relationships can show important trends in the operations of and/or the investments made by the firm.

Solution to quiz number twenty-six – Fundamentals of accounting theory

* The three fundamental elements of accounting theory are assets, liabilities and owners' equity.

* Measurement may be defined as the use of a currency during an accounting and/or financial function.

* Classification and coding may be defined as the separation of financial transactions into a number of specific functions, usually eight (8) or a basic minimum of four (4) in the government of Canada.

* Recording may be defined as maintaining a set of data records of transactions occurring in a firm in words and currency by type(s) of classification. Reporting may be defined as producing a set of condensed information of recorded transactions in a format that is conducive to decision-making by the reader of the same information.

* Accruals may be defined as the matching of the use and ownership of information as it occurs in a firm rather than the spending or receipt of cash associated with a specific economic event. Prudence and probity comprise the combination of that generally accepted accounting principle of overestimating expenses and underestimating revenues. This accounting principle is also called conservatism.

* PSAAB means the Public Sector Accounting and Auditing Board.

Solution to quiz number twenty-seven – Inventory

* Lower; End; Net realizable value; Unit cost.

Solution to quiz number twenty-eight – Income Statement

Income Statement

Fees Income		38,000
Expenses:	Nil	Nil
Supplies Expense	16,000	Nil
Salaries Expense	12,000	Nil
Miscellaneous Expense	7,000	Nil
Total Expenses		35,000
Net Income		3,000

Solution to quiz number twenty-nine

Balance Sheet

ASSETS:	Nil
Current Assets	Nil
Cash	6,000
Accounts Receivable	3,000
Supplies	1,000
Total Current Assets	10,000
Fixed Assets:	Nil
Equipment	14,000
TOTAL ASSETS	**24,000**
LIABILITIES AND OWNERS' EQUITY:	Nil
Current Liabilities:	Nil
Notes Payable	1,500
Accounts Payable	2,500
Total Current Liabilities	4,000
Long Term Liabilities:	Nil
Mortgage Payable	12,000
Total Liabilities	16,000
Capital	8,000
TOTAL LIABILITIES & OWNERS' EQUITY	**24,000**

Solution to quiz number thirty – Closing Entries

Closing Entries

20—			
Dec. 31	Fees Earned	43,000	Nil
	Other Income	20,000	Nil
	Rev. & Exp. Summary	nil	63,000
	Rev. & Exp. Summary	27,000	Nil
	Salary Expense		21,000
	Rent Expense		1,500
	Supplies Expense		2,500
	Depreciation Exp. Computer		1,300
	Office Expense		700

Solutions to Problems

Solution to Problem A – Posting closing entries to ledger accounts

Revenue and Expense Summary			Rent Expense	
4,000	|	6,455	4,000 |	4,000
2,225	|			
150	|			
80	|			

Advertising Expense			Utilities Expense	
2,225	|	2,225	150 |	150

Miscellaneous Expense		
80	|	80

Solution to problem number B --- Owners' Equity, Etc....

* Because the capital account remains the same unless drawings have been taken. Usually any net income or loss (the difference between total income and total expenses for the accounting period under consideration) is added to or subtracted from retained earnings, which in turn is also added to the owners' equity account in total.

* The two major kinds of owners' equity accounts used during an accounting period are capital and retained earnings. Generally in a public sector organization there may be no retained earnings since most public sector firms are non-profit making. Also, the taxpayer investment represents the amount of taxes appropriated by Parliament to a set of programs so that monies may be spent on goods and services for the public and any user fees have been recovered in the process.

* Because in essence any set of activities during an accounting period which transpired may result in some sort of income or expense. The difference has an impact on capital, since the company's capital has been used to generate a profit or loss.

* The balance left in the temporary revenue and expense summary represents the difference between the total of expenses and the total of all revenues incurred by the firm in the accounting period under review. This balance is then transferred to the retained earnings account, the latter of which has a direct impact on the capital account.

* The purpose of striking a post closing trial balance is to make sure that any errors made in the closing entries are noted and corrected.

* Step 1: Enter original data, Step 2: Journalize, Step 3: Post, Step 4: Prove Ledger, Step 5: Trial Balance, Step 6: Make closing entries

Solution to problem number C --- Fundamental elements of accounting

* The fundamental elements of accounting are assets, liabilities and owners' equity.

* A business needs complete accounting records to provide the reader and/or decision maker with a timely, accurate and complete record of the costs associated with the operational, statistical and financial activities of the firm during the accounting period under review.

* A chartered accountant, a designated accountancy professional, is usually a member of the Institute of Chartered Accountants of England and Wales or Scotland or a member of the Canadian Institute of Chartered Accountants. His or her duties include public accounting, auditing and the statutory authority to comment on or sign the audited statement of a firm. A certified management accountant, also a designated professional, is usually a member of the Chartered Management Accountants of the United Kingdom, the Society of Management Accountants of Canada, or the Institute of Management Accountants in the United States. His or her duties focus on managerial accounting. A certified general accountant, also a designated accounting professional, is a member of the Certified General Accountants of Canada. His or her duties may in-

clude public accounting, auditing and managerial accounting.

* An asset is what a firm owns. [The second part of this answer depends on the mix of participants].

* An expense is what a company uses. [Part of this answer depends on the mix of participants].

* A liability is that which a firm owes. [The remainder of this answer depends on the mix in the class].

* A revenue is what a company earns. [The remainder of this answer depends on the mix of participants].

* Owners' equity is what is left over from assets after liabilities are subtracted. It can also be called the stockholders' equity or Investment in Canada.

* Monsieur Filbert's owners' equity is $ 70,000. N. B. Assets – Liabilities = Owners' Equity.

* We need a balance sheet to present in an orderly fashion the asset, liabilities and owners' equity of a business at a particular point in time.

* An accounting item, common to balance sheet and income statement, is the retained earnings, which represents the difference between income and expenses, either for one accounting period stated as net income or net loss.

Solution to problem L-B 1 – Language of business, part 1

This solution to this problem depends mainly on the mix of participants attending.

Solution to problem number L-B 2 – Language of business, part 2

This solution to this problem depends mainly on the mix of participants attending.

Solution to problem number D – McGrunder's Trucking

McGrunder's Trucking

Balance Sheet

As At December 31, 2XX1

ASSETS			LIABILITIES AND OWNERS' EQUITY		
Cash	$	230	Accounts Payable:		
Bank: Caisse Populaire		6,770	Rhona Hardware Supply	$	3,560
Accounts Receivable		2,900	Grand & Toy Office Supply		260
Total Current Assets	$	9,900	Loans Pay: TD Canada Trust		30,000
Office Furniture	$ 6,585		Total Current Liabilities		33,820
Toyota Truck	10,850		Mortgage Payable: BNS		100,000
Off. Bldgs. & Garage 150,000			Owners' Equity:		
Total Fixed Assets		167,435	Sean McGrunder, Capital		43,515
TOTAL ASSETS		$ 177,335	TOTAL LIAB. & OWNRS. EQTY.		$ 177,335

Solution to problem number E – Francine Jardine, CGA

Changed accounting equation:

	Assets	–	Liabilities	=	Owners' Equity
	$ 109,050	–	$ 4,400	=	$ 104,650

Francine Jardine, Certified General Accountant

Balance Sheet

As At January 15, 2XX2

ASSETS			LIABILITIES & OWNERS' EQUITY		
Cash	$	100			
Banque Nationale		3,350	Accounts Payable: Grand & Toy	$	500
Acc. Rec.: Gov't. of Quebec		2,500	Accounts Payable: The Brick		2,850
Inventory: Supplies		9,000	Wages Payable		1,050
Total Current Assets		14,950	Total Current Liabilities		4,400
Toyota Camry		32,750	Owners' Equity:		
Furniture & Fixtures		2,850	Francine Jardine, Capital		101,350
Computer		3,500	Net Income (Ret. Erngs.)		3,300
Premises		55,000	Total Owners' Equity		104,650
Total Fixed Assets		94,100			
TOTAL ASSETS		$ 109,050	TOT. LIAB. & OWNRS. EQTY.		$ 109,050

Solution to Problem F – Passport Office

*   The owner of this business is the Department of Foreign Affairs in the government of Canada.

*   The business has $ 3,500 in cash.

*   The government of Canada owes $ 25.00 to the business.

*   The firm owns no computer equipment.

*   The recorded value of the printing equipment is $ 6,100.

*   The total value of the assets owned by the business is $ 10,975.

*   The business owes money to Grand and Toy and The Queen's Printer.

*   Each creditor is owed $ 40 and $ 1,200 respectively.

*   The business owns $ 9,735 of equity in the assets.

*   The balance sheet was prepared as at January 31, 2XX1.

*   The accounting equation for the Passport Office:

Assets	-	Liabilities	=	Owners' Equity
$ 10,975	-	$ 1,240	=	$ 9,735

Solution to problem number G – Queen's Printer

* The accounting equation for the Queen's Printer:

Assets - Liabilities = Owners' Equity
$ 5,985 - $ 815   = $ 5,170

The Queen's Printer

Balance Sheet

As At June 30, 2XX1

ASSETS		LIABILITIES & INVESTMENT IN CANADA	
Cash	$ 2,800	Accounts Payable:	
Accounts Receivable:		Grand and Toy	$ 345
Canadian Public Service School	110	Toshiba	470
The Passport Office	275	Total Liabilities	815
Inventory: Supplies	250	Investment in Canada	5,170
Total Current Assets	3,435		
Computer	1,950		
Other Equipment	600		
Total Fixed Assets	2,550		
TOTAL ASSETS	$ **5,985**	TOTAL LIAB. & INV. IN CAN. $ **5,985**	

Solution to problem number H – Role of an accountant

* The role of an accountant in a business is to maintain an accurate, a complete and a timely set of records of all business transactions. He or she must also produce a set of financial reports at the end of each accounting period under consideration.

* The answers provided to this question depend upon the mix of participants in each course, working group or workshop.

Solution to problem number I – Classified ads

* The answers to each question depend on the mix of participants in each course, working group or workshop.

Solution to problem number J – Community Garage, Part 1

* Accounting equation for Community Garage:

$$\text{Assets} = \text{Liabilities \& Owners' Equity}$$
$$690,000 = 450,000 + 240,000$$

Community Garage

Balance Sheet

As At April 30, 2XX1

ASSETS		LIABILITIES & OWNERS' EQUITY	
Bank of Nova Scotia	$ 90,000	Accounts Payable:	
Total Current Assets	90,000	Robert Jackson	$ 10,000
Goodwill	50,000	Total Current Liabilities	$ 10,000
Fixed Assets: Building	350,000	Long Term Note Payable:	
Fixed Assets: Land	150,000	Michel Jacques	440,000
Fixed Assets: Equipment	50,000	Total Liabilities	450,000
Total Fixed Assets	550,000	Rosalind Moreau, Capital	240,000
TOTAL ASSETS	$ 690,000	TOTAL LIAB. & OWNRS.EQTY.	$ 690,000

Solution to problem number K – Community Garage, part 2

* Firm's account balance at the Bank of Nova Scotia on May 31, 2XX1 is as follows:

Bank of Nova Scotia

Bal May 1, 2XX1	90,000	JE No. 1	10,000
J E No. 2	20,000	JE No. 3	10,000
J E No. 4	1,000	JE No. 5	5,000
Total	111,000	To balance	86,000
Balance carried forward	86,000	Total	111,000

Community Garage

Balance Sheet

As At May 31, 2XX1

ASSETS		LIABILITIES & OWNERS' EQUITY		
Bank of Nova Scotia	$ 86,000	Accounts Payable:		
Total Current Assets	$ 86,000	Rhona Construction	$ 10,000	
Goodwill	50,000	Bank Street Chrysler	45,000	
Building	370,000	Total Accounts Payable	$ 55,000	
Land	150,000	Long Term Note Payable:		
Equipment	50,000	Michel Jacques	440,000	
Tow Truck	50,000	Total Liabilities	495,000	
Total Fixed Assets	620,000	Rosalind Moreau, Capital	261,000	
TOTAL ASSETS	$ 756,000	TOT. LIAB. & OWNRS' EQTY.	$ 756,000	

Solution to problem number L – Sean Higgins

	Assets		Equals	Liabilities	Plus	Owners' Equity
	Cash	Equipment		Acc. Pay.		S. Higgins, Capital
Opening Bal	900	5000		3000		2900
A		200		200		
B	1000					1000
C	-300			-300		
D	-60					-60
E	-100	100				
F	50	-50				
TOTAL	1490	5250		2900		3840

Solution to problem number M – Transactions and fundamental elements

* The examples suggested by the class participants will depend on the mix of attendees in each relevant course or workshop.

* When an owner invests cash in a business the fundamental elements will increase.

* When cash is received on an accounts receivable the fundamental elements will remain unchanged.

* When an owner withdraws cash from a business the fundamental elements decrease.

* Expenses incurred decrease the owners' equity because expenses **use** part of the equity in a business.

* When cash sales are made the fundamental elements increase.

* A balance sheet is prepared at a specific point in time. An income statement covers a specific accounting period being reported on. The balance sheet shows all the 'open' accounts in a firm. At the end of a specific accounting period being reported on, an income statement closes all revenue and expense accounts into a revenue and expense summary then into one retained earnings account, the latter whose balance is eventually either added to or subtracted from the owners' equity. Both a balance sheet and an income statement are affected by the income or loss generated by a company.

* One statement covers only a specific point in time; whilst the other statement covers an entire accounting period. Both types of information these statements provide are needed by the reader and/or the decision maker.

* The income or loss generated by a firm during an accounting period under review which is being reported on by means of the information presented by both kinds of financial statements.

Solution to problem number N – Debit and credit entries

What Happened	Account Debited	What Happened	Account Credited
Asset increased	Cash	Asset decreased	Inventory: Tools
Liability decreased	Accounts Payable	Asset decreased	Cash
Asset increased	Cash	Asset decreased	Accounts Receivable
Asset increased	Inventory: Tools	Liability increased	Accounts Payable
Asset decreased	Cash	Liability decreased	Accounts Payable
Asset increased	Inventory: Supply	Asset decreased	Cash
Asset increased	Cash	Asset decreased	Accounts Receivable
Asset increased	Inventory	Asset decreased	Cash
Ownrs' equty decr	Wages Expense	Asset decreased	Cash

Debit Entry / *Credit Entry*

Solution to problem number L-B3 – Language of business, part 3

* The solutions suggested to this problem depend partially on the mix, experience and expertise of the participants' course or workshop being conducted at the time.

Solution to problem number O – Effect on accounting equation: A = L + OE

Debit Entry / *Credit Entry*

What happened?	Account debited?	What happened?	Account credited?
A+	Equipment	L+	Acc. Pay.: Staples
A+	Acc Rec T. Lindsay	OE+	Sales Revenue
OE-	Rent Expense	A-	Cash
A+	Cash	OE+	Sales Revenue
A+	Cash	A-	Acc Rec T Lindsay
A+	Cash	OE+	M. Peters, Capital
A+	Cash	OE+	Sales Revenue
OE-	Telephone Exp.	A-	Cash
A+	Acc Rec Mmrl Univ	OE+	Sales Revenue

Solution to problem P – Scratch and Dent Store, St. John

* Total reduction on cost of carload of 500 freezers = 500 x 200 = $100,000. Reduction on cost of sale of 400 freezers = Zero, as the reduction is given on a minimum of a carload of 500 freezers. Reduction on cost of sale 400 + 20% or 480 freezers is also Zero, as reduction applies to 500 freezers. Therefore, if an increased cost of sales' dollars, as a result of a gradual increase in sales, and the gross profit on sales is greater than the loss resulting from not receiving reduction in cost by ordering a carload of freezers, the company should order a carload of freezers.

Solution to problem number Q – Poonabit Shoe Store

* Creating the batch against the sales revenue account resulting in a net sales figure prevents the store manager from knowing exactly how revenues were lost from the bulk of the sales returns.

* The accountant could set up a sales return account in the firm's general ledger.

* Sales returns are [($ 565,000 divided by 2,450,000) multiplied by 100] = 23.06%. If the gross margin on the cost of sales is anywhere near to or less than 23.0%, the sales returns are too high. Do a similar comparison as just was done to determine if they were excessive. Find out if the item produced has become shoddy, or if the trend towards customers purchasing this product is falling off. A marked reduction, therefore, in the production of this item, or an increase in the level of quality control of the end product, could go a long way towards reducing the amount of returned goods. Or it may be the ease with which the customers can return this product should be curtailed.

Solution to problem number R – Sources and uses of funds: ABC Co.

Table R-1 Balance Sheets of ABC Co. (values in 000's of dollars)

	Year 1	Year 2	Year 3	Year 4
Assets:	Nil	Nil	Nil	Nil
Cash	100	200	Nil	100
Loans Receivable	50	110	Nil	60
Acc. Receivable	40	42	Nil	2
Inventories	80	110	Nil	30
Fixed Assets	90	95	Nil	5
Depreciation	(30)	(34)	4	Nil
Total Assets	*330*	*523*		
Lblts & Own Eqty	Nil	Nil	Nil	Nil
Acc. Payable	45	46	1	Nil
Notes Payable	45	45	Nil	Nil
Long Term Debt	20	210	190	Nil
Owners' Equity	220	222	2	Nil
Ttl Lb.& Ow. Ety.	*330*	*523*		

Table R-2 Percentages of Sources and Uses of Funds for ABC Co.

	Thousands of Dollars	**Percentage**
Sources:	Nil	Nil
Depreciation	4	2.03%
Accounts Payable	1	0.075%
Long Term Debt	190	96.72%
Owners' Equity	2	1.18%
Total Sources	197	100.00%
Uses:	Nil	Nil
Cash	100	50.76%
Loans Receivable	60	30.46%
Accounts Receivable	2	1.02%
Inventories	30	15.23%
Fixed Assets	5	2.53%
Total Uses	197	100.00%

Table R-4 Ranking Of Sources And Uses Of Funds For ABC Co.

Rank	Source	Percentage	Rank	Use	Percentage
1	Long Term Debt	96.72	1	Cash	50.19
2	Depreciation	2.03	2	Loans Recvble.	30.46
3	Owners' Equity	1.18	3	Inventories	15.47
4	Acc. Pay.	0.07	4	Fixed Assets	2.53

* The ABC Co. funds the greater percentage of its operations (96.72%) with long term debt. A little more than half (50.19%) is kept in cash and 30.46% on loans. It is unlikely that the return on the investment on the loans outstanding would be as great as the percentage of interest paid to finance its long term debt. In addition, if the cash is held in a bank, the return on funds held in a current and/or savings account, or even in short term debt would generate a return again as high as the percentage of interest most likely levied on the long term debt. ABC Co's funding policies, mainly in the way it dispenses these funds afterwards, needs much to be desired.

Solution to problem number S – Cash required

* Step 1: Cash turnover = 360 days/Cash cycle = 360 days/60 = 6.

* Step 2: Minimum cash required = Annual/expenditures = $ 2,000,000/6 = $ 333,333.

Solution to problem number T – Cash surplus or deficit: Almonte Engineering Works

* Net cash flow = Receipts – Payments: $ 100,000 - $ 60,000 = $40,000.

* Finding cash = Net cash flow + Beginning or opening cash: = $ 40,000 + $ 10,000 = $ 50,000.

* Cash surplus or deficit = Ending cash + Cash reserve: $ 50,000 + $5,000 = $ 55,000.

Therefore, the Almonte Engineering Works has a surplus of $ 33,000 in that particular month.

Solution to problem number AA – Halifax Distributing

* Halifax Distributing: Annual truck depreciation: [$ 65,000 - $ 5,000 = $ 60,000/5] = $ 12,000.

* Therefore, truck depreciation expense for 2XX6 = 9/12 of $ 12,000 = $ 9,000.

* The monthly truck depreciation expense is $ 1,000.

* Balance in accumulated depreciation – delivery truck account at end of 2XX7: = Accumulated depreciation for 2XX6 + accumulated depreciation for 2XX7 = [$ 9,000 + $ 12,000 = $ 21,000].

* Balance in accumulated depreciation for 2XX6: $ 9,000

* Unexpired cost as at Dec 31, 2006 = $ 65,000 - $ 9,000 = $ 56,000.

* Unexpired cost as at Dec 31, 2007 = $ 56,000 - $ 12,000 = $ 44,000.

Solution to problem number LB-4 – Language of business, part 4

* The solutions provided to this problem will depend mainly on the mix, experience and expertise of the participants at the relevant course or workshop at the time.

Solution to problem number LB-5 – Language of business, part 5

* See solution for Problem number LB-4

Solution to problem number BB – Rustic Furniture Store

Rustic Furniture Store

Saskatoon, Saskatchewan

Analysis Of Probable Bad Debt Losses

Credit Sales	2,000,000	3,000,000	4,000,000	4,500,000	Nil
Grs. Smtd. Prft.	500,000	750,000	1,000,000	1,125,000	Nil
Less: Bad Debts	(500,000)	(30,000)	(20,000)	(22,500)	Nil
Net Smtd. Prft.	Nil	720,000	880,000	1,102,500	Choice

Solution to problem number CC – Crown Assets Disposal

Crown Assets Disposal, PWGSC, government of Canada

Sault Ste Marie, Ontario

Alternate Service Delivery for Delivery Truck – Per Unit Cost of operating delivery truck

Operating costs for 2XX5/2XX6:

Depreciation	$ 40,000
Fuel and other expenses	20,000
Insurance	4,400
License	900
Storage	4,800
Drivers' salaries and benefits	133,000
Total operating costs 2XX5/2XX6	$ 203,100

Therefore, operating costs per kilometre = $ 203,100/400,000 = $ .50775 cents per kilometre.

Operating costs per stop: = $ 203,100/250,000 = $ .8124 cents per stop.

Rental expense from National (Tilden) Rent-A-Truck:

Annual charge	$ 12,000
1st 50,000 kilometres @ $ 1.60 per km =	80,000
Next 50,000 kilometres @ $ 1.40 per km =	70,000
Remaining 345,000 kilometres @ $ 1.20 per km	414,000

Total annual cost of rental from National $ 449,500 versus total operating costs of $203,100. Rental from National cost per stop = $ 1.798 per stop.

Rental expenses from Acme Delivery Services: Including pick up and delivery in any area: 250,000 stops at $ 3.00 per stop: $ 750,000.

Conclusively, based on the above analysis, the service should remain with Crown Assets Disposal.

Solutions to problem number DD – FIS accounting standards: Weckworth's Clothiers

Weckworth's Clothiers

Projected Expenses For 200X7

Actual Spent For Nine Months

Advertising	22,080.00
Salaries And Wages	261,370.00
Supplies Used	13,160.00
Sub-Total	296,610.00

	Weckworth's Clothiers		Comparative Industry Based on Weckworth	
	%	Actual $	%	Actual $
Percentage Spent On items:				
Advertising	4.2	52,750	3.0	37,769
Supplies Used	0.7	8,790	1.0	12,557
Salaries And Wages	15.5	194,680	19.5	244,920
	20.4	256,220	23.5	295,246
Left to spend on remaining exps	79.6		76.5	

* Average left to spend on remaining expenses: $[79.6 + 76.5]/2 = 78.1\%$

* Based on Weckworth's Clothiers dollar expenditure for 2007 to date:

   $= 20.4\% \times \$296,610 \ = \ \$60,508.44 \ \times \ 78.1 \ = \ \$4,725,709.17$

Therefore, Weckworth's Clothiers may need an additional approximately $ 4,800,000.00 more in expenditure to complete 2007.

Solution to problem number LB-6 – Language of business, part 6

* The solutions which may be provided to this problem depend mainly on the mix, experience and expertise of the participants in attendance at the particularly delivery of the relevant course or workshop.

Solution to problem number EE – Regal Parking Lot

* This is clearly a problem of a lack of proper internal control. There is no back up person or system covering the attendant. This assumes that the back up individual and the attendant are not working in collusion.

* The manager of the parking lot may: (a) place a machine in the parking lot's attendant's booth which issues a ticket at the time the customer's vehicle leaves the parking lot; and (b) may calculate the amount of money the customer has to pay. These tickets and receipts issued for cash received should both be pre-numbered by the machine, not by the attendant.

* Alternatively, a barrier should be installed at the entrance to the parking lot with a machine which issues tickets. The customer's vehicle should not be able to leave the lot unless he or she places the ticket in another machine, receives a ticket for which he or she has paid the required amount, and the receipt from the paid ticket used to clear the barrier at the exit to the parking lot. This system should be totally mechanized with controls to prevent manipulation by the attendant.

* To determine if a special weekly rate should be established, find out immediately two things: (1) How much the neighbouring malls are charging for their weekly rates; and (2) How much the market will bear for a special weekly rate. Then calculate the amount for a special weekly rate which does not make the parking lot operate at a loss of money and/or customers to the competition should the rate set be too high or two low.

Solution to problem number FF – Northern Supermarket

* Cash receipts should never be kept overnight in a safe. That practice courts disaster. Ask the cashier, while accompanied by a guard, having obtained the commensurate approval to hire the guard's services, to deposit the receipts in the overnight deposit safe which most banks make accessible via one or more of their outside building walls.

* Acquire the necessary executive approval for, request and engage the services of an armoured courier service such as Brinks or Wells Fargo to collect the cash receipts.

Solution to problem number GG – Safeguarding monies

*   Hire a payroll preparation service such as a local financial institution. Submit the required pay information to the bank and ask it to prepare the necessary pay envelopes. Then hire the services of an armoured car firm to pick up the pay envelopes from the bank and deliver them to the branches of the school. As the pay packets are being distributed to the school's employees, use two or more individuals, most likely other armoured service employees, other than those directly involved with handing out the pay packets, after the receipt of each recipient's signature, to assist in the authentication of the school employees' identifications and signature. In addition, hire additional armed security guards to monitor the distribution of pay envelopes.

Solution to problem number HH – Shipment of water coolers

*   Sales discount to be received in the invoice is paid within 30 days: 2% of $ 360,000 = $ 7,200. Compare this with: 6% interest on $ 300,000 for 20 days [20/365 x 6 x 100 x $ 300,000] = $ 986.30.

*   Since it would appear that savings could be as much as [$ 6,000.00 - $ 986.30] or $ 5,013.70, Mr. Warren may be well advised to accept the sales discount.

Solution to problem number II – Tugs and Lighters Canada

2XX1

April 15 Dr. Operating Expense	$ 2,500		B11A/B12A	11XX
Dr.GST Refundable Advance	125		G111	8171
Cr. Accounts Payable		$ 2,625	R 300	8299

To record the purchase and receipt of supplies plus GST levied from Marine Merchants Ltd. on April 15, 2XX1.

April 25 Dr. Accounts Payable	$ 2,625	21111 R300 8299
Cr. Receiver General Payment Control Account	$ 2,625	62DDD R300 6299

To record the settlement of invoice for $ 2,625 (including 5% GST) with Marine Merchants Ltd. on April 25, 2XX1.

Solution to problem number JJ – Greenhouses Canada

2XX6

April 01 Dr. Building		$ 500,000
HST Refundable Advance		65,000
Cr. Receiver General Payment Control Account		$ 565,000

To record purchase of a building on April 01, 2XX6, with payment and HST (13%) also recorded.

2XX6

Sept 30 Dr. Amortization Expense – Building	$ 25,000
Cr. Accumulated Amortization – Building	$ 25,000

To record amortization of building for a 6-month period from April 01, 2XX6 to Sept 30, 2XX6.

2XX7

March 31 Dr. Accumulated Amortization – Building	$ 50,000
Receiver General – Deposit Control Account	150,000
Accounts Receivable – Private Parks	186,000
Loss On Sale Of Building	150,000
Cr. Building	$ 500,000
HST Refundable Advance (13%)	36,000

To record sale of a building on September 30, 2XX6 for $ 300,000, $150,000 received in cash, the remainder to be settled later on.

2XX7

June 05 Dr. Salaries And Wages Expense	$ 35,000
Employee Benefit Plan	15,000
Cr. Accrued Salaries, Wages And Benefits	$ 50,000

To accrue salaries, wages and benefits of $ 50,000 on June 05, 2XX7 which are payable at the end of the ensuring pay period on June 15, 2XX7.

Solutions to Case Studies

Solution to case study number one – Morris Fenty's bowling alley and the bank

* The bank would request a list of assets and liabilities of the business before it makes a decision because: From this list would be seen the total current assets and liabilities, giving the bank a picture of the company's working capital, its liquidity and owners' equity situation in detail.

* Morris Fenty should have submitted a balance sheet, a cash flow statement, an income statement and a sources and uses statement.

* The bank may also consider a business plan, a cash flow budget, a marketing plan, an operating budget, and a statement of how Morris Fenty proposes to finance the additional capital expenditure needed to construct the four additional lanes.

Solution to case study number two – Gaspe Gift and Flower shop and its working capital

* Not really. As it stands, the flower shop is not only in a deficit liquid situation [$ 2,500 – $ 6,500 = ($ 4,000)], but most of its working capital is tied up in $ 15,500 of inventories, $ 15,000 of which are for sale.

Solution to case study number three – Oak Bay Cleaners and Window Washers

* Types of revenues: window washing; window repair; and probably miscellaneous revenue.

* Types of expenses: wages incurred; cleaning supplies used; cleaning

equipment used: depreciation of cleaning equipment; repair supplies used; and miscellaneous expenses.

* Expenses should never be netted out against revenues, creating a sort of 'hash' total or account balance.

* Various expense and revenue accounts should be separated so that each type of expense and each type of revenue may be monitored separately. Purchases returns accounts and sales allowed discounts should be also created and expenses like salaries and wages should be accounted for separately in order that any statutory deductions may be accounted for, reported to and settled periodically with Canada Revenue Agency.

* Keep journals and ledgers, the latter with individual accounts, which may include those for the bank, any accounts receivable and/or payable, inventories, fixed assets and the owners' equity, to show any capital the owner(s) may provide to the business to maintain its operational viability.

Solution to case study number four – Jean Phillipe and the Mayfair Dress Shoppe

* The security of regular employment and a probable regular pay cheque; and not being liable for the losses of the Dress Shoppe.

* Independence, in order to escape the possible cloying influence of a master-servant relationship often foisted by an employer on an employee.

* Advantage: Will probably reap the benefits of ownership; Disadvantage: May have to suffer the pangs of complete liability that can befall a sole business owner, unless the firm is incorporated as a business with limited liability.

* Cash for working capital, including inventories, and fixed assets.

* Enough to support items mentioned in the previous answer.

* Investigate similar businesses; collate the necessary information; compare and contrast; and then execute.

* Other sources may include: friends, relatives, business associates and the general public.

* Janine is the most likely person to lose money.

Solution to case study number five --- Jean and Vincento

* Jean's business depends more on his skill, but is also more labour intensive.

* Vincente's business also depends on his skill. However, operating an auto repair maintenance facility is more machine intensive than labour intensive.

* So on the face of it, at first blush; it would appear that Vincente's firm would need more capital.

Solution to case study number six – Anderson at Acadia

* Not so feasible an idea. In partnerships of three, invariably, two of the partners, even after starting with the best of intentions, but mostly in times of crises, will "gang up" on the third member of the partnership.

* The individual(s) who has (have) invested the greater percentage in the partnership, especially if the partnership agreement has stated that the partners would share in the profits and/or losses according to their percentage of contribution to the partnership.

* If the firm were a registered as a company with limited liability. Then the onus would be on the company itself instead of only Mr. Andrews.

Solution to case study number seven – HR Management

* At some level the human resource manager must put some trust in the information which he/she receives from the applicant to support the job application.

* The human resource manager can do one of five or all of the following: He/she can either call at random, not necessarily all of them, but one or more of the references the applicant has supplied. Or he/she can ask the references to submit actual letters of reference. Or he/she can call individuals at the applicant's last place(s) of employment who would know of the applicant's true experience and/or expertise, and not necessarily those names supplied by the applicant. Or he/she may ask the second set of references to supply letters of reference. Or he/she may contact

the educational and professional institutions from which the applicant has said that he/she has obtained the relevant educational qualifications or professional designations so as to verify their accuracy.

Solution to case study number eight – Maria Corleone's Bakery

* Significant changes include: an increase in the amount of the mortgage due; a reduction in the current liabilities; a decrease in Maria Corleone's capital investment; an increase in the amount of cash available to the company; and a decrease in the amount of accounts receivable.

* A continual decrease in Maria Corleone's capital and an increase in the size of the mortgage.

* A proper set of income statements should be kept detailing revenues and expenses.

* Maria Corleone should desist from making drawings on owners' equity. She may, however, make these drawings from any income the bakery makes.

* Funding by incurring long term debt should be curtailed.

* The markets for its products and the company's pricing strategy should be also analyzed.

Solution to case study number nine – Auditor's Report

* During an audit of a firm's books, an independent verification of the balances found in the accounts payable and accounts receivable sub ledgers contribute to effective internal control.

* This may not be necessary, unless there exists a trend or pattern of continuous differences between the firm's balances in the various accounts and that held by the customers. Otherwise, a cut off method where accounts will be investigated may be based on the size and/or age of the particular account.

Solution to case study number ten – Situation, GAAP, Statutory Authority, Accounting Method

Situation	GAAP Principle	Statutory Authority	Accounting Method
Mistake of a 0.05 cent error repeats itself 50 times on a regular basis	Consistency	Not applicable	Analysis and reversal
Contract for a 25K is struck	Not applicable	Fin. Admin. Act.	Not applicable
Budgetary expense exceeds budgetary revenue significantly	Conservatism	Not applicable	Not applicable

Solution to case study number eleven – BNA and CRF

* The CRF and how it functions in the government of Canada was not really affected by the repatriation of the Canadian Constitution.

* The Governor General is very important to the availability of funds when Supply is generated. If a budget is not voted by Parliament, the Governor General through an Order-in-Council may authorize a Special Warrant, making available the necessary funds to carry on the business of government. At the time, the size of the CRF is temporarily increased.

* The Minister of Finance is ultimately responsible for the current level of the CRF, at times borrowing the necessary funding either internally or externally.

Solution to case study number twelve – Ice Roads

* Yes, ice roads may be recorded as fixed assets in the books of the Canadian Coast Guard or Fisheries and Oceans Canada or the government of Canada, as long as the asset involved has an estimated useful life of more than one year.

* These assets would be more than likely subject to amortization.

* The financial policy and rule making organizations most likely to provide the guiding policies within the government of Canada are *the Canadian Institute of Chartered Accountants, the Public Sector Accounting and Auditing Board, and the Treasury Board of Canada.*

Solution to case study number thirteen – Westminster Model

* The very high level organization in a government adapting the Westminster Model such as Canada which may seem to have the same dual roles in the appointment and hiring process is the human resource section of the government's civil or public service commission.

* A deputy minister is officially a hired public servant.

* A reasonable reaction would be to replace the missing employees with public servants via the official hiring and firing process.

Solution to case study number fourteen – Department QRS

* The resulting role play may depend on the mix, experience and expertise of the participants.

* Specifically: strategic management may be compared to the Fiscal Plan; management control to the Annual Reference Level Update (ARLU), and operational control to The Estimates.

Solution to case study number fifteen – MacGregor's Automobile Repair Shop

* MacGregor should hire either a bookkeeper or an accountant to create a complete set of accounting records, at a minimum journals and ledgers for the business so as to help him with this important decision.

Solution to case study to number sixteen – Inter Provincial Trucking

* Equipment wears out, thus creating more annual expense for the company and needs to be replaced, causing a need for capital expenditure. A set of records based on the life cycle of each bit of equipment in the company may be necessary.

* A detailed record of each asset in a fixed asset sub-ledger should be kept.

Solution to case study number seventeen - PWGSC Coding Block

* PWGSC has developed a standardized coding block with a limited size of 22 digits. This coding block is always in a state of redevelopment because of the need for constant flexibility in the classification and coding system of the government of Canada.

* Oracle may be similar in some respects as a private sector developed system such as GMAX and SAP. CDFS has however been designed and developed by PWGSC. Its predecessor was named FINCON, or FINFO according to Correctional Services Canada.

* Computer generated tables and files are used.

* These apparent 'missing' fields may be calculated and or derived by way of imposed coding and by the use of computer generated tables and files.

Solutions to Projects

Solution to project number one – Eaton Employment Service

Dr. Cash	2,400	
Dr. Accounts Receivable	905	
Dr. Fixed Assets	1,595	
Cr. Accounts Payable		430
Cr. Owners' Equity		4,470

To make opening entries recording company's assets, liabilities and owners' equity as at October 1, 2XX1.

Cash	Acc.Rec.: Le Roi	Acc. Rec.: Tyres Inc.	Furniture	Office Eqpt.
Oct 1 2400	160	525	150	380		1,270		325	
nil	560		2,005		750	200 560
Oct 5 2,400	600				
nil	160				
Oct 11 5,900| 130				
Oct 18 850| 150				
nil	100				
Oct 23 150| 230				
Oct 26 1,800| 120				
Oct 30 600|				

Rent Expense	J. Sauve: Drawings	Advertising Expense
Oct 1 160		Oct 8 600|	Oct 9 160	
nil	Oct 25 100		Oct 30 120	

Hydro Expense	Acc. Pay. L.Pariseau	J. Sauve, Capital
Oct 29 230		Oct 12 130	Oct 16 430	|Oct 1 4,470

Sales	Acc. Rec: Rex Co. Ltd.	Telephone Expense
nil	240	Oct 1 240		Oct 27 150|

nil	2,400
nil	5,900
nil	2,005
nil	850
nil	600
nil	1,800

Eaton Employment Service

Working Papers, As At October 01, 2XX1

Trial Balance; Income Statement; Balance Sheet

Accounts	Trial Balance	Income Statement	Balance Sheet
Cash	11,890	nil	11,890
Acc. Rec.: Le Roi	375	nil	375
Acc. Rec.: Tyres	2,385	nil	2,385
J. Sauve, Drawings	700	nil	700
Advertising Exp.	280	280	nil
Rent Expense	160	160	nil
Hydro Expense	230	230	nil
Acc Pay L. Pariseau	(850)	nil	(850)
J. Sauve, Capital	(4,470)	nil	(4,470)
Sales	(13,795)	(13,795)	nil
Telephone Exp	150	150	nil
Acc Rec: Rex Ltd.	240	nil	240
Furniture	1,820	nil	1,820
Office Equipment	885	nil	885
Sub-Totals	nil	(12,975)	12,975
Balancing items:	nil	nil	nil
Inc. for Oct., 2XX1	nil	12,975	(12,975)
Grand Totals	nil	nil	nil

Eaton Employment Service
Income Statement
For The Period October 01 to 31, 2XX1

Income:	$	$
Sales	13,795	-
Total Income	-	13,795
Expenses:	-	-
Advertising Expense	280	nil
Hydro Expense	230	nil
Rent Expense	160	nil
Telephone Expense	150	nil
Total Expenses		820
Net Income For Oct, 2XX1		12,975

Balance Sheet
As At October 31, 2XX1

ASSETS:	$	LIAB & OWN. EQTY.	$
Cash	11,890	Acc Pay L. Pariseau	850
Acc Rec: Le Roi & Co.	375	Total Liabilities	850
Acc Rec: Tyres Inc.	2,385	Owners' Equity:	nil
Acc Rec: Rex Ltd	240	Retained earnings	12,975
Total Acc. Rec.	3,000	J. Sauve, Capital	3,770
Fixed Assets:	nil	Total Owners Eqty.	16,745
Furniture	1,820		
Office Equipment	885		
Total Fixed Assets	2705		
TOTAL ASSETS	17,595	TOTAL LIAB. & O.E.	17,595

Solution to project number two – Department PQR

*   No accounting entries are required when: Parliament votes appropriations; Treasury Board approves allotments; or when funds are committed under Section 32 of the *Financial Administration Act.*

*   Calculation of Investment in Canada:

Accounts	Balances
Cash	5,000
Imprest Cash	20,000
Departmental Bank Account	150,000
Receiver General Deposit Control	750,000
Receiver General Payment Control	(310,000)
Receiver General Payroll Control	(350,000)
Receiver General IS Debit Control	800,000
Receiver General IS Credit Control	(300,000)
Receiver General Foreign Exchange Ctr.	15,000
Other Control Accounts	780,000
Accounts Payable: Rhona Hardware	(500,000)
Land And Buildings	2,600,000
Furniture And Fixtures	500,000
Computers	700,000
Accrued Salaries	(2,300,000)
Accum. Amort. – Land And Buildings	(700,000)
Accum. Amort. – Furniture & Fixtures	(210,000)
Accum. Amort. – Computers	(250,000)
Office Supplies Inventory	210,000
Materiel Inventory	850,000
Work In Progress Inventory	950,000
Finished Goods Inventory	850,000
Prepaid Rent	895,000
Prepaid Insurance	485,000
Accrued Vacation Liability	(2,500,000)
Investment In Canada	(3,140,000)
TOTAL	NIL

* Required adjusting entries:

Dr. Computers	250,000	
Cr: Accounts Payable – Dell Computers		250,000

Purchased computer system on credit from Dell Computers.

Dr. Salaries Expense	370,000	
Cr. Accrued Salaries		370,000

To accrue the bi-weekly salary bill.

Dr. Accrued Salaries	368,857	
Cr. RG Payroll Control Account		368,857

To pay the actual bi-weekly salary bill.

Dr. Accounts Receivable – OGD Dept X	2,500,000	
Dr. Accounts Receivable – BC Govt.	1,600,000	
Cr. Non-Tax Revenue		4,100,000

Sales for cash and credit to Department PX ($ 2,500,000) and the British Columbia government ($ 1,600,000) respectively.

Dr. Bad Debts Expense	1,517,000	
Cr. Allowance For Doubtful Accounts		1,517,000

37% of receivables (37% of $ 4,100,000) proves uncollectible.

Dr. Amortization Expense: Land & Buildings	44,000	
Dr. Amortization Expense: Furniture & Fixtures	55,000	
Dr. Amortization Expense: Computers	140,000	
Cr. Accumulated Amortization: Land & Buildings		44,000
Cr. Accumulated Amortization: Furniture & Fixtures		55,000
Cr. Accumulated Amortization: Computers		140,000

To record amortization of fixed assets for one fiscal year.

Dr. Material Supplies Inventory	600,000	
Cr. Receiver General Payment Control Account		300,000
Cr. Accounts Payable: Rhona Hardware		300,000
Dr. Accounts Payable: Rhona Hardware	100,000	
Cr. Receiver General Payment Control Account		100,000

Purchase of supplies from and partial settlement of account with Rhona Hardware.

Dr. Materials Used [Expense]	930,000	
Cr. Materiel Inventory		930,000

Calculation of materials used during fiscal year as follows:

Materiel inventory as at April 1, 2XX7	$ 850,000
Add: Purchases	600,000
Total available for use	1,450,000
Transfers to Work In Progress	(150,000)
Amount left after transfers	1,300,000
Less: balance as at 31/12/2XX8	(370,000)
Amount used during fiscal year	930,000

Dr. Finished Goods Inventory	700,000	
Cr. Work In Progress Inventory	700,000	

Calculation of amounts transferred to finished goods inventory as follows:

Work In Progress Inventory as at 1/4/2XX7	950,000
Add: transfers from materiel inventory	150,000
Total available for use	1,100,000
Less: balance as at 31/12/2XX8	(400,000)
Amount transferred to Finished Goods	700,000

Dr. Cost of goods available for sale	1,050,000	
Cr. Finished goods inventory		1,050,000

Calculation of amounts transferred to cost of goods available for sale as follows:

Finished goods inventory as at April 01, 2XX7	850,000
Add: transfers from work in progress inventory	700,000
Total available for use	1,550,000
Less: balance as at December 31, 2XX8	(500,000)
Transfers to cost of goods available for sale	1,050,000

Journal Entries Comprising Prepaid Items

Dr. Accrued Salaries	368,857	
Cr. Receiver General Payroll Control Account		368,857

Acual payroll paid as per paylist from PWGSC.

Dr. Office Supplies Inventory	80,000	
Cr. R.G. Payment Control		80,000

Purchase of supplies inventory for cash.

Dr. Office Supplies Expense	120,000	
Cr. Office Supplies Inventory		120,000

Usage of office supplies inventory

Dr. Prepaid Rent   250,000
   Cr. R. G. Payment Control   250,000
Prepayment of rent

Dr. Rent Expense   350,000
   Cr. Prepaid Rent   350,000
Usage of rent expense

Dr. Prepaid Insurance   360,000
   Cr. R, G, Payment Control   360,000
Prepayment of insurance

Dr. Insurance Expense   250,000
   Cr. Prepaid Insurance   250,000
Usage of insurance expense.

Other adjusting journal entries

Dr. Computers   250,000
   Cr. Accounts Payable – Dell Computers   250,000
Purchased computer system on credit from Dell Computers

Dr. Salaries Expense   370,000
   Cr. Accrued Salaries   370,000
To accrue the bi-weekly salary bill

Dr. Accounts Receivable – OGD Dept X   2,500,000
   Accounts Receivable – BC Govt.   1,600,000
   Cr. Non-tax revenue   4,100,000
Sales for cash and credit to Dept X ($ 2,500,000) and the BC Government
respectively ($ 1,600,000)

Dr. Bad Debts Expense   1,517,000
   Cr. Allowance for Doubtful Accounts   1,517,000
37% of Receivables (37% of $4,100,000) proves uncollectible

Dr. Amortization Expense: Land & Bldgs.   44,000
   Amortization Expense: Furn & Fxtrs   55,000
   Amortization Expense: Computers   140,000
   Cr. Accm. Amort: Land & Bldgs   44,000
      Accm. Amort: Furn & Fxtrs   55,000
      Accm. Amort: Computers   140,000
To record amortization of assets for one year

Dr. Material Supplies Inventory   600,000
   Cr. RG Payment Control Account   300,000
      Acc. Pay. Rhona Hardware   300,000
Dr. Acc. Pay. Rhona Hardware   100,000
   Cr., RG Payment Control Account   100,000

Purchase of supplies and partial settlement of account with Rhona

Dr: Materials Used [Expense]	930,000	
Cr. Material Inventory		930,000

Calculation of materials used during the fiscal year as follows:

Material inventory as at April 1, 2XX7	850,000	
Add: Purchases	600,000	
Total available for use		1,450,000
Less: Transfers to Work in Progress		-150,000
Amount left after transfers		1,300,000
Less: Balance as at March 31, 2XX8		-370,000
Amount used during fiscal year		930,000

Dr. Finished Goods Inventory	700,000
Cr. Work in Progress Inventory	700,000

Calculation of amounts transferred to finished goods inventory as follows:

Work in Progress Invenory as at April 1, 2XX7	950,000
Add: transfers from materiel inventory	150,000
Total available for use	1,100,000
Less: Balance as at March 31, 2XX8	-400,000
Amount transferred to Finished Goods	700,000

Dr. Cost of goods available for sale	1,050,000	
Cr. Finished goods inventory		1,050,000

Calculation of amounts transferred to cost of goods available for sale as follows:

Finished goods inventory as at April 1, 2XX7	850,000
Add: transfers from work in progress inventory	700,000
Total available for use	1,550,000
Less: balance as at December 31, 2XX8	-500,000
Transfers to cost of goods available for use	1,050,000

Dr. Salaries and wages expense	40,000	
Fixed assets – furniture and fixtures	20,000	
Supplies expense	15,000	
Cr. PAYE		75,000

To set up the PAYE liability as at March 31, 2XX8.

* Ledger (T) accounts:

			Balance
Cash			
5,000			5,000

Imprest Cash			Balance
20,000			20,000

Departmental Bank Account
150,000 | 150,000

Receiver General Deposit Control
750,000 | 750,000

Acc. Rec. OGD Department X
2,500,000 | 2,500,000

Acc. Rec. British Columbia Government
1,600,000 | 1,600,000

Non-Tax Revenue
| 4,100,000 4,100,000

Acc. Pay. Dell Computers
| 250,000 250,000

Acc. Pay. Rhona Hardware
100,000 | 500,000
| 300,000 700,000

Materials Used [Expense]
930,000 | 930,000

Bad Debts Expense
1,517,000 | 1,517,000

Allowance for Doubtful Accounts
| 1,517,000 1,517,000

Cost of Goods Available
1,050,000 | 1,050,000

Receiver General Payment Control
| 310,000
| 100,000
| 360,000
| 80,000
| 250,000
| 300,000 1,400,000

Receiver General Payroll Control
| 350,000
| 368,857 718,857

Receiver General Foreign Xchange Cntrl
15,000 | 15,000

Other Control Accounts
780,000 | 780,000

Fixed Assets: Land and Buildings
2,600,000 | 2,600,000

Receiver General IS Debit Control Account
800,000 | 800,000

Receiver General IS Credit Control Account
| 300,000 300,000

* Ledger (T) accounts (continued):

Fixed Assets: Furniture & Fixtures

500,000	
20,000	**520,000**

Fixed Assets: Computers

700,000	
250,000	**950,000**

Amortization Expense: Land & Buildings

44,000	**44,000**

Amortization Expense: Furniture & Fixtures

55,000	**55,000**

Amortization Expense: Computers

140,000	**140,000**

Accumulated Amortization: Land & Bldgs

	700,000	
	44,000	**744,000**

Accumulated Amortization: Furn & Fxtrs

	210,000	
	55,000	**265,000**

Accumulated Amortization: Computers

	250,000	
	140,000	**390,000**

Accrued Salaries

368,857	2,300,000	
	370,000	**2,301,143**

Prepaid Rent

895,000	350,000	
250,000		**795,000**

Prepaid Insurance

485,000	250,000	
360,000		**595,000**

Materiel Inventory

850,000	930,000	
600,000		**520,000**

Work-in-Progress Inventory

950,000	700,000	**250,000**

Finished Goods Inventory

850,000	1,050,000	
700,000		**500,000**

Office Supplies Inventory

210,000	120,000	
80,000		**170,000**

Accrued Vacation Liability

2,500,000	**2,500,000**

Salaries and Wages Expense

40,000		
370,000		**410,000**

Rent Expense

350,000	**350,000**

Insurance Expense

250,000	**250,000**

Office Supplies Expense

120,000	
15,000	**135,000**

Payable-At-Year-End

75,000	**75,000**

Investment in Canada

3,140,000	**3,140,000**

Department PQR   **Working Papers**   **R. C. Number 203578**

For Fiscal Year Ending March 31, 2XX8

Accounts Title	Adjusted Trial Balance Dr.	Adjusted Trial Balance Cr.	Income Statement Dr.	Income Statement Dr.	Balance Sheet Dr.	Balance Sheet Cr.
Cash	5,000				5,000	
Imprest Cash	20,000				20,000	
Departmental Bank Account	150,000				150,000	
Acc. Rec. OGD Department X	2,500,000				2,500,000	
Acc. Rec. B. C. Government	1,600,000				1,600,000	
Non-Tax Revenue		4,100,000		4,100,000		
Acc. Pay. Dell Computers		250,000				250,000
Acc. Pay. Rhona Hardware		700,000				700,000
Materials Used [Expense]	930,000		930,000			
Bad Debts Expense	1,517,000		1,517,000			
Receiver General Deposit Control	750,000				750,000	
Allowance For Doubtful Accounts		1,517,000				1,517,000
Cost Of Goods Available For Sale	1,050,000		1,050,000			
Receiver General Payment Control		1,400,000				1,400,000
Receiver General Payroll Control		718,857				718,857
Receiver General Forgn Xchnge Control	15,000				15,000	
Receiver General IS Debit Control	800,000				800,000	
Receiver General IS Credit Control		300,000				300,000
Other Control Accounts	780,000				780,000	
Fixed Assets: Land and Buildings	2,600,000				2,600,000	
Fixed Assets: Furniture & Fixtures	520,000				520,000	
Fixed Assets: Computers	950,000				950,000	
Amort 'Expense: Land & Buildings	44,000		44,000			
Amort Expense: Furniture & Fixures	55,000		55,000			
Amort Expense: Computers	140,000		140,000			
Accum. Amort: Land & Buildings		744,000				744,000
Accum. Amort: Furniture & Fixtures		265,000				265,000
Accum. Amort: Computers		390,000				390,000
Accrued Salaries		2,301,143				2,301,143
Prepaid Rent	795,000				795,000	
Prepaid Insurance	595,000				595,000	
Materiel Inventory	520,000				520,000	
Work in Progress Inventory	250,000				250,000	
Finished Goods Inventory	500,000				500,000	
Office Supplies Inventory	170,000				170,000	
Accrued Vacation Liability		2,500,000				2,500,000
Payable-At-Year-End [PAYE]		75,000				75,000
Investment in Canada		3,140,000				3,140,000
Salaries and Wages Expense	410,000		410,000			
Rent expense	350,000		350,000			
Office Supplies Expense	135,000					
Insurance Expense	250,000		250,000			
Sub-Total Expenses			4,881,000			
Net Loss for 2XX7/2XX8			-781,000		781,000	
Totals	18,401,000	18,401,000	4,100,000	4,100,000	14,301,000	14,301,000

Department PQR – R. C. Number 203578

Income Statement For Fiscal Year Ending March 31, 2XX8

	$	$	$
Income:			
Non-Tax Revenue		4,100,000	
Total Income			4,100,000
Less: Cost of Goods Sold			-1,050,000
Net Income			3,050,000
Expenses:			
Material Used (Expense)	930,000		
Bad Debts Expense	1,517,000		
Amortization Expense: Land & Bldgs	44,000		
Amortization Expense: Furn, & Fxtrs.	55,000		
Amortization Expense: Computers	140,000		
Rent Expense	350,000		
Insurance Expense	250,000		
Office Supplies Expense	135,000		
Salaries and Wages Expense	410,000		
Total Expenses			*3,831,000*
Net Loss for Fiscal Year 2XX7/2XX8			*-781,000*

Department PQR – R. C. Number 203578

Balance Sheet As At March 31, 2XX8

Assets:	$	$	$
Current Assets:			
Cash and Bank			
Cash	5,000		
Imprest Cash	20,000		
Departmental Bank Account	150,000		
Receiver General Deposit Control Account	750,000		
Receiver General Payment Control Account		1,400,000	
Receiver General Payroll Control Account		718,857	
Receiver General IS Debit Control Account	800,000		
Receiver General IS Credit Control Account		300,000	
Receiver General Foreign Exchange Control Account	15,000		
Other Control Accounts	780,000		
Sub-Total Cash and Bank		101,143	
Accounts Receivable – OGD X	2,500,000		
Accounts Receivable – British Columbia Government	1,600,000		
Less: Allowance for Doubtful Accounts	-1,517,000		
Net Accounts Receivable		2,583,000	

Prepaid Insurance	595,000		
Prepaid Rent	795,000		
Sub-Total Prepaids		1,390,000	
Materiel Inventory	520,000		
Work in Progress Inventory	250,000		
Finished Goods Inventory	500,000		
Office Supplies Inventory	170,000		
Sub-Total Inventory		1,440,000	
Total Current Assets		5,514,143	
Fixed Assets:			
Land and Buildings	2,600,000		
Less: Accumulated Amortization	-744,000		
Furniture and Fixtures	520,000		
Less: Accumulated Amortization	-265,000		
Computers	950,000		
Less: Accumulated Amortization	-390,000		
Total Fixed Assets		2,671,000	
Total Assets			**8,185,143**
Liabilities and Owners' Equity:			
Current Liabilities:			
Accounts Payable – Dell Computers	250,000		
Accounts Payable – Rhona Hardware	700,000		
Payable-At-Year-End [PAYE]	75,000		
Accrued Salaries	2,301,143		
Total Current Liabilities		3,326,143	
Long Term Liabilities:			
Accrued Vacation Liability	2,500,000		
Total Long Term Liabilities		2,500,000	
Owners' Equity:			
Investment in Canada	3,140,000		
Less: Loss for Fiscal Year 2XX1/2XX2	-781,000		
Net Owners' Equity		2,359,000	
Total Liabilities and Owners' Equity			**8,185,143**

Bibliography

Accountable Advance Regulations, Receiver General for Canada

Accounting and Financial Systems, Receiver General for Canada

Accounting Standards, 1.1., 1.2., 1.3., 3.1., Treasury Board of Canada

Annual Reference Level Update (ARLU) System – User Guide, August, 2006, Treasury Board Secretariat

Annual Report to Parliament, 1984, Office of the Auditor General for Canada

Annual Report to Parliament, 2005, Office of the Auditor General for Canada

Atack, Jim, Ph. D., Headley, Glyden O., CMA, *"Have Accountants Failed Government,"* Cost and Management Accounting, January, 1984

"Bank Facilities System (BFS) and Departments", Receiver General for Canada Manual, Chapter 5, Treasury Board of Canada

Blake, J. D.: *"The Concise Guide to Interpreting Accounts"*, 1st Edition, von-Nostrand, Reinhart, London, 1989

Blazenko, G. and Scott, W. R., *"A Model of Standard Setting and Auditing"*, Contemporary Accounting Research, Fall, 1968, pages 68 to 92.

Brown, Richard, Ed., *"A History of Accounting and Accountants"*, Edinburgh, 1905

Calhoun, George M., *"The Business Life of Ancient Athens"*, Chicago, University of Chicago Press, 1926

Canada-Aboriginal Peoples Roundtable Follow-up Session on Accountability, *Summary of Outcomes,* January 25 – 26, 2005, Ottawa, Canada

Castle, E. F., and Owens, N. P. [Revised by Geoffrey Whitehead, B. Sc. (Econ)], *Principles of Accounts, 9th Edition,* The M & E Handbook Series, Pitman Publishing, United Kingdom

Chapter 5, "Bank *Facilities System (BFS) and Departments"; Chapter 10, "Departmental and Central Accounting Entities under Full FIS"*, Receiver General for Canada Manual, Treasury Board of Canada

Chart of Accounts for the Financial Reporting Authority for Fiscal Year, 2004-2005, Treasury Board of Canada

Chart of Accounts Manual, Treasury Board of Canada

Charko, Phil, Ph. D., Headley, Glyden O., CMA, Johri, Hari, Ph. D., *"Transfer Pricing in the Public Sector"*, Cost and Management Accounting, July/August, 1991

Chiera, Edward, *"They Wrote on Clay"*, Chicago: University of Chicago Press, 1938

CICA Handbook, Canadian Institute of Chartered Accountants, Toronto

Comptrollership Manual, Treasury Board of Canada

Debt Write-off Regulations, 1994 (Pursuant to Section 25(1) of the Financial Administration Act, Receiver General for Canada

Departmental and Agency Financial Statements, Treasury Board Accounting Standard, 1.2, Treasury Board of Canada

Donaldson, Ian R., Mallin, Chris, A. *"The Business of Accounting and Finance Blueprint"*, Blackwell Business, Great Britain, 1993

Financial Administration Act, Section 34(b)

Financial Information Strategy Manual, Treasury Board of Canada

FIS Transition Protocol, Treasury Board of Canada

Glauthier, M. W. E. and Underdown, B, *Accounting Theory and Practice,* 4th Edition, London: Pitman, 1991

Greysbeck, John Bart, *Ancient Double Entry Bookkeeping: Luca Pacioli's Treatise.* Denver: University of Colorado, 1914

Groppelli, A. A., and Nikbath, Ehsan, *Business Review Books, Finance,* Barron's Educational Series, Hauppage, New York, U. S. A., 2000

Kaulea, Henry J., *Elements of Accounting,* Gregg Publishing, 1959

Keister, Orville R., *Commercial Record-Keeping in Ancient Mesopotamia"*, Accounting Review 38 (April, 1963), pp 371-376.

Littleton, A. C., *Accounting Evolution to 1900,* New York: American Institute Publishing Co., 1933

"Payables at Year-End (PAYE) for FIS and non-FIS departments", Information Bulletin of January 27, 2000, Treasury Board of Canada

Pergallo, Edward: *Origin and Evolution of Double Entry Bookkeeping: A Study of Italian Practice from the Fourteenth Century,* New York: American Publishing Institute, Co., 1938

Policy on the Application of the Goods and Services Tax and the Harmonized Sales Tax in the Departments and Agencies of the government of Canada for FIS Compliant Departments and Agencies, Treasury Board of Canada

Policy on Classification and Coding of Financial Transactions, Treasury Board of Canada

Policy on Specified Purpose Accounts – Appendix A Sections 2, 4, 6 and 7, Treasury Board of Canada

PSAAC Handbook, Canadian Institute of Chartered Accountants, Toronto, Canada

Public Accounts of Canada, 2005-2006, Receiver General for Canada

Report of the Committee on the Modernization of Comptrollership, Ottawa, Ontario, Canada

Report on Plans and Priorities, 2004-2005, Treasury Board of Canada

Rickwood, C. Thomas, A., *An Introduction to Financial Accounting,* 1st Edition, Maidenhead: McGraw-Hill, 1992

Securities Act, Revised Statutes of Ontario, 1990, Volume 11, Chapter 5, Toronto, Ontario

Scott, William R., *Financial Accounting Theory,* 2nd Edition, Prentice Hall, Canada

The Free Dictionary, by Farlex

The Financial Statements of Canada, 2005, 2006, Receiver General for Canada

Weber, Charles, *The Evolution of Direct Costing,* Urbana Centre for International Education and Research in Accounting, 1966

Wikipedia, *The Free Encyclopedia*